Learning jQuery

Third Edition

Create better interaction, design, and web development
with simple JavaScript techniques

Jonathan Chaffer

Karl Swedberg

[PACKT] open source✻

PUBLISHING   community experience distilled

BIRMINGHAM - MUMBAI

Learning jQuery
Third Edition

Copyright © 2011 Packt Publishing

First published: September 2011

Production Reference: 1160911

Published by Packt Publishing Ltd.
Livery Place
35 Livery Street
Birmingham B3 2PB, UK..

ISBN 978-1-84951-654-9

www.packtpub.com

Cover Image by Karl Swedberg (kswedberg@gmail.com)

Credits

Authors
Jonathan Chaffer

Karl Swedberg

Reviewers
Kaiser Ahmed

Kevin Boudloche

Carlos Estebes

Acquisition Editor
Sarah Cullington

Development Editor
Roger D'souza

Technical Editors
Llewellyn F. Rozario

Azharuddin Sheikh

Project Coordinator
Srimoyee Ghoshal

Proofreader
Linda Morris

Indexers
Tejal Daruwale

Rekha Nair

Graphics
Nilesh Mohite

Production Coordinators
Aparna Bhagat

Prachali Bhiwandkar

Cover Work
Aparna Bhagat

Prachali Bhiwandkar

Foreword

I feel honored knowing that Karl Swedberg and Jonathan Chaffer undertook the task of writing Learning jQuery. As the first book about jQuery, it set the standard that other jQuery—and, really, other JavaScript books in general—have tried to match. It's consistently been one of the top selling JavaScript books since its release, in no small part due to its quality and attention to detail.

I'm especially pleased that it was Karl and Jonathan who wrote the book as I already knew them so well and knew that they would be perfect for the job. Being part of the core jQuery team, I've had the opportunity to come to know Karl quite well over the past couple years, and especially within the context of his book writing effort. Looking at the end result, it's clear that his skills as both a developer and a former English teacher were perfectly designed for this singular task.

I've also had the opportunity to meet both of them in person, a rare occurrence in the world of distributed Open Source projects, and they continue to be upstanding members of the jQuery community.

The jQuery library is used by so many different people in the jQuery community. The community is full of designers, developers, people who have experience programming, and those who don't. Even within the jQuery team, we have people from all backgrounds providing their feedback on the direction of the project. There is one thing that is common across all of jQuery's users, though: We are a community of developers and designers who want JavaScript development to be made simple.

It's almost a cliché, at this point, to say that an open source project is community-oriented, or that a project wants to focus on helping new users get started. However, it's not just an empty gesture for jQuery; it's the liquid-oxygen fuel for the project. We actually have more people in the jQuery team dedicated to managing the jQuery community, writing documentation, or writing plugins than actually maintaining the core code base. While the health of the library is incredibly important, the community surrounding that code is the difference between a floundering, mediocre project and one that will match and exceed your every need.

How we run the project, and how you use the code, is fundamentally very different from most open source projects—and most JavaScript libraries. The jQuery project and community is incredibly knowledgeable; we understand what makes jQuery a different programming experience and do our best to pass that knowledge on to fellow users.

The jQuery community isn't something that you can read about to understand; it's something that you actually have to participate in for it to fully sink in. I hope that you'll have the opportunity to partake in it. Come join us in our forums, mailing lists, and blogs and let us help guide you through the experience of getting to know jQuery better.

For me, jQuery is much more than a block of code. It's the sum total of experiences that have transpired over the years in order to make the library happen. The considerable ups and downs, the struggle of development together with the excitement of seeing it grow and succeed. Growing close with its users and fellow team members, understanding them and trying to grow and adapt.

When I first saw this book talk about jQuery and discuss it like a unified tool, as opposed to the experiences that it's come to encapsulate for me, I was both taken aback and excited. Seeing how others learn, understand, and mold jQuery to fit them is much of what makes the project so exhilarating.

I'm not the only one who enjoys jQuery on a level that is far different from a normal tool-user relationship. I don't know if I can properly encapsulate why this is, but I've seen it time and time again—the singular moment when a user's face lights up with the realization of just how much jQuery will help them.

There is a specific moment where it just clicks for a jQuery user, when they realize that this tool that they were using was in fact much, much more than just a simple tool all along—and suddenly their understanding of how to write dynamic web applications completely shifts. It's an incredible thing, and absolutely my favorite part of the jQuery project.

I hope you'll have the opportunity to experience this sensation as well.

John Resig

Creator of jQuery

About the Authors

Jonathan Chaffer is a member of Rapid Development Group, a web development firm located in Grand Rapids, Michigan. His work there includes overseeing and implementing projects in a wide variety of technologies, with an emphasis in PHP, MySQL, and JavaScript. He also leads on-site training seminars on the jQuery framework for web developers.

In the open-source community, Jonathan has been very active in the Drupal CMS project, which has adopted jQuery as its JavaScript framework of choice. He is the creator of the Content Construction Kit, a popular module for managing structured content on Drupal sites. He is responsible for major overhauls of Drupal's menu system and developer API reference.

Jonathan lives in Grand Rapids with his wife, Jennifer.

I would like to thank Jenny for her tireless enthusiasm and support, Karl for the motivation to continue writing when the spirit is weak, and the Ars Technica community for constant inspiration toward technical excellence. In addition, I'd like to thank Mike Henry and the Twisted Pixel team for producing consistently entertaining distractions in between writing sessions.

Karl Swedberg is a web developer at Fusionary Media in Grand Rapids, Michigan, where he spends much of his time making cool things happen with JavaScript. As a member of the jQuery team, Karl is responsible for maintaining the jQuery API site at `api.jquery.com`. He also publishes tutorials on his blog, `learningjquery.com`, and presents at workshops and conferences. When he isn't coding, Karl likes to hang out with his family, roast coffee in his garage, and exercise at the local cross-fit gym.

I wish to thank my wife, Sara, and my two children, Benjamin and Lucia, for all the joy that they bring into my life. Thanks also to Jonathan Chaffer for his patience and his willingness to write this book with me.

Many thanks to John Resig for creating the world's greatest JavaScript library and to all the others who have contributed their code, time, and expertise to the project. Thanks to the folks at Packt Publishing, the technical reviewers of this book, the jQuery Cabal, and the many others who have provided help and inspiration along the way.

About the Reviewers

Kaiser Ahmed is a professional web developer. He has gained his Bachelor's Degree from Khulna University of Engineering and Technology (KUET). He is also a co-founder of fully outsourcing company CyberXpress.Net Inc based on Bangladesh.

He has a wide breadth of technical skills, Internet knowledge, and experience across the spectrum of online development in the service of building and improving online properties for multiple clients. He enjoys creating site architecture and infrastructure, backend development using open source toolset (PHP, MySQL, Apache, Linux, and others (that is LAMP)), frontend development with CSS and HTML/XHTML.

He would like to thank his loving wife, Maria Akter, for her support.

Kevin Boudloche is a web developer out of Mississippi. He has been building web pages as a hobby for more than eight years and for three years professionally. Kevin's primary focus is front-end development and web application development.

Carlos Estebes is the founder of Ehxioz (http://ehxioz.com/) a Los Angeles-based software development startup that specializes in developing modern web applications and utilizing the latest web development technologies & methodologies. He has over 10 years of web development experience and holds a BSc in Computer Science from California State University, Los Angeles.

www.PacktPub.com

Support files, eBooks, discount offers and more

You might want to visit www.PacktPub.com for support files and downloads related to your book.

Did you know that Packt offers eBook versions of every book published, with PDF and ePub files available? You can upgrade to the eBook version at www.PacktPub.com and as a print book customer, you are entitled to a discount on the eBook copy. Get in touch with us at service@packtpub.com for more details.

At www.PacktPub.com, you can also read a collection of free technical articles, sign up for a range of free newsletters and receive exclusive discounts and offers on Packt books and eBooks.

http://PacktLib.PacktPub.com

Do you need instant solutions to your IT questions? PacktLib is Packt's online digital book library. Here, you can access, read and search across Packt's entire library of books.

Why subscribe?

- Fully searchable across every book published by Packt
- Copy and paste, print and bookmark content
- On demand and accessible via web browser

Free access for Packt account holders

If you have an account with Packt at www.PacktPub.com, you can use this to access PacktLib today and view nine entirely free books. Simply use your login credentials for immediate access.

Table of Contents

Preface

In 2005, inspired by pioneers in the field such as Dean Edwards and Simon Willison, John Resig put together a set of functions to make it easy to programmatically find elements on a web page and assign behaviors to them. By the time he first publicly announced his project in January 2006, he had added DOM modification and basic animations. He gave it the name jQuery to emphasize the central role of finding, or querying, parts of a web page and acting on them with JavaScript. In the few short years since then, jQuery has grown in its feature set, improved in its performance, and gained widespread adoption by many of the most popular sites on the Internet. While Resig remains the lead developer of the project, jQuery has blossomed, in true open-source fashion, to the point where it now boasts a core team of top-notch JavaScript developers, as well as a vibrant community of thousands of developers.

The jQuery JavaScript library can enhance your websites regardless of your background. It provides a wide range of features, an easy-to-learn syntax, and robust cross-platform compatibility in a single compact file. What's more, hundreds of plugins have been developed to extend jQuery's functionality, making it an essential tool for nearly every client-side scripting occasion.

Learning jQuery Third Edition provides a gentle introduction to jQuery concepts, allowing you to add interactions and animations to your pages—even if previous attempts at writing JavaScript have left you baffled. This book guides you past the pitfalls associated with Ajax, events, effects, and advanced JavaScript language features, and provides you with a brief reference to the jQuery library to return to again and again.

What This Book Covers

In *Chapter 1, Getting Started*, you'll get your feet wet with the jQuery JavaScript library. The chapter begins with a description of jQuery and what it can do for you. It then walks you through downloading and setting up the library, as well as writing your first script.

In *Chapter 2, Selecting Elements*, you'll learn how to use jQuery's selector expressions and DOM traversal methods to find elements on the page, wherever they may be. You'll use jQuery to apply styling to a diverse set of page elements, sometimes in a way that pure CSS cannot.

In *Chapter 3, Handling Events*, you'll use jQuery's event-handling mechanism to fire off behaviors when browser events occur. You'll see how jQuery makes it easy to attach events to elements unobtrusively, even before the page finishes loading. Also, you'll get an overview of deeper topics, such as event bubbling, delegation, and namespacing.

In *Chapter 4, Styling and Animating*, you'll be introduced to jQuery's animation techniques and see how to hide, show, and move page elements with effects that are both useful and pleasing to the eye.

In *Chapter 5, Manipulating the DOM*, you'll learn how to change your page on command. This chapter will teach you how to alter the very structure of an HTML document, as well as its content, on the fly.

In *Chapter 6, Sending Data with Ajax*, you'll discover the many ways in which jQuery makes it easy to access server-side functionality without resorting to clunky page refreshes. With the basic components of the library well in hand, you will be ready to explore how the library can expand to fit your needs.

In *Chapter 7, Using Plugins*, will show you how to find, install, and use plugins, including the powerful jQuery UI plugin library.

In *Chapter 8, Developing Plugins*, you'll learn how to take advantage of jQuery's impressive extension capabilities to develop your own plugins from the ground up. You'll create your own utility functions, add jQuery object methods, and discover the jQuery UI widget factory. Next, you'll take a second tour through jQuery's building blocks, learning more advanced techniques.

In *Chapter 9, Advanced Selectors and Traversing*, you'll refine your knowledge of selectors and traversals, gaining the ability to optimize selectors for performance, manipulate the DOM element stack, and write plugins that expand selecting and traversing capabilities.

In *Chapter 10, Advanced Events*, you'll dive further into techniques such as delegation and throttling that can greatly improve event handling performance. You'll also create custom and special events that add even more capabilities to the jQuery library.

In *Chapter 11, Advanced Effects*, you'll fine-tune the visual effects jQuery can provide by crafting custom easing functions and reacting to each step of an animation. You'll gain the ability to manipulate animations as they occur, and schedule actions with custom queuing.

In *Chapter 12, Advanced DOM Manipulation*, you'll get more practice modifying the DOM, with techniques such as attaching arbitrary data to elements. You'll also learn how to extend the way jQuery processes CSS properties on elements.

In *Chapter 13, Advanced Ajax*, you'll achieve a greater understanding of Ajax transactions, including the jQuery deferred object system for handling data that may become available at a later time.

In *Appendix A, JavaScript Closures*, you'll gain a solid understanding of closures in JavaScript—what they are and how you can use them to your advantage.

In *Appendix B, Testing JavaScript with QUnit*, you'll learn about the QUnit library for unit testing of JavaScript programs. This library will add to your toolkit for developing and maintaining highly sophisticated web applications.

In *Appendix C, Quick Reference*, you'll get a glimpse of the entire jQuery library, including every one of its methods and selector expressions. Its easy-to-scan format is perfect for those moments when you know what you want to do, but you're just unsure about the right method name or selector.

What you need for this book

In order to run the example code demonstrated in this book, you need a modern web browser such as Mozilla Firefox, Apple Safari, Google Chrome, or Microsoft Internet Explorer.

To experiment with the examples and to work on the chapter-ending exercises, you will also need:

- A basic text editor
- Web development tools for the browser such as Firebug (as described in *Chapter 1* in the *Development Tools* section)
- The full code package for each chapter, which includes a copy of the jQuery library (seen in the following *Downloading the example code* section)

Additionally, to run some of the Ajax examples in *Chapter 6* and beyond, you will need a PHP-enabled web server.

Who this book is for

This book is for web designers who want to create interactive elements for their designs, and for developers who want to create the best user interface for their web applications. Basic JavaScript programming knowledge is required. You will need to know the basics of HTML and CSS, and should be comfortable with the syntax of JavaScript. No knowledge of jQuery is assumed, nor is experience with any other JavaScript libraries required.

By reading this book, you will become familiar with the functionality and syntax of jQuery 1.6.x, the latest version at the time of writing.

History of the jQuery project

This book covers the functionality and syntax of jQuery 1.6.x, the latest version at the time of writing. The premise behind the library—providing an easy way to find elements on a web page and manipulate them—has not changed over the course of its development, but some syntax details and features have. This brief overview of the project history describes the most significant changes from version to version, which may prove helpful to readers working with legacy versions of the library.

- **Public Development Phase**: John Resig first made mention of an improvement on Prototype's *Behavior* library in August of 2005. This new framework was formally released as jQuery on January 14, 2006.

- **jQuery 1.0** (August 2006): This, the first stable release of the library, already had robust support for CSS selectors, event handling, and AJAX interaction.

- **jQuery 1.1** (January 2007): This release streamlined the API considerably. Many rarely-used methods were combined, reducing the number of methods to learn and document.

- **jQuery 1.1.3** (July 2007): This minor release contained massive speed improvements for jQuery's selector engine. From this version on, jQuery's performance would compare favorably to its fellow JavaScript libraries such as Prototype, Mootools, and Dojo.

- **jQuery 1.2** (September 2007): XPath syntax for selecting elements was removed in this release, as it had become redundant with the CSS syntax. Effect customization became much more flexible in this release, and plugin development became easier with the addition of **namespaced events**.

- **jQuery UI** (September 2007): This new plugin suite was announced to replace the popular, but aging, Interface plugin. A rich collection of prefabricated widgets was included, as well as a set of tools for building sophisticated elements such as drag-and-drop interfaces.

- **jQuery 1.2.6** (May 2008): The functionality of Brandon Aaron's popular Dimensions plugin was brought into the main library.

- **jQuery 1.3** (January 2009): A major overhaul of the selector engine (**Sizzle**) provided a huge boost to the library's performance. **Event delegation** became formally supported.

- **jQuery 1.4** (January 2010): This version, perhaps the most ambitious update since 1.0, brought many performance improvements to DOM manipulation, as well as a large number of new or enhanced methods to nearly every aspect of the library. Version 1.4 was accompanied by fourteen days of announcements and videos on a dedicated website, `http://jquery14.com/`.

- **jQuery 1.4.2** (February 2010): Two new event delegation methods, `.delegate()` and `.undelegate()`, were added, and jQuery's entire event system saw a comprehensive overhaul for more flexible use and greater cross-browser consistency.

- **jQuery Mobile** (August 2010): The jQuery Project publicly outlined its strategy, research, and UI designs for mobile web development with jQuery and a new mobile framework at `http://jquerymobile.com/`.

- **jQuery 1.5** (January 2011): The Ajax component underwent a major rewrite, adding greater extensibility and performance. Additionally, jQuery 1.5 included an implementation of the Promise pattern for handling queues of both synchronous and asynchronous functions.

- **jQuery 1.6** (May 2011): The Attribute component was rewritten to more accurately reflect the distinction between HTML attributes and DOM properties. Also, the Deferred object, which was introduced in jQuery 1.5, received two new methods: `.always()` and `.pipe()`.

Historical Details

Release notes for older jQuery versions can be found on the project's website at `http://jquery.org/history`.

Conventions

In this book, you will find a number of styles of text that distinguish between different kinds of information. Here are some examples of these styles, and an explanation of their meaning.

Code words in text are shown as follows: "This code illustrates that we can pass any kind of expression into the `console.log()` method."

A block of code is set as follows:

```
$('button.show-details').click(function() {
  $('div.details').show();
});
```

When we wish to draw your attention to a particular part of a code block, the relevant lines or items are set in bold:

```
$('#switcher-narrow').bind('click', function() {
  $('body').removeClass().addClass('narrow');
});
```

New terms and **important words** are shown in bold. Words that you see on the screen, in menus or dialog boxes for example, appear in the text like this: "The **Console** tab will be of most frequent use to us while learning jQuery, as shown in the following screenshot".

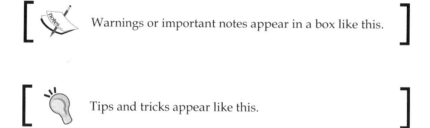

Warnings or important notes appear in a box like this.

Tips and tricks appear like this.

Reader feedback

Feedback from our readers is always welcome. Let us know what you think about this book—what you liked or may have disliked. Reader feedback is important for us to develop titles that you really get the most out of.

To send us general feedback, simply send an e-mail to feedback@packtpub.com, and mention the book title via the subject of your message.

If there is a book that you need and would like to see us publish, please send us a note in the **SUGGEST A TITLE** form on www.packtpub.com or e-mail suggest@packtpub.com.

If there is a topic that you have expertise in and you are interested in either writing or contributing to a book, see our author guide on www.packtpub.com/authors.

Customer support

Now that you are the proud owner of a Packt book, we have a number of things to help you to get the most from your purchase.

Downloading the example code

You can download the example code files for all Packt books you have purchased from your account at `http://www.PacktPub.com`. If you purchased this book elsewhere, you can visit `http://www.PacktPub.com/support` and register to have the files e-mailed directly to you.

Errata

Although we have taken every care to ensure the accuracy of our content, mistakes do happen. If you find a mistake in one of our books—maybe a mistake in the text or the code—we would be grateful if you would report this to us. By doing so, you can save other readers from frustration and help us improve subsequent versions of this book. If you find any errata, please report them by visiting `http://www.packtpub.com/support`, selecting your book, clicking on the **errata submission form** link, and entering the details of your errata. Once your errata are verified, your submission will be accepted and the errata will be uploaded on our website, or added to any list of existing errata, under the Errata section of that title. Any existing errata can be viewed by selecting your title from `http://www.packtpub.com/support`.

Piracy

Piracy of copyright material on the Internet is an ongoing problem across all media. At Packt, we take the protection of our copyright and licenses very seriously. If you come across any illegal copies of our works, in any form, on the Internet, please provide us with the location address or website name immediately so that we can pursue a remedy.

Please contact us at `copyright@packtpub.com` with a link to the suspected pirated material.

We appreciate your help in protecting our authors, and our ability to bring you valuable content.

Questions

You can contact us at `questions@packtpub.com` if you are having a problem with any aspect of the book, and we will do our best to address it.

Getting Started

1

Today's World Wide Web is a dynamic environment, and its users set a high bar for both style and function of sites. To build interesting, interactive sites, developers are turning to JavaScript libraries such as jQuery to automate common tasks and simplify complicated ones. One reason for jQuery's popularity is its ability to assist in a wide range of tasks.

It can seem challenging to know where to begin because jQuery performs so many different functions. Yet, there is a coherence and symmetry to the design of the library; many of its concepts are borrowed from the structure of **HTML** and **Cascading Style Sheets (CSS)**. The library's design lends itself to a quick start for designers with little programming experience as many of them have more experience with these technologies than they do with JavaScript. In fact, in this opening chapter, we'll write a functioning jQuery program in just three lines of code. On the other hand, experienced programmers will also be aided by this conceptual consistency, as we'll see in the later, more advanced chapters.

So let's look at what jQuery can do for us.

What jQuery does

The jQuery library provides a general-purpose abstraction layer for common web scripting, and is, therefore, useful in almost every scripting situation. Its extensible nature means that we could never cover all possible uses and functions in a single book, as plugins are constantly being developed to add new abilities. The core features, though, assist us in accomplishing the following tasks:

- Access elements in a document: Without a JavaScript library, web developers often need to write many lines of code to traverse the **Document Object Model (DOM)** tree and locate specific portions of an HTML document's structure. With jQuery, developers have a robust and efficient selector mechanism at their disposal, making it easy to retrieve the exact piece of the document that needs to be inspected or manipulated.

```
$('div.content').find('p');
```

- Modify the appearance of a web page: CSS offers a powerful method of influencing the way a document is rendered, but it falls short when web browsers do not all support the same standards. With jQuery, developers can bridge this gap, relying on the same standards support across all browsers. In addition, jQuery can change the classes or individual style properties applied to a portion of the document even after the page has been rendered.

```
$('ul > li:first').addClass('active');
```

- Alter the content of a document: Not limited to mere cosmetic changes, jQuery can modify the content of a document itself with a few keystrokes. Text can be changed, images can be inserted or swapped, lists can be reordered, or the entire structure of the HTML can be rewritten and extended—all with a single easy-to-use **Application Programming Interface (API)**.

```
$('#container').append('<a href="more.html">more</a>');
```

- Respond to a user's interaction: Even the most elaborate and powerful behaviors are not useful if we can't control when they take place. The jQuery library offers an elegant way to intercept a wide variety of events, such as a user clicking on a link, without the need to clutter the HTML code itself with event handlers. At the same time, its event-handling API removes browser inconsistencies that often plague web developers.

```
$('button.show-details').click(function() {
  $('div.details').show();
});
```

- Animate changes being made to a document: To effectively implement such interactive behaviors, a designer must also provide visual feedback to the user. The jQuery library facilitates this by providing an array of effects such as fades and wipes, as well as a toolkit for crafting new graphic displays.

```
$('div.details').slideDown();
```

- Retrieve information from a server without refreshing a page: This code pattern has become known as **Ajax**, which originally stood for **asynchronous JavaScript and XML**, but has since come to represent a much greater set of technologies for communicating between the client and the server. The jQuery library removes the browser-specific complexity from this responsive, feature-rich process, allowing developers to focus on the server-end functionality.

```
$('div.details').load('more.html #content');
```

- Simplify common JavaScript tasks: In addition to all of the document-specific features of jQuery, the library provides enhancements to basic JavaScript constructs such as iteration and array manipulation.

```
$.each(obj, function(key, value) {
  total += value;
});
```

Downloading the example code

You can download the example code files for all Packt books you have purchased from your account at http://www.PacktPub.com. If you purchased this book elsewhere, you can visit http://www.PacktPub.com/support and register to have the files e-mailed directly to you.

Why jQuery works well

With the resurgence of interest in dynamic HTML comes a proliferation of JavaScript frameworks. Some are specialized, focusing on just one or two of the above tasks. Others attempt to catalog every possible behavior and animation, and serve these all up pre-packaged. To maintain the wide range of features outlined above while remaining relatively compact, jQuery employs several strategies:

- Leverage knowledge of CSS: By basing the mechanism for locating page elements on **CSS selectors**, jQuery inherits a terse, yet legible, way of expressing a document's structure. The jQuery library becomes an entry point for designers who want to add behaviors to their pages because a prerequisite for doing professional web development is to have knowledge of CSS syntax.

- Support extensions: In order to avoid *feature creep*, jQuery relegates special-case uses to **plugins**. The method for creating new plugins is simple and well-documented, which has spurred the development of a wide variety of inventive and useful modules. Most of the features in the basic jQuery download are internally realized through the plugin architecture, and can be removed if desired, yielding an even smaller library.

- Abstract away browser quirks: An unfortunate reality of web development is that each browser has its own set of deviations from published standards. A significant portion of any web application can be relegated to handle features differently on each platform. While the ever-evolving browser landscape makes a perfectly browser-neutral code base impossible for some advanced features, jQuery adds an **abstraction layer** that normalizes the common tasks, reducing the size of code while tremendously simplifying it.

- Always work with sets: When we instruct jQuery, "Find all elements with the class `collapsible` and hide them," there is no need to loop through each returned element. Instead, methods such as `.hide()` are designed to automatically work on sets of objects instead of individual ones. This technique, called **implicit iteration**, means that many looping constructs become unnecessary, shortening code considerably.

- Allow multiple actions in one line: To avoid overuse of temporary variables or wasteful repetition, jQuery employs a programming pattern called **chaining** for the majority of its methods. This means that the result of most operations on an object is the object itself, ready for the next action to be applied to it.

These strategies have kept the jQuery package slim—roughly 30 KB, compressed—while at the same time providing techniques to keep our custom code that uses the library compact.

The elegance of the library comes about partly by design, and partly due to the evolutionary process spurred by the vibrant community that has sprung up around the project. Users of jQuery gather to discuss not only the development of plugins, but also enhancements to the core library. The users and developers also assist in continually improving the official project documentation, which can be found at `http://api.jquery.com`.

Despite all of the efforts required to engineer such a flexible and robust system, the end product is free for all to use. This open source project is dually licensed under the **MIT License** (to permit free use of jQuery on any site and facilitate its use within proprietary software) and the **GNU Public License** (appropriate for inclusion in other GNU-licensed open-source projects).

Our first jQuery-powered web page

Now that we have covered the range of features available to us with jQuery, we can examine how to put the library into action. To get started, we need a copy of jQuery.

Downloading jQuery

No installation is required. To use jQuery, we just need a publicly available copy of the file, whether that copy is on an external site or our own. As JavaScript is an interpreted language, there is no compilation or build phase to worry about. Whenever we need a page to have jQuery available, we will simply refer to the file's location from a `<script>` element in the HTML document.

The official jQuery website (http://jquery.com/) always has the most up-to-date, stable version of the library, which can be downloaded right from the home page of the site. Several versions of jQuery may be available at any given moment; the most appropriate for us as site developers will be the latest uncompressed version of the library. This can be replaced with a compressed version in production environments.

As jQuery's popularity has grown, companies have made the file freely available through their **Content Delivery Networks** (**CDN**s). Most notably, Google (http://code.google.com/apis/ajaxlibs/documentation/), and Microsoft (http://www.asp.net/ajax/cdn) offer the file on powerful, low-latency servers distributed around the world for fast download regardless of the user's location. While a CDN-hosted copy of jQuery has speed advantages due to server distribution and caching, using a local copy can be convenient during development. Throughout this book we'll use a copy of the file stored on our own system, which will allow us to run our code whether we're connected to the Internet or not.

Setting up jQuery in an HTML document

There are three pieces to most examples of jQuery usage: the HTML document, CSS files to style it, and JavaScript files to act on it. For our first example, we'll use a page with a book excerpt that has a number of classes applied to portions of it. This page includes a reference to the latest version of the jQuery library, which we have downloaded, renamed `jquery.js`, and placed in our local project directory, as follows:

```html
<!DOCTYPE html>

<html lang="en">
  <head>
    <meta charset="utf-8">
    <title>Through the Looking-Glass</title>

    <link rel="stylesheet" href="01.css">

    <script src="jquery.js"></script>
    <script src="01.js"></script>
  </head>

  <body>
    <h1>Through the Looking-Glass</h1>
    <div class="author">by Lewis Carroll</div>

    <div class="chapter" id="chapter-1">
      <h2 class="chapter-title">1. Looking-Glass House</h2>
```

```
        <p>There was a book lying near Alice on the table,
          and while she sat watching the White King (for she
          was still a little anxious about him, and had the
          ink all ready to throw over him, in case he fainted
          again), she turned over the leaves, to find some
          part that she could read,
          <span class="spoken">
            "&mdash;for it's all in some language I don't know,"
          </span>
          she said to herself.
        </p>
        <p>It was like this.</p>
        <div class="poem">
          <h3 class="poem-title">YKCOWREBBAJ</h3>
          <div class="poem-stanza">
            <div>sevot yhtils eht dna ,gillirb sawT'</div>
            <div>;ebaw eht ni elbmig dna eryg diD</div>
            <div>,sevogorob eht erew ysmim llA</div>
            <div>.ebargtuo shtar emom eht dnA</div>
          </div>
        </div>
        <p>She puzzled over this for some time, but at last
          a bright thought struck her.
          <span class="spoken">
            "Why, it's a Looking-glass book, of course! And if
            I hold it up to a glass, the words will all go the
            right way again."
          </span>
        </p>
        <p>This was the poem that Alice read.</p>
        <div class="poem">
          <h3 class="poem-title">JABBERWOCKY</h3>
          <div class="poem-stanza">
            <div>'Twas brillig, and the slithy toves</div>
            <div>Did gyre and gimble in the wabe;</div>
            <div>All mimsy were the borogoves,</div>
            <div>And the mome raths outgrabe.</div>
          </div>
        </div>
      </div>
    </body>
  </html>
```

File Paths

The actual layout of files on the server does not matter. References from one file to another just need to be adjusted to match the organization we choose. In most examples in this book, we will use relative paths to reference files (`../images/foo.png`) rather than absolute paths (`/images/foo.png`). This will allow the code to run locally without the need for a web server.

Immediately following the normal HTML preamble, the stylesheet is loaded. For this example, we'll use the following:

```
body {
  background-color: #fff;
  color: #000;
  font-family: Helvetica, Arial, sans-serif;
}
h1, h2, h3 {
  margin-bottom: .2em;
}
.poem {
  margin: 0 2em;
}
.highlight {
  background-color: #ccc;
  border: 1px solid #888;
  font-style: italic;
  margin: 0.5em 0;
  padding: 0.5em;
}
```

After the stylesheet is referenced, the JavaScript files are included. It is important that the script tag for the jQuery library be placed before the tag for our custom scripts; otherwise, the jQuery framework will not be available when our code attempts to reference it.

Throughout the rest of this book, only the relevant portions of HTML and CSS files will be printed. The files in their entirety are available at the book's companion website `http://book.learningjquery.com`.

Now we have a page that looks similar to the following screenshot:

Through the Looking-Glass

by Lewis Carroll

1. Looking-Glass House

There was a book lying near Alice on the table, and while she sat watching the White King (for she was still a little anxious about him, and had the ink all ready to throw over him, in case he fainted again), she turned over the leaves, to find some part that she could read, "—for it's all in some language I don't know," she said to herself.

It was like this.

YKCOWREBBAJ
sevot yhtils eht dna ,gillirb sawT'
;ebaw eht ni elbmig dna eryg diD
,sevogorob eht erew ysmim llA
.ebargtuo shtar emom eht dnA

She puzzled over this for some time, but at last a bright thought struck her. "Why, it's a Looking-glass book, of course! And if I hold it up to a glass, the words will all go the right way again."

This was the poem that Alice read.

JABBERWOCKY
'Twas brillig, and the slithy toves
Did gyre and gimble in the wabe;
All mimsy were the borogoves,
And the mome raths outgrabe.

We will use jQuery to apply a new style to the poem text.

 This example is to demonstrate a simple use of jQuery. In real-world situations, this type of styling could be performed purely with CSS.

Adding our jQuery code

Our custom code will go in the second, currently empty, JavaScript file which we included from the HTML using `<script src="01.js"></script>`. For this example, we only need three lines of code, as follows:

```
$(document).ready(function() {
  $('div.poem-stanza').addClass('highlight');
});
```

Finding the poem text

The fundamental operation in jQuery is selecting a part of the document. This is done with the `$()` function. Typically, it takes a string as a parameter, which can contain any CSS selector expression. In this case, we wish to find all of the `<div>` elements in the document that have the `poem-stanza` class applied to them, so the selector is very simple. However, we will cover much more sophisticated options through the course of the book. We will step through many ways of locating parts of a document in *Chapter 2, Selecting Elements*.

When called, the `$()` function returns a new **jQuery object instance**, which is the basic building block we will be working with from now on. This object encapsulates zero or more DOM elements, and allows us to interact with them in many different ways. In this case, we wish to modify the appearance of these parts of the page, and we will accomplish this by changing the classes applied to the poem text.

Injecting the new class

The `.addClass()` method, like most jQuery methods, is named self-descriptively; it applies a CSS class to the part of the page that we have selected. Its only parameter is the name of the class to add. This method, and its counterpart, `.removeClass()`, will allow us to easily observe jQuery in action as we explore the different selector expressions available to us. For now, our example simply adds the `highlight` class, which our stylesheet has defined as italicized text with a gray background and a border.

Note that no iteration is necessary to add the class to all the poem stanzas. As we discussed, jQuery uses **implicit iteration** within methods such as `.addClass()`, so a single function call is all it takes to alter all of the selected parts of the document.

Executing the code

Taken together, `$()` and `.addClass()` are enough for us to accomplish our goal of changing the appearance of the poem text. However, if this line of code is inserted alone in the document header, it will have no effect. JavaScript code is generally run as soon as it is encountered in the browser, and at the time the header is being processed, no HTML is yet present to style. We need to delay the execution of the code until after the DOM is available for our use.

With the `$(document).ready()` construct, jQuery allows us to schedule function calls for firing once the DOM is loaded — without necessarily waiting for images to fully render. While this event scheduling is possible without the aid of jQuery, `$(document).ready()` provides an especially elegant cross-browser solution that:

- Uses the browser's native DOM ready implementations when available and adds a `window.onload` event handler as a safety net

- Allows for multiple calls to `$(document).ready()` and executes them in the order in which they are called
- Executes functions passed to `$(document).ready()` even if they are added after the browser event has already occurred
- Handles the event scheduling asynchronously to allow scripts to delay it if necessary
- Simulates a DOM ready event in some older browsers by repeatedly checking for the existence of a DOM method that typically becomes available at the same time as the DOM

The `.ready()` method's parameter can accept a reference to an already defined function, as shown in the following code snippet:

```
function addHighlightClass()  {
    $('div.poem-stanza').addClass('highlight');
}


$(document).ready(addHighlightClass);
```

Shorter way to call

Listing 1.1

However, as demonstrated in the original version of the script, and repeated in Listing 1.2, as follows, the method can also accept an **anonymous function** (sometimes also called a **lambda function**), as follows:

```
$(document).ready(function() {
    $('div.poem-stanza').addClass('highlight');
});
```

Listing 1.2

This anonymous function idiom is convenient in jQuery code for methods that take a function as an argument when that function isn't reusable. Moreover, the **closure** it creates can be an advanced and powerful tool. However, it may also have unintended consequences and ramifications on memory use, if not dealt with carefully. The topic of closures is discussed fully in *Appendix A, JavaScript Closures*.

The finished product

Now that our JavaScript is in place, the page looks similar to the following screenshot:

Through the Looking-Glass

by Lewis Carroll

1. Looking-Glass House

There was a book lying near Alice on the table, and while she sat watching the White King (for she was still a little anxious about him, and had the ink all ready to throw over him, in case he fainted again), she turned over the leaves, to find some part that she could read, "—for it's all in some language I don't know," she said to herself.

It was like this.

YKCOWREBBAJ

sevot yhtils eht dna ,gillirb sawT'
;ebaw eht ni elbmig dna eryg diD
,sevogorob eht erew ysmim llA
.ebargtuo shtar emom eht dnA

She puzzled over this for some time, but at last a bright thought struck her. "Why, it's a Looking-glass book, of course! And if I hold it up to a glass, the words will all go the right way again."

This was the poem that Alice read.

JABBERWOCKY

'Twas brillig, and the slithy toves
Did gyre and gimble in the wabe;
All mimsy were the borogoves,
And the mome raths outgrabe.

The poem stanzas are now italicized and enclosed in boxes, as specified by the `01.css` stylesheet, due to the insertion of the `highlight` class by the JavaScript code.

Plain JavaScript vs. jQuery

Even a task as simple as this can be complicated without jQuery at our disposal. In plain JavaScript, we could add the `highlighted` class as shown in the following code snippet: *\ Much more complicated*

```
window.onload = function() {
  var divs = document.getElementsByTagName('div');
  for (var i = 0; i < divs.length; i++) {
    if (hasClass(divs[i], 'poem-stanza')
      && !hasClass(divs[i], 'highlight')) {
      divs[i].className += ' highlight';
```

```
    }
  }

  function hasClass( elem, cls ) {
    var reClass = new RegExp(' ' + cls + ' ');
    return reClass.test(' ' + elem.className + ' ');
  }
};
```

Listing 1.3

Despite its length, this solution does not handle many of the situations that jQuery takes care of for us in Listing 1.2, such as the following:

- Properly respecting other `window.onload` event handlers
- Acting as soon as the DOM is ready
- Optimizing element retrieval and other tasks with modern DOM methods

We can see that our jQuery-driven code is easier to write, simpler to read, and faster to execute than its plain JavaScript equivalent.

Development tools

As this code comparison has shown, jQuery code is typically shorter and clearer than its basic JavaScript equivalent. However, this doesn't mean we will always write code that is free from bugs, or that we will intuitively understand what is happening on our pages at all times. Our jQuery coding experience will be much smoother with the assistance of standard development tools.

High-quality development tools are available in all modern browsers. We can feel free to use the environment that is most comfortable to us. Options include:

- The Internet Explorer Developer Tools:
  `http://msdn.microsoft.com/en-us/library/dd565628.aspx`
- The Safari Web Inspector:
  `http://developer.apple.com/technologies/safari/developer-tools.html`
- The Chrome Developer Tools:
  `http://code.google.com/chrome/devtools/`
- Firebug for Firefox: `http://getfirebug.com/`

Each of these toolkits offers similar development features, including:

- The ability to explore and modify aspects of the DOM
- Investigating the relationship between CSS and its effect on page presentation
- Convenient tracing of script execution through special methods
- Pausing execution of running scripts and inspecting variable values

While the details of these features vary from one browser to the next, the general concepts remain constant. In this book, some examples will require the use of one of these toolkits; we will use Firebug for these demonstrations, but development tools for other browsers are fine alternatives.

Firebug

✓ use installed

Up-to-date instructions for installing and using Firebug can be found on the project's home page at `http://getfirebug.com/`. The tool is too involved to explore in great detail here, but a survey of some of the most relevant features will be useful to us.

Understanding these screenshots

Firebug is a quickly-evolving project, so the following screenshots may not exactly match your environment. Some of the labels and buttons are provided by the optional **FireQuery** add-on: `http://firequery.binaryage.com/`.

When Firebug is activated, a new panel appears offering information about the current page.

In the default **HTML** tab of this panel, we can see a representation of the page structure on the left side, and details of the selected element (such as the CSS rules that apply to it) on the right side. This tab is especially useful for investigating the structure of the page and debugging CSS issues, as shown in the following screenshot:

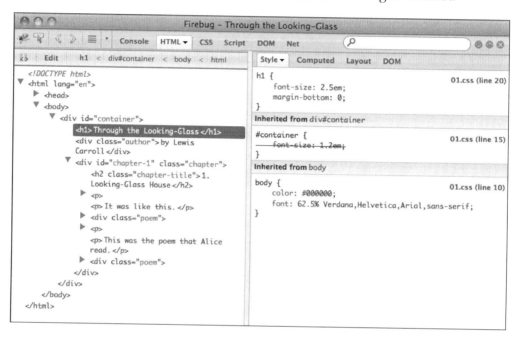

The **Script** tab allows us to view the contents of all loaded scripts on the page, as shown in the preceding screenshot. By clicking on a line number, we can set a breakpoint; when the script reaches a line with a breakpoint, it will pause until we resume execution with a button click. On the right side of the page, we can enter a list of variables and expressions we wish to know the value of at any time.

by clicking on [>] in Script tab

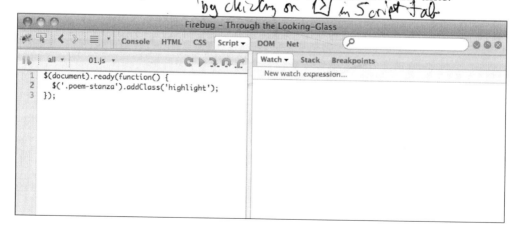

The **Console** tab will be of most frequent use to us while learning jQuery, as shown in the following screenshot. A field at the bottom of the panel allows us to enter any JavaScript statement, and the result of the statement is then presented in the panel:

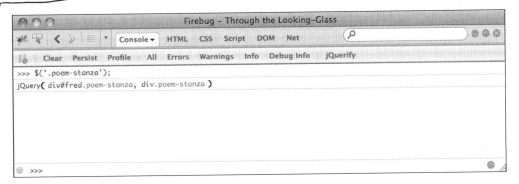

In this example, we have performed the same jQuery selector as in Listing 1.2, but have not performed any action on the selected elements. Even so, the statement gives us interesting information. We see that the result of the selector is a jQuery object pointing to two .poem-stanza elements on the page. We can use this console feature to quickly try out jQuery code at any time, right from within the browser.

In addition, we can interact with this console directly from our code, using the console.log() method, as follows:

```
$(document).ready(function() {
  console.log('hello');
  console.log(52);
  console.log($('div.poem-stanza'));
});
```

Listing 1.4

This code illustrates that we can pass any kind of expression into the `console.log()` method. Simple values such as strings and numbers are printed directly, and more complicated values such as jQuery objects are nicely formatted for our inspection, as shown in the following screenshot:

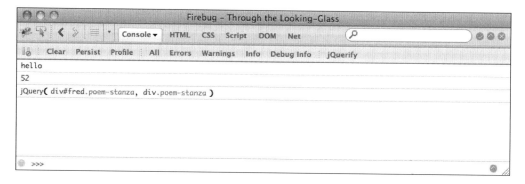

This `console.log()` function (which works in each of the browser developer tools we mentioned) is a convenient alternative to the JavaScript `alert()` function, and will be very useful as we test our jQuery code.

Summary

We now have an idea of why a developer would choose to use a JavaScript framework rather than writing all code from scratch, even for the most basic tasks. We also have seen some of the ways in which jQuery excels as a framework, why we might choose it over other options, and in general which tasks jQuery makes easier.

In this chapter, we have learned how to make jQuery available to JavaScript code on our web page, use the `$()` function to locate a part of the page that has a given class, call `.addClass()` to apply additional styling to this part of the page, and invoke `$(document).ready()` to cause this code to execute upon the loading of the page. We have also explored the development tools we will be relying on when writing, testing, and debugging our jQuery code.

The simple example we have been using demonstrates how jQuery works, but is not very useful in real-world situations. In the next chapter, we will expand on the code here by exploring jQuery's sophisticated selector language, finding practical uses for this technique.

2
Selecting Elements

The jQuery library harnesses the power of Cascading Style Sheets (CSS) **selectors** to let us quickly and easily access elements or groups of elements in the Document Object Model (DOM). In this chapter, we will explore a few of these selectors, as well as jQuery's own **custom selectors**. We'll also look at jQuery's **DOM traversal methods** that provide even greater flexibility for getting what we want.

The Document Object Model

One of the most powerful aspects of jQuery is its ability to make selecting elements in the DOM easy. The Document Object Model serves as the interface between JavaScript and a web page; it provides a representation of the source HTML as a network of objects rather than as plain text.

This network takes the form of a "family tree" of elements on the page. When we refer to the relationships that elements have with one another, we use the same terminology that we use when referring to family relationships: parents, children, and so on. A simple example can help us understand how the family tree metaphor applies to a document, as follows:

```
<html>
  <head>
    <title>the title</title>
  </head>
  <body>
    <div>
      <p>This is a paragraph.</p>
      <p>This is another paragraph.</p>
      <p>This is yet another paragraph.</p>
    </div>
  </body>
</html>
```

Here, `<html>` is the **ancestor** of all the other elements; in other words, all the other elements are **descendants** of `<html>`. The `<head>` and `<body>` elements are not only descendants, but **children** of `<html>`, as well. Likewise, in addition to being the ancestor of `<head>` and `<body>`, `<html>` is also their **parent**. The `<p>` elements are children (and descendants) of `<div>`, descendants of `<body>` and `<html>`, and **siblings** of each other, as shown in the following diagram:

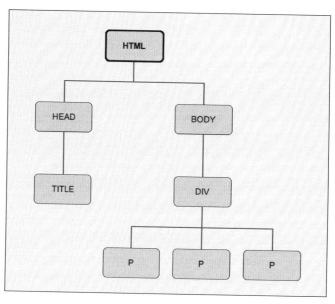

To help visualize the family tree structure of the DOM, you can use a number of software tools, such as the Firebug plugin for Firefox, or the Web Inspector in Safari or Chrome.

With this tree of elements at our disposal, we'll be able to use jQuery to efficiently locate any set of elements on the page. Our tools to achieve this are jQuery selectors and traversal methods.

An important point to note, before we begin, is that the resulting set of elements from selectors and methods is always wrapped in a **jQuery object**. These jQuery objects are very easy to work with when we want to actually do something with the things that we find on a page. We can easily bind **events** to these objects and add slick **effects** to them, as well as **chain** multiple modifications or effects together. Nevertheless, jQuery objects are different from regular DOM elements or node lists, and as such do not necessarily provide the same methods and properties for some tasks. In the final part of this chapter, therefore, we will look at ways to directly access the DOM elements that are wrapped in a jQuery object.

The $() function

No matter which type of selector we want to use in jQuery, we always start with the same function: $(). This function typically accepts a CSS selector as its sole parameter, and serves as a factory, returning a new jQuery object pointing to the corresponding elements on the page. Just about anything that can be used in a stylesheet can also be passed as a string to this function, allowing us to apply jQuery methods to the matched set of elements.

Making jQuery play well with other JavaScript libraries

In jQuery, the dollar sign $ is simply an "alias" for jQuery. As a $() function is very common in JavaScript libraries, conflicts could arise if more than one of these libraries were being used in a given page. We can avoid such conflicts by replacing every instance of $ with jQuery in our custom jQuery code. Additional solutions to this problem are addressed in *Chapter 10, Advanced Events*.

The three primary building blocks of selectors are **tag name**, **ID**, and **class**. They can be used either on their own or in combination with others. The following simple examples illustrate how these three selectors appear in code:

Selector Type	CSS	jQuery	What It Does
Tag name	p { }	$('p')	Selects all paragraphs in the document
ID	#some-id { }	$('#some-id')	Selects the single element in the document that has an ID of some-id
Class	.some-class { }	$('.some-class')	Selects all elements in the document that have a class of some-class

(handwritten annotations: "w — begin w '#'" near the ID row; "— begin '.'" near the Class row)

As mentioned in *Chapter 1, Getting Started*, when we call methods of a jQuery object, the elements referred to by the selector we passed to $() are looped through automatically and implicitly. Therefore, we can usually avoid **explicit iteration**, such as a for loop, that is so often required in DOM scripting.

Now that we have covered the basics, we're ready to start exploring some more powerful uses of selectors.

CSS selectors

The jQuery library supports nearly all of the selectors included in CSS specifications 1 through 3, as outlined on the World Wide Web Consortium's site: `http://www.w3.org/Style/CSS/specs`. This support allows developers to enhance their websites without worrying about which browsers (particularly Internet Explorer 6) might not understand advanced selectors, as long as the browsers have JavaScript enabled.

Progressive enhancement

Responsible jQuery developers should always apply the concepts of **progressive enhancement** and **graceful degradation** to their code, ensuring that a page will render as accurately, even if not as beautifully, with JavaScript disabled as it does with JavaScript turned on. We will continue to explore these concepts throughout the book.

To begin learning how jQuery works with CSS selectors, we'll use a structure that appears on many websites, often for navigation: the nested, unordered list:

```
<ul id="selected-plays">
  <li>Comedies
    <ul>
      <li><a href="/asyoulikeit/">As You Like It</a></li>
      <li>All's Well That Ends Well</li>
      <li>A Midsummer Night's Dream</li>
      <li>Twelfth Night</li>
    </ul>
  </li>
  <li>Tragedies
    <ul>
      <li><a href="hamlet.pdf">Hamlet</a></li>
      <li>Macbeth</li>
      <li>Romeo and Juliet</li>
    </ul>
  </li>
  <li>Histories
    <ul>
      <li>Henry IV (<a href="mailto:henryiv@king.co.uk
        ">email</a>)
        <ul>
          <li>Part I</li>
          <li>Part II</li>
        </ul>
```

```
        <li><a href="http://www.shakespeare.co.uk/henryv.htm">
          Henry V
        </a></li>
        <li>Richard II</li>
      </ul>
    </li>
  </ul>
```

Notice that the first `<ul>` has an ID of `selected-plays`, but none of the `<li>` tags have a class associated with them. Without any styles applied, the list looks similar to the following screenshot:

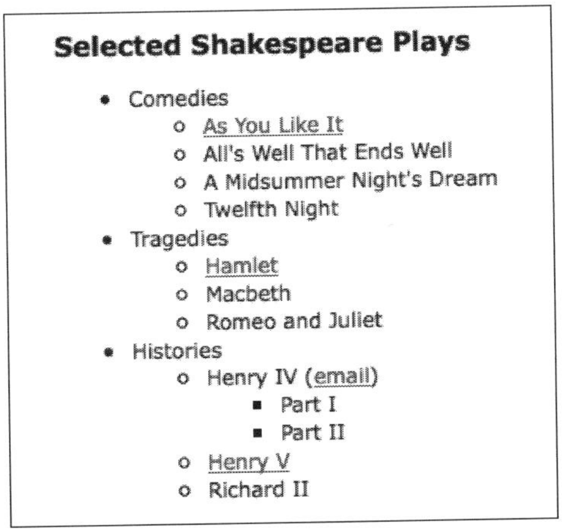

Selected Shakespeare Plays

- Comedies
    - As You Like It
    - All's Well That Ends Well
    - A Midsummer Night's Dream
    - Twelfth Night
- Tragedies
    - Hamlet
    - Macbeth
    - Romeo and Juliet
- Histories
    - Henry IV (email)
        - Part I
        - Part II
    - Henry V
    - Richard II

The nested list appears as we would expect it to — a set of bulleted items arranged vertically and indented according to their level.

Styling list-item levels

Let's suppose that we want the top-level items, and only the top-level items, to be arranged horizontally. We can start by defining a `horizontal` class in the stylesheet:

```
.horizontal {
  float: left;
  list-style: none;
  margin: 10px;
}
```

The `horizontal` class floats the element to the left of the one following it, removes the bullet from it if it's a list item, and adds a 10-pixel margin on all sides of it.

Rather than attaching the `horizontal` class directly in our HTML, we'll add it dynamically to the top-level list items only—**Comedies**, **Tragedies**, and **Histories**—to demonstrate jQuery's use of selectors, as follows:

```
$(document).ready(function() {
  $('#selected-plays > li').addClass('horizontal');
});
```

Listing 2.1

As discussed in *Chapter 1*, we begin the jQuery code by calling `$(document).ready()`, which runs the function passed to it as soon as the DOM has loaded but not before.

The second line uses the **child combinator** (>) to add the `horizontal` class to all top-level items only. In effect, the selector inside the `$()` function is saying, "Find each list item (`li`) that is a child (>) of the element with an ID of `selected-plays` (`#selected-plays`)."

With the class now applied, the rules defined for that class in the stylesheet take effect. Now our nested list looks similar to the following screenshot:

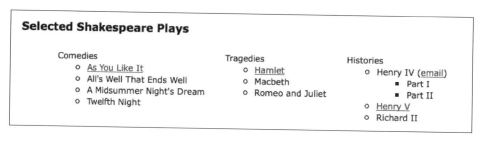

Styling all of the other items—those that are not in the top level—can be done in a number of ways. As we have already applied the `horizontal` class to the top-level items, one way to select all sub-level items is to use a **negation pseudo-class** to identify all list items that do not have a class of `horizontal`. Note the addition of the third line of code:

```
$(document).ready(function() {
  $('#selected-plays > li').addClass('horizontal');
  $('#selected-plays li:not(.horizontal)').addClass('sub-level');
});
```

Listing 2.2

This time we are selecting every list item (`<li>`) that:

- Is a descendant of the element with an ID of `selected-plays`
- (`#selected-plays`)
- Does not have a class of `horizontal` (`:not(.horizontal)`)

When we add the `sub-level` class to these items, they receive the shaded background defined in the stylesheet. Now the nested list looks similar to the following screenshot:

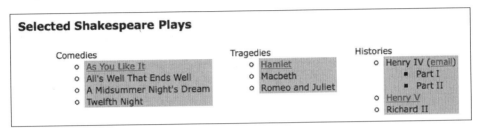

Attribute selectors

Attribute selectors are a particularly helpful subset of CSS selectors. They allow us to specify an element by one of its HTML attributes, such as a link's `title` attribute or an image's `alt` attribute. For example, to select all images that have an `alt` attribute, we write the following:

```
$('img[alt]')
```

Attribute selectors accept a wildcard syntax inspired by regular expressions for identifying the value at the beginning (`^`) or ending (`$`) of a string. They can also take an asterisk (`*`) to indicate the value at an arbitrary position within a string or an exclamation mark (`!`) to indicate a negated value.

Styling links

Let's say we want to have different styles for different types of links. We first define the styles in our stylesheet, as follows:

a = anchor

```
a {
  color: #00c;
}
a.mailto {
  background: url(images/mail.png) no-repeat right top;
  padding-right: 18px;
}
```

```
a.pdflink {
  background: url(images/pdf.png) no-repeat right top;
  padding-right: 18px;
}
a.henrylink {
  background-color: #fff;
  padding: 2px;
  border: 1px solid #000;
}
```

Then, we add the three classes—`mailto`, `pdflink`, and `henrylink`—to the appropriate links using jQuery.

To add a class for all e-mail links, we construct a selector that looks for all anchor elements (a) with an `href` attribute (`[href]`) that begins with `mailto:` (`^="mailto:"`), as follows:

```
$(document).ready(function() {
  $('a[href^="mailto:"]').addClass('mailto');
});
```

Listing 2.3

Because of the rules defined in the page's stylesheet, an envelope image appears after all `mailto:` links on the page, as shown in the following screenshot:

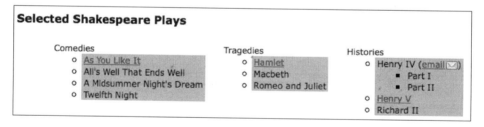

To add a class for all links to PDF files, we use the dollar sign rather than the caret symbol. This is because we're selecting links with an `href` attribute that ends with `.pdf`, as follows:

```
$(document).ready(function() {
  $('a[href^="mailto:"]').addClass('mailto');
  $('a[href$=".pdf"]').addClass('pdflink');
});
```

Listing 2.4

The stylesheet rule for the newly-added `pdflink` class causes an Adobe Acrobat icon to appear after each link to a PDF document, as shown in the following screenshot:

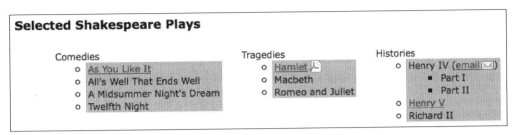

Attribute selectors can be combined as well. We can, for example, add a `henrylink` class for all links with an `href` value that both starts with `http` and contains **henry** anywhere:

```
$(document).ready(function() {
  $('a[href^="mailto:"]').addClass('mailto');
  $('a[href$=".pdf"]').addClass('pdflink');
  $('a[href^="http"][href*="henry"]')
    .addClass('henrylink');
});
```

Listing 2.5

With the three classes applied to the three types of links, we should see the following:

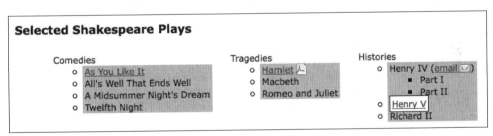

In the preceding screenshot, note the PDF icon to the right of the **Hamlet** link, the envelope icon next to the **email** link, and the white background and black border around the **Henry V** link.

Custom selectors

To the wide variety of CSS selectors, jQuery adds its own custom selectors. These custom selectors enhance the already impressive capabilities of CSS selectors to locate page elements in new ways.

Performance note

When possible, jQuery uses the native DOM selector engine of the browser to find elements. This extremely fast approach is not possible when custom jQuery selectors are used. For this reason, it is recommended to avoid frequent use of custom selectors when a native option is available and performance is very important.

Most of the custom selectors allow us to pick certain elements out of a line-up, so to speak. Typically used following a CSS selector, this kind of custom selector identifies elements based on their positions within the previously-selected group. The syntax is the same as the **CSS pseudo-class** syntax, where the selector starts with a colon (:). For example, to select the second item from a set of `<div>` elements with a class of `horizontal`, we write the following code:

```
$('div.horizontal:eq(1)')
```

Note that `:eq(1)` selects the second item in the set because JavaScript array numbering is **zero-based**, meaning that it starts with 0. In contrast, CSS is **one-based**, so a CSS selector such as `$('div:nth-child(1)')` would select all `div` selectors that are the first child of their parent (in this case, however, we would probably use `$('div:first-child')` instead).

Styling alternate rows

Two very useful custom selectors in the jQuery library are `:odd` and `:even`. Let's take a look at how we can use one of them for basic table striping, given the following tables:

```
<h2>Shakespeare's Plays</h2>
<table>
  <tr>
    <td>As You Like It</td>
    <td>Comedy</td>
    <td></td>
  </tr>
  <tr>
    <td>All's Well that Ends Well</td>
    <td>Comedy</td>
    <td>1601</td>
```

```
    </tr>
    <tr>
      <td>Hamlet</td>
      <td>Tragedy</td>
      <td>1604</td>
    </tr>
    <tr>
      <td>Macbeth</td>
      <td>Tragedy</td>
      <td>1606</td>
    </tr>
    <tr>
      <td>Romeo and Juliet</td>
      <td>Tragedy</td>
      <td>1595</td>
    </tr>
    <tr>
      <td>Henry IV, Part I</td>
      <td>History</td>
      <td>1596</td>
    </tr>
    <tr>
      <td>Henry V</td>
      <td>History</td>
      <td>1599</td>
    </tr>
</table>
<h2>Shakespeare's Sonnets</h2>
<table>
    <tr>
      <td>The Fair Youth</td>
      <td>1-126</td>
    </tr>
    <tr>
      <td>The Dark Lady</td>
      <td>127-152</td>
    </tr>
    <tr>
      <td>The Rival Poet</td>
      <td>78-86</td>
    </tr>
</table>
```

With minimal styles applied from our stylesheet, these headings and tables appear quite plain. The table has a solid white background, with no styling separating one row from the next:

Shakespeare's Plays

As You Like It	Comedy	
All's Well that Ends Well	Comedy	1601
Hamlet	Tragedy	1604
Macbeth	Tragedy	1606
Romeo and Juliet	Tragedy	1595
Henry IV, Part I	History	1596
Henry V	History	1599

Shakespeare's Sonnets

The Fair Youth	1–126
The Dark Lady	127–152
The Rival Poet	78–86

Now we can add a style to the stylesheet for all table rows, and use an `alt` class for the odd rows:

```
tr {
  background-color: #fff;
}
.alt {
  background-color: #ccc;
}
```

Finally, we write our jQuery code, attaching the class to the odd-numbered table rows (`<tr>` tags):

```
$(document).ready(function() {
  $('tr:even').addClass('alt');
});
```

Listing 2.6

But wait! Why use the `:even` selector for odd-numbered rows? Well, just as with the `:eq()` selector, the `:even` and `:odd` selectors use JavaScript's native zero-based numbering. Therefore, the first row counts as 0 (even) and the second row counts as 1 (odd), and so on. With this in mind, we can expect our simple bit of code to produce tables that look similar to the following screenshot:

Shakespeare's Plays

As You Like It	Comedy	
All's Well that Ends Well	Comedy	1601
Hamlet	Tragedy	1604
Macbeth	Tragedy	1606
Romeo and Juliet	Tragedy	1595
Henry IV, Part I	History	1596
Henry V	History	1599

Shakespeare's Sonnets

The Fair Youth	1–126
The Dark Lady	127–152
The Rival Poet	78–86

Note that for the second table, this result may not be what we intend. As the last row in the **Plays** table has the "alternate" gray background, the first row in the **Sonnets** table has the plain white background. One way to avoid this type of problem is to use the `:nth-child()` selector instead, which counts an element's position relative to its parent element, rather than relative to all the elements selected so far. This selector can take either a number, `odd`, or `even` as its argument.

```
$(document).ready(function() {
  $('tr:nth-child(odd)').addClass('alt');
});
```

Listing 2.7

As before, note that `:nth-child()` is the only jQuery selector that is one-based. To achieve the same row striping as we did above—except with consistent behavior for the second table—we need to use `odd` rather than `even` as the argument. With this selector in place, both tables are now striped nicely, as shown in the following screenshot:

Shakespeare's Plays

As You Like It	Comedy	
All's Well that Ends Well	Comedy	1601
Hamlet	Tragedy	1604
Macbeth	Tragedy	1606
Romeo and Juliet	Tragedy	1595
Henry IV, Part I	History	1596
Henry V	History	1599

Shakespeare's Sonnets

The Fair Youth	1–126
The Dark Lady	127–152
The Rival Poet	78–86

For one final custom-selector touch, let's suppose for some reason we want to highlight any table cell that referred to one of the **Henry** plays. All we have to do—after adding a class to the stylesheet to make the text bold and italicized (`.highlight {font-weight: bold; font-style: italic;}`)—is add a line to our jQuery code, using the `:contains()` selector, as shown in the following code snippet:

```
$(document).ready(function() {
    $('tr:nth-child(odd)').addClass('alt');
    $('td:contains(Henry)').addClass('highlight');
});
```

Listing 2.8

So, now we can see our lovely striped table with the **Henry** plays prominently featured:

Shakespeare's Plays

As You Like It	Comedy	
All's Well that Ends Well	Comedy	1601
Hamlet	Tragedy	1604
Macbeth	Tragedy	1606
Romeo and Juliet	Tragedy	1595
Henry IV, Part I	History	1596
Henry V	History	1599

Shakespeare's Sonnets

The Fair Youth	1–126
The Dark Lady	127–152
The Rival Poet	78–86

It's important to note that the `:contains()` selector is case-sensitive. Using `$('td:contains(henry)')` instead, without the uppercase "H," would select no cells.

Admittedly, there are ways to achieve the row striping and text highlighting without jQuery—or any client-side programming, for that matter. Nevertheless, jQuery, along with CSS, is a great alternative for this type of styling in cases where the content is generated dynamically and we don't have access to either the HTML or server-side code.

Form selectors

The capabilities of custom selectors are not limited to locating elements based on their position. For example, when working with forms, jQuery's custom selectors and complementary CSS3 selectors can make short work of selecting just the elements we need. The following table describes a handful of these **form selectors:**

Selector	Match
`:input`	Input, textarea, select, and button elements
`:button`	Button elements and input elements with a `type` attribute equal to `button`
`:enabled`	Form elements that are enabled
`:disabled`	Form elements that are disabled
`:checked`	Radio buttons or checkboxes that are checked
`:selected`	Option elements that are selected

As with the other selectors, form selectors can be combined for greater specificity. We can, for example, select all checked radio buttons (but not checkboxes) with `$('input[type="radio"]:checked')` or select all password inputs and disabled text inputs with `$('input[type="password"], input[type="text"]:disabled')`. Even with custom selectors, we use the same basic principles of CSS to build the list of matched elements.

We have only scratched the surface of available selector expressions here. We will dive further into the topic in *Chapter 9, Advanced Selectors and Traversing*.

DOM traversal methods

The jQuery selectors that we have explored so far allow us to select a set of elements as we navigate across and down the DOM tree and filter the results. If this were the only way to select elements, then our options would be quite limited (although, frankly, the selector expressions are robust in their own right, especially when compared to the regular DOM scripting options). There are many occasions when selecting a parent or ancestor element is essential; that is where jQuery's DOM traversal methods come into play. With these methods at our disposal, we can go up, down, and all around the DOM tree with ease.

Some of the methods have a nearly identical counterpart among the selector expressions. For example, the line we first used to add the alt class, $('tr:even'). addClass('alt'), could be rewritten with the .filter() method as follows:

```
$('tr').filter(':even').addClass('alt');
```

For the most part, however, the two ways of selecting elements complement each other. Furthermore, the .filter() method in particular has enormous power because it can take a function as its argument. The function allows us to create complex tests for whether elements should be kept in the matched set. Let's suppose, for example, we want to add a class to all external links. jQuery has no selector for this sort of case. Without a filter function, we'd be forced to explicitly loop through each element, testing each one separately. With the following **filter function**, however, we can still rely on jQuery's implicit iteration and keep our code compact:

```
$('a').filter(function() {
  return this.hostname && this.hostname != location.hostname;
}).addClass('external');
```

Listing 2.9

The second line filters the set of <a> elements by two criteria:

1. They must have a href attribute with a domain name (this.hostname). We use this test to exclude mailto links, for instance.

2. The domain name that they link to (again, this.hostname) must not match (!=) the domain name of the current page (location.hostname).

More precisely, the .filter() method iterates through the matched set of elements, calling the function once for each, and testing the return value. If the function returns false, then the element is removed from the matched set. If it returns true, then the element is kept, as follows:

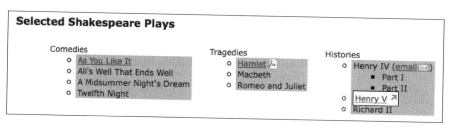

In the next section, we'll take another look at our striped tables to see what else is possible with traversal methods.

Styling specific cells

Earlier we added a `highlight` class to all cells containing the text **Henry**. To style the cell next to each cell containing **Henry**, we can begin with the selector that we have already written, and simply call the `.next()` method on the result, as follows:

```
$(document).ready(function() {
  $('td:contains(Henry)').next().addClass('highlight');
});
```

Listing 2.10

The tables should now look similar to the following screenshot:

Shakespeare's Plays

As You Like It	Comedy	
All's Well that Ends Well	Comedy	1601
Hamlet	Tragedy	1604
Macbeth	Tragedy	1606
Romeo and Juliet	Tragedy	1595
Henry IV, Part I	*History*	1596
Henry V	*History*	1599

Shakespeare's Sonnets

The Fair Youth	1–126
The Dark Lady	127–152
The Rival Poet	78–86

The `.next()` method selects only the very next sibling element. To highlight all of the cells following the one containing **Henry**, we could use the `.nextAll()` method instead:

```
$(document).ready(function() {
  $('td:contains(Henry)').nextAll().addClass('highlight');
});
```

Listing 2.11

As the cells containing **Henry** are in the first column of the table, this code causes the rest of the cells in these rows to be highlighted, as shown in the following screenshot:

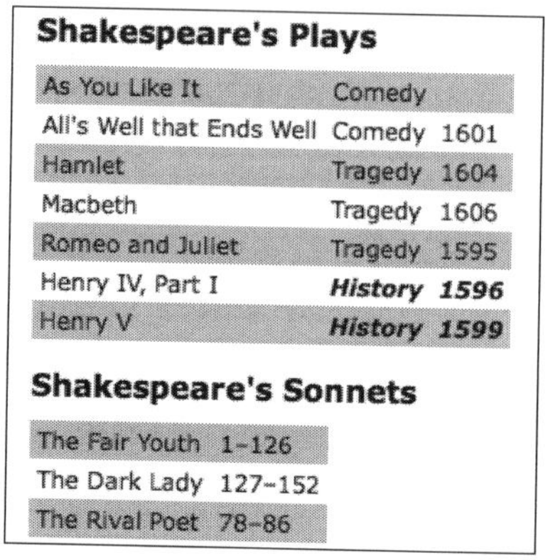

As we might expect, the .next() and .nextAll() methods have counterparts: .prev() and .prevAll(). Additionally, .siblings() selects all other elements at the same DOM level, regardless of whether they come before or after the previously selected element.

To include the original cell (the one that contains **Henry**) along with the cells that follow, we can add the .andSelf() method, as follows:

```
$(document).ready(function() {
  $('td:contains(Henry)').nextAll().andSelf()
    .addClass('highlight');
});
```

Listing 2.12

With this modification in place, all of the cells in the row get the styling offered by the highlight class, as follows:

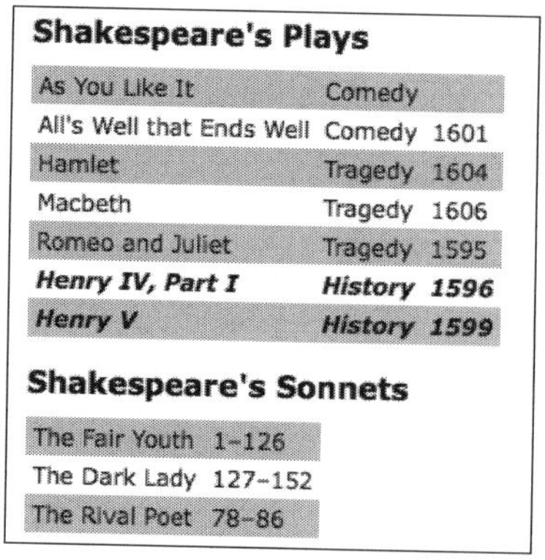

To be sure, there are a multitude of selector and traversal-method combinations by which we can select the same set of elements. Here, for example, is another way to select every cell in each row where at least one of the cells contains **Henry**:

```
$(document).ready(function() {
  $('td:contains(Henry)').parent().children()
    .addClass('highlight');
});
```

Listing 2.13

Here, rather than traversing across to sibling elements, we travel up one level in the DOM to the `<tr>` with `.parent()` and then select all of the row's cells with `.children()`.

Chaining

The traversal method combinations that we have just explored illustrate jQuery's **chaining** capability. With jQuery, it is possible to select multiple sets of elements and do multiple things with them, all within a single line of code. This chaining not only helps keep jQuery code concise, but it also can improve a script's performance when the alternative is to re-specify a selector.

How chaining works

We will explore how chaining is implemented in greater detail later. For now, just realize that almost all jQuery methods return a jQuery object, and so can have more jQuery methods applied to the result.

It is also possible to break a single line of code into multiple lines for greater readability. For example, a single chained sequence of methods could be written as one line:

```
$('td:contains(Henry)').parent().find('td:eq(1)')
  .addClass('highlight').end().find('td:eq(2)')
  .addClass('highlight');
```

Listing 2.14

Or as seven lines:

```
$('td:contains(Henry)') // Find every cell containing "Henry"
  .parent() // Select its parent
  .find('td:eq(1)') // Find the 2nd descendant cell
  .addClass('highlight') // Add the "highlight" class
```

```
.end() // Return to the parent of the cell containing "Henry"
.find('td:eq(2)') // Find the 3rd descendant cell
.addClass('highlight'); // Add the "highlight" class
```

Listing 2.15

Admittedly, the DOM traversal in this example is circuitous to the point of absurdity. We certainly wouldn't recommend using it, as there are clearly simpler, more direct methods at our disposal. The point of the example is simply to demonstrate the tremendous flexibility that chaining affords us.

Chaining can be like speaking a whole paragraph's worth of words in a single breath—it gets the job done quickly, but it can be hard for someone else to understand. Breaking it up into multiple lines and adding judicious comments can save more time in the long run.

Accessing DOM elements

Every selector expression and most jQuery methods return a jQuery object. This is almost always what we want, because of the implicit iteration and chaining capabilities that it affords.

Still, there may be points in our code when we need to access a **DOM element** directly. For example, we may need to make a resulting set of elements available to another JavaScript library. Additionally, we might need to access an element's tag name, which is available as a **property** of the DOM element. For these admittedly rare situations, jQuery provides the .get() method. To access the first DOM element referred to by a jQuery object, we would use .get(0). If the DOM element is needed within a loop, then we would use .get(index). So, if we want to know the tag name of an element with id="my-element", we would write the following code snippet:

```
var myTag = $('#my-element').get(0).tagName;
```

For even greater convenience, jQuery provides a shorthand for .get(). Instead of writing the preceding line, we can use square brackets immediately following the selector:

```
var myTag = $('#my-element')[0].tagName;
```

It's no accident that this syntax appears to treat the jQuery object as an array of DOM elements; using the square brackets is like peeling away the jQuery wrapper to get at the node list, and including the **index** (in this case, 0) is like plucking out the DOM element itself.

Summary

With the techniques that we have covered in this chapter, we should now be able to locate sets of elements on the page in a variety of ways. In particular, we learned how to style top-level and sub-level items in a nested list by using basic **CSS selectors**, apply different styles to different types of links by using **attribute selectors**, add rudimentary striping to a table by using either the **custom jQuery selectors** :odd and :even or the advanced CSS selector :nth-child(), and highlight text within certain table cells by **chaining** jQuery methods.

So far, we have been using the $(document).ready() method to add a class to a matched set of elements. In the next chapter, we'll explore ways in which to add a class in response to a variety of user-initiated events.

Further reading

The topic of selectors and traversal methods will be explored in more detail in *Chapter 9*. A complete list of jQuery's selectors and traversal methods is available in *Appendix C* of this book, in *jQuery Reference Guide*, or in the official jQuery documentation at http://api.jquery.com/.

Exercises

To complete these exercises, you will need the index.html file for this chapter, as well as the finished JavaScript code as found in complete.js. These files can be downloaded from the Packt Publishing web site at http://www.packtpub.com/support.

Challenge exercises may require use of the official jQuery documentation at http://api.jquery.com/.

1. Add a class of special to all of the <li> elements at the second level of the nested list.

2. Add a class of year to all of the table cells in the third column of a table.

3. Add the class special to the first table row that has the word **Tragedy** in it.

4. Challenge: Select all of the list items (<li>s) containing a link (<a>). Add the class afterlink to the sibling list items that follow the ones selected.

5. Challenge: Add the class tragedy to the closest ancestor <ul> of any .pdf link.

3
Handling Events

JavaScript has several built-in ways of reacting to user interaction and other events. To make a page dynamic and responsive, we need to harness this capability so that we can, at the appropriate times, use the jQuery techniques we have learned so far and the other tricks we'll learn later. While we could do this with vanilla JavaScript, jQuery enhances and extends the basic event handling mechanisms to give them a more elegant syntax, while at the same time making them more powerful.

Performing tasks on page load

We have already seen how to make jQuery react to the loading of a web page. The `$(document).ready()` event handler can be used to fire off a function's worth of code, but there's a bit more to be said about it.

Timing of code execution

In *Chapter 1, Getting Started*, we noted that `$(document).ready()` was jQuery's primary way to perform tasks on page load. It is not, however, the only method at our disposal. The native `window.onload` event can achieve a similar effect. While the two methods are similar, it is important to recognize their difference in timing, even though it can be quite subtle depending on the number of resources being loaded.

The `window.onload` event fires when a document is completely downloaded to the browser. This means that every element on the page is ready to be manipulated by JavaScript, which is a boon for writing featureful code without worrying about load order.

On the other hand, a handler registered using `$(document).ready()` is invoked when the DOM is completely ready for use. This also means that all elements are accessible by our scripts, but does not mean that every associated file has been downloaded. As soon as the HTML has been downloaded and parsed into a DOM tree, the code can run.

Style loading and code execution

To ensure that the page has also been styled before the JavaScript code executes, it is a good practice to place `<link rel="stylesheet">` and `<style>` tags prior to `<script>` tags within the document's `<head>` element.

Consider, for example, a page that presents an image gallery; such a page may have many large images on it, which we can hide, show, move, and otherwise manipulate with jQuery. If we set up our interface using the `onload` event, users will have to wait until each and every image is completely downloaded before they can use those features. Even worse, if behaviors are not yet attached to elements that have default behaviors (such as links), user interactions could produce unintended outcomes. However, when we use `$(document).ready()` for the setup, the interface is ready to use earlier with the correct behavior.

What is loaded and what is not?

Using `$(document).ready()` is almost always preferable to using an `onload` handler, but we need to keep in mind that because supporting files may not have loaded, attributes such as image height and width are not necessarily available at this time. If these are needed, we may, at times, also choose to implement an `onload` handler (or more likely, use jQuery to bind a handler to the `load` event); the two mechanisms can coexist peacefully.

Multiple scripts on one page

The traditional mechanism for registering event handlers through JavaScript (rather than adding handler attributes right in HTML) is to assign a function to the DOM element's corresponding attribute. For example, suppose we had defined the function:

```
function doStuff() {
  // Perform a task...
}
```

We could then either assign it within our HTML markup:

```
<body onload="doStuff();">
```

Or, we could assign it from within JavaScript code:

```
window.onload = doStuff;
```

Both of these approaches will cause the function to execute when the page is loaded. The advantage of the second is that the behavior is more cleanly separated from the markup.

Referencing vs. calling functions

Note here, that when we assign a function as a handler, we use the function name but omit the trailing parentheses. With the parentheses, the function is called immediately; without, the name simply identifies, or **references** the function, and can be used to call it later.

With one function, this strategy works quite well. However, suppose we have a second function:

```
function doOtherStuff() {
  // Perform another task...
}
```

We could then attempt to assign this function to run on page load:

```
window.onload = doOtherStuff;
```

However, this assignment trumps the first one. The `.onload` attribute can only store one function reference at a time: so we can't add this to the existing behavior.

The `$(document).ready()` mechanism handles this situation gracefully. Each call to the method adds the new function to an internal queue of behaviors; when the page is loaded all of the functions will execute. The functions will run in the order in which they were registered.

To be fair, jQuery doesn't have a monopoly on workarounds to this issue. We can write a JavaScript function that forms a new function that calls the existing `onload` handler, then calls a passed-in handler. This approach avoids conflicts between rival handlers like `$(document).ready()` does, but lacks some of the other benefits we have discussed. In modern browsers, including Internet Explorer 9, the `DOMContentLoaded` event can be triggered with the W3C standard `document.addEventListener()` method. However, if we need to support older browsers as well, jQuery handles the inconsistencies that these browsers present so that we don't have to.

Shortcuts for code brevity

The $(document).ready() construct is actually calling the .ready() method on a jQuery object we've constructed from the document DOM element. The $() function provides a shortcut for us as this is a common task. When we pass in a function as the argument, jQuery performs an implicit call to .ready(). For the same result as shown in the following code snippet:

```
$(document).ready(function() {
  // Our code here...
});
```

We can also write the following code:

```
$(function() {
  // Our code here...
});
```

While this other syntax is shorter, the longer version makes code more descriptive about what it is doing. For this reason, we will use the longer syntax throughout this book.

Passing an argument to the .ready() callback

In some cases, it may prove useful to use more than one JavaScript library on the same page. As many libraries make use of the $ identifier (as it is short and convenient), we need a way to prevent collisions between these uses.

Fortunately, jQuery provides a method called jQuery.noConflict() to return control of the $ identifier back to other libraries. Typical usage of jQuery.noConflict() is as follows:

```
<script src="prototype.js"></script>
<script src="jquery.js"></script>
<script>
  jQuery.noConflict();
</script>
<script src="myscript.js"></script>
```

First, the other library (Prototype in this example) is included. Then, jQuery itself is included, taking over $ for its own use. Next, a call to .noConflict() frees up $, so that control of it reverts to the first included library (Prototype). Now in our custom script, we can use both libraries—but whenever we want to use a jQuery method, we need to write jQuery instead of $ as an identifier.

The `.ready()` method has one more trick up its sleeve to help us in this situation. The callback function we pass to it can take a single parameter: the jQuery object itself. This allows us to effectively rename it without fear of conflicts, as shown in the following code snippet:

```
jQuery(document).ready(function($) {
  // In here, we can use $ like normal!
});
```

Or, using the shorter syntax we learned in the preceding code:

```
jQuery(function($) {
  // Code that uses $.
});
```

Simple events

There are many other times, apart from the loading of the page, at which we might want to perform a task. Just as JavaScript allows us to intercept the page load event with `<body onload="">` or `window.onload`, it provides similar hooks for user-initiated events such as mouse clicks (`onclick`), form fields being modified (`onchange`), and windows changing size (`onresize`). When assigned directly to elements in the DOM, these hooks have similar drawbacks to the ones we outlined for `onload`. Therefore, jQuery offers an improved way of handling these events as well.

A simple style switcher

To illustrate some event handling techniques, suppose we wish to have a single page rendered in several different styles based on user input. We will allow the user to click buttons to toggle between a normal view, a view in which the text is constrained to a narrow column, and a view with large print for the content area.

Progressive enhancement

In a real-world example, a good web citizen will employ the principle of **progressive enhancement** here. The style switcher should either be hidden when JavaScript is unavailable or, better yet, should still function through links to alternative versions of the page. For the purposes of this tutorial, we'll assume that all users have JavaScript turned on.

The HTML markup for the style switcher is as follows:

```html
<div id="switcher" class="switcher">
  <h3>Style Switcher</h3>
  <button id="switcher-default">
    Default
  </button>
  <button id="switcher-narrow">
    Narrow Column
  </button>
  <button id="switcher-large">
    Large Print
  </button>
</div>
```

Combined with the rest of the page's HTML markup and some basic CSS, we get a page that looks like the following screenshot:

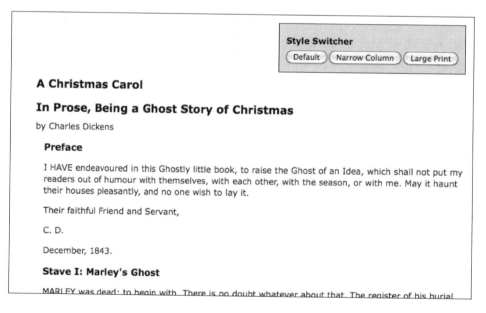

To begin, we'll make the **Large Print** button operate. We need a bit of CSS to implement our alternative view of the page, as shown in the following code snippet:

```css
body.large .chapter {
  font-size: 1.5em;
}
```

Our goal, then, is to apply the `large` class to the `<body>` tag. This will allow the stylesheet to reformat the page appropriately. Using what we learned in *Chapter 2, Selecting Elements*, the following is the statement needed to accomplish this:

```
$('body').addClass('large');
```

However, we want this to occur when the button is clicked, not when the page is loaded as we have seen so far. To do this, we'll introduce the `.bind()` method. This method allows us to specify any DOM event, and to attach a behavior to it. In this case, the event is called `click`, and the behavior is a function consisting of our preceding one-liner:

```
$(document).ready(function() {
  $('#switcher-large').bind('click', function() {
    $('body').addClass('large');
  });
});
```

Listing 3.1

Now when the button gets clicked, our code runs, and the text is enlarged, as shown in the following screenshot:

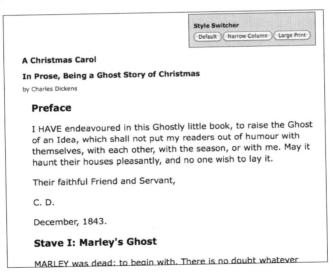

That's all there is to binding a behavior to an event. The advantages we discussed with the .ready() method apply here, as well. Multiple calls to .bind() coexist nicely, appending additional behaviors to the same event as necessary.

This is not necessarily the most elegant or efficient way to accomplish this task. As we proceed through this chapter, we will extend and refine this code into something we can be proud of.

Enabling the other buttons

We now have a **Large Print** button that works as advertised, but we need to apply similar handling to the other two buttons (**Default** and **Narrow Column**) to make them perform their tasks. This is straightforward; we use .bind() to add a click handler to each of them, removing and adding classes as necessary. The new code reads as shown in the following code snippet:

```
$(document).ready(function() {
  $('#switcher-default').bind('click', function() {
    $('body').removeClass('narrow');
    $('body').removeClass('large');
  });
  $('#switcher-narrow').bind('click', function() {
    $('body').addClass('narrow');
    $('body').removeClass('large');
  });
  $('#switcher-large').bind('click', function() {
    $('body').removeClass('narrow');
    $('body').addClass('large');
  });
});
```

Listing 3.2

This is combined with a CSS rule for the narrow class:

```
body.narrow .chapter {
  width: 250px;
}
```

Now, after clicking the **Narrow Column** button, its corresponding CSS is applied and the text gets laid out differently:

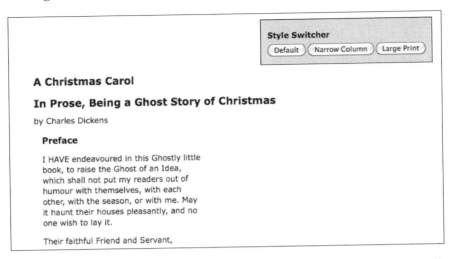

Clicking on **Default** removes both class names from the `<body>` tag, returning the page to its initial rendering.

Event handler context

Our switcher is behaving correctly, but we are not giving the user any feedback about which button is currently active. Our approach for handling this will be to apply the `selected` class to the button when it is clicked, and remove this class from the other buttons. The `selected` class simply makes the button's text bold:

```
.selected {
  font-weight: bold;
}
```

We could accomplish the preceding class modification by referring to each button by ID and applying or removing classes as necessary, but instead we'll explore a more elegant and scalable solution that exploits the **context** in which event handlers run.

When any event handler is triggered, the keyword `this` refers to the DOM element to which the behavior was attached. Earlier we noted that the `$()` function could take a DOM element as its argument; this is one of the key reasons that facility is available. By writing `$(this)` within the event handler, we create a jQuery object corresponding to the element, and can act on it just as if we had located it with a CSS selector.

With this in mind, we can write the following code snippet:

```
$(this).addClass('selected');
```

Placing this line in each of the three handlers will add the class when a button is clicked. To remove the class from the other buttons, we can take advantage of jQuery's implicit iteration feature, and write the following code snippet:

```
$('#switcher button').removeClass('selected');
```

This line removes the class from every button inside the style switcher.

We should also add the class to the **Default** button when the document is ready. So, placing these in the correct order, we have the following code snippet:

```
$(document).ready(function() {
  $('#switcher-default')
  .addClass('selected')
  .bind('click', function() {
    $('body').removeClass('narrow');
    $('body').removeClass('large');
    $('#switcher button').removeClass('selected');
    $(this).addClass('selected');
  });
  $('#switcher-narrow').bind('click', function() {
    $('body').addClass('narrow');
    $('body').removeClass('large');
    $('#switcher button').removeClass('selected');
    $(this).addClass('selected');
  });
  $('#switcher-large').bind('click', function() {
    $('body').removeClass('narrow');
    $('body').addClass('large');
    $('#switcher button').removeClass('selected');
    $(this).addClass('selected');
  });
});
```

Listing 3.3

Now the style switcher gives appropriate feedback.

Generalizing the statements by using the handler context allows us to be yet more efficient. We can factor the highlighting routine out into a separate handler, as shown in Listing 3.4, because it is the same for all three buttons:

```
$(document).ready(function() {
  $('#switcher-default')
  .addClass('selected')
  .bind('click', function() {
    $('body').removeClass('narrow').removeClass('large');
  });
  $('#switcher-narrow').bind('click', function() {
    $('body').addClass('narrow').removeClass('large');
  });
  $('#switcher-large').bind('click', function() {
    $('body').removeClass('narrow').addClass('large');
  });

  $('#switcher button').bind('click', function() {
    $('#switcher button').removeClass('selected');
    $(this).addClass('selected');
  });
});
```

Listing 3.4

This optimization takes advantage of three jQuery features we have discussed. First, **implicit iteration** is, once again, useful when we bind the same `click` handler to each button with a single call to `.bind()`. Second, **behavior queuing** allows us to bind two functions to the same click event, without the second overwriting the first. Lastly, we're using jQuery's **chaining** capabilities to collapse the adding and removing of classes into a single line of code each time.

Further consolidation

The code optimization we've just completed is an example of **refactoring**—modifying existing code to perform the same task in a more efficient or elegant way. To explore further refactoring opportunities, let's look at the behaviors we have bound to each button. The `.removeClass()` method's parameter is optional; when omitted, it removes all classes from the element. We can streamline our code a bit by exploiting this feature, as follows:

```
// work in progress
$(document).ready(function() {
  $('#switcher-default')
```

```
    .addClass('selected')
    .bind('click', function() {
      $('body').removeClass();
    });
    $('#switcher-narrow').bind('click', function() {
      $('body').removeClass().addClass('narrow');
    });
    $('#switcher-large').bind('click', function() {
      $('body').removeClass().addClass('large');
    });

    $('#switcher button').bind('click', function() {
      $('#switcher button').removeClass('selected');
      $(this).addClass('selected');
    });
  });
```

Listing 3.5

Note that the order of operations has changed a bit to accommodate our more general class removal; we need to execute `.removeClass()` first so that it doesn't undo the `.addClass()` we perform in the same breath.

 We can only safely remove all classes because we are in charge of the HTML in this case. When we are writing code for reuse (such as for a plugin), we need to respect any classes that might be present and leave them intact.

Now, we are executing some of the same code in each of the buttons' handlers. This can be easily factored out into our general button `click` handler, as shown in the following code snippet:

```
$(document).ready(function() {
  $('#switcher-default').addClass('selected');

  $('#switcher button').bind('click', function() {
    $('body').removeClass();
    $('#switcher button').removeClass('selected');
    $(this).addClass('selected');
  });

  $('#switcher-narrow').bind('click', function() {
    $('body').addClass('narrow');
  });
```

```
  $('#switcher-large').bind('click', function() {
    $('body').addClass('large');
  });
});
```

Listing 3.6

Note that we need to move the general handler above the specific ones now. The `.removeClass()` needs to happen before the `.addClass()`, and we can count on this because jQuery always triggers event handlers in the order in which they were registered. Finally, we can get rid of the specific handlers entirely by, once again, exploiting **event context**. As the context keyword `this` gives us a DOM element rather than a jQuery object, we can use native DOM properties to determine the ID of the element that was clicked. We can, thus, bind the same handler to all the buttons and within the handler perform different actions for each button, as follows:

```
$(document).ready(function() {
  $('#switcher-default').addClass('selected');

  $('#switcher button').bind('click', function() {
    var bodyClass = this.id.split('-')[1];

    $('body').removeClass().addClass(bodyClass);

    $('#switcher button').removeClass('selected');
    $(this).addClass('selected');
  });
});
```

Listing 3.7

The value of the `bodyClass` variable will be `default`, `narrow`, or `large`, depending on which button is clicked. Here, we are departing somewhat from our previous code in that we are adding a `default` class to the `<body>` when the user clicks `<button id="switcher-default">`. While we do not need this class applied, it isn't causing any harm either, and the reduction of code complexity more than makes up for an unused class name.

Shorthand events

Binding a handler for an event (like a simple `click` event) is such a common task that jQuery provides an even terser way to accomplish it; **shorthand event methods** work in the same way as their `.bind()` counterparts with a few less keystrokes.

For example, our style switcher could be written using `.click()` instead of `.bind()` as shown in the following code snippet:

```
$(document).ready(function() {
  $('#switcher-default').addClass('selected');

  $('#switcher button').click(function() {
    var bodyClass = this.id.split('-')[1];

    $('body').removeClass().addClass(bodyClass);

    $('#switcher button').removeClass('selected');
    $(this).addClass('selected');
  });
});
```

Listing 3.8

Shorthand event methods, such as this, exist for all standard DOM events, as shown in the following list:

- blur
- change
- click
- dblclick
- error
- focus
- keydown
- keypress
- keyup
- load
- mousedown
- mousemove
- mouseout
- mouseover
- mouseup
- resize

- scroll
- select
- submit
- unload

Each shortcut method binds a handler to the event with the corresponding name.

Compound events

Most of jQuery's event-handling methods correspond directly to native DOM events. A handful, however, are custom handlers added for convenience and cross-browser optimization. One of these, the .ready() method, we have discussed in detail already. Others, including .mouseenter(), .mouseleave(), .focusin(), and .focusout(), normalize proprietary Internet Explorer events of the same name. Two custom jQuery handlers, .toggle() and .hover(), are referred to as **compound event handlers** because they intercept combinations of user actions, and respond to them using more than one function.

Showing and hiding advanced features

Suppose that we wanted to be able to hide our style switcher when it is not needed. One convenient way to hide advanced features is to make them collapsible. We will allow one click on the label to hide the buttons, leaving the label alone. Another click on the label will restore the buttons. We need another class to handle the hidden buttons, as follows:

```
.hidden {
  display: none;
}
```

We could implement this feature by storing the current state of the buttons in a variable, and checking its value each time the label is clicked to know whether to add or remove the hidden class on the buttons. We could also directly check for the presence of the class on a button, and use this information to decide what to do. Instead, jQuery provides the .toggle() method, which performs this housekeeping task for us.

Toggle effect

There are in fact two `.toggle()` methods defined by jQuery. For information on the effect method of this name (which is distinguished by different argument types), see: `http://api.jquery.com/toggle/`

The `.toggle()` event method takes two or more arguments, each of which is a function. The first click on the element causes the first function to execute; the second click triggers the second function, and so forth. Once each function has been invoked, the cycle begins again from the first function. With `.toggle()`, we can implement our collapsible style switcher quite easily:

```
$(document).ready(function() {
  $('#switcher h3').toggle(function() {
    $('#switcher button').addClass('hidden');
  }, function() {
    $('#switcher button').removeClass('hidden');
  });
});
```

Listing 3.9

After the first click, the buttons are all hidden:

And a second click returns them to visibility:

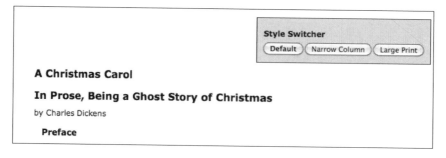

Once again, we rely on implicit iteration; this time, to hide all the buttons in one fell swoop without requiring an enclosing element.

For this specific case, jQuery provides another mechanism for the collapsing we are performing. We can use the `.toggleClass()` method to automatically check for the presence of the class before applying or removing it:

```
$(document).ready(function() {
  $('#switcher h3').click(function() {
    $('#switcher button').toggleClass('hidden');
  });
});
```

Listing 3.10

In this case, `.toggleClass()` is probably the more elegant solution, but `.toggle()` is, in general, a versatile way to perform two or more different actions in alternation.

Highlighting clickable items

In illustrating the ability of the `click` event to operate on normally non-clickable page elements, we have crafted an interface that gives few hints that the style switcher label—actually just an `<h3>` element—is actually a live part of the page, awaiting user interaction. To remedy this, we can give it a rollover state, making it clear that it interacts in some way with the mouse:

```
.hover {
  cursor: pointer;
  background-color: #afa;
}
```

The CSS specification includes a pseudo-class called `:hover`, which allows a stylesheet to affect an element's appearance when the user's mouse cursor hovers over it. In Internet Explorer 6, this capability is restricted to link elements, so we can't use it for other items when we need to support this legacy browser. More importantly, in keeping with **progressive enhancement**, we only want to style the `<h3>` as clickable if we have made it clickable with our jQuery code. Fortunately, jQuery's `.hover()` method allows us to use JavaScript to change an element's styling—and indeed, perform any arbitrary action—both when the mouse cursor enters the element and when it leaves the element.

The `.hover()` method takes two function arguments, just as in our preceding `.toggle()` example. In this case, the first function will be executed when the mouse cursor enters the selected element, and the second is fired when the cursor leaves. We can modify the classes applied to the buttons at these times to achieve a rollover effect, as follows:

```
$(document).ready(function() {
  $('#switcher h3').hover(function() {
    $(this).addClass('hover');
  }, function() {
    $(this).removeClass('hover');
  });
});
```

Listing 3.11

We once again use implicit iteration and event context for short, simple code. Now when hovering over the `<h3>`, we see our class applied in the following screenshot:

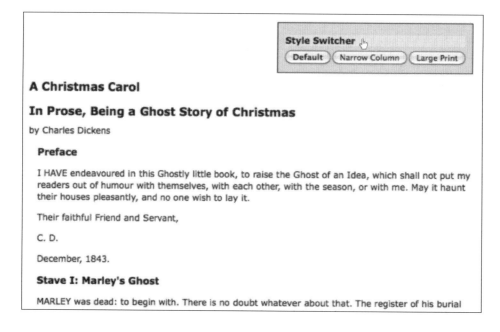

The use of `.hover()` also means we avoid headaches caused by **event propagation** in JavaScript. To understand this, we need to take a look at how JavaScript decides which element gets to handle a given event.

The journey of an event

When an event occurs on a page, an entire hierarchy of DOM elements gets a chance to handle the event. Consider a page model similar to the following screenshot:

```
<div class="foo">
  <span class="bar">
    <a href="http://www.example.com/">
      The quick brown fox jumps over the lazy dog.
    </a>
  </span>
  <p>
    How razorback-jumping frogs can level six piqued gymnasts!
  </p>
</div>
```

We then visualize the code as a set of nested elements, as shown in the following figure:

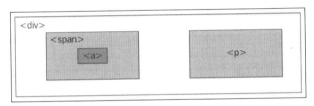

For any event, there are multiple elements that could logically be responsible for reacting. When the link on this page is clicked, for example, the `<div>`, `<span>`, and `<a>` all should get the opportunity to respond to the click. After all, the three are all under the user's mouse cursor at the time. The `<p>` element, on the other hand, is not part of this interaction at all.

One strategy for allowing multiple elements to respond to a user interaction is called **event capturing**. With event capturing, the event is first given to the most all-encompassing element, and then to successively more specific ones. In our example, this means that first the `<div>` gets passed the event, then the `<span>`, and finally, the `<a>`, as illustrated in the following diagram:

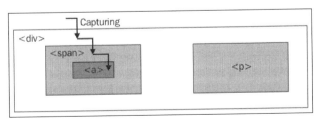

Technically, in browser implementations of event capturing, specific elements are registered to listen for events that occur among their descendants. The approximation provided here is close enough for our needs.

The opposite strategy is called **event bubbling**. The event gets sent to the most specific element, and after this element has an opportunity to react, the event **bubbles up** to more general elements. In our example, the `<a>` would be handed the event first, and then the `<span>` and `<div>` in that order, as illustrated in the following diagram:

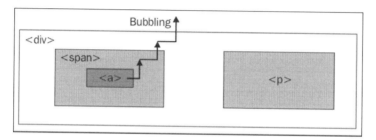

Unsurprisingly, different browser developers originally decided on different models for event propagation. The DOM standard that eventually developed thus specified that both strategies should be used: first the event is **captured** from general elements to specific ones, and then the event **bubbles** back up to the top of the DOM tree. Event handlers can be registered for either part of the process.

Not all browsers have been updated to match this new standard, and in those that support capturing it typically must be specifically enabled. To provide cross-browser consistency, therefore, jQuery always registers event handlers for the bubbling phase of the model. We can always assume that the most specific element will get the first opportunity to respond to any event.

Side effects of event bubbling

Event bubbling can cause unexpected behavior, especially when the wrong element responds to a `mouseover` or `mouseout`. Consider a `mouseout` event handler attached to the `<div>` in our example. When the user's mouse cursor exits the `<div>`, the `mouseout` handler is run as anticipated. As this is at the top of the hierarchy, no other elements get the event. On the other hand, when the cursor exits the `<a>` element, a `mouseout` event is sent to that. This event will then bubble up to the `<span>` and then to the `<div>`, firing the same event handler. This bubbling sequence is likely not desired.

The `mouseenter` and `mouseleave` events, either bound individually or combined in the `.hover()` method, are aware of these bubbling issues, and when we use them to attach events, we can ignore the problems caused by the wrong element getting a `mouseover` or `mouseout` event.

The `mouseout` scenario illustrates the need to constrain the scope of an event. While `.hover()` handles this specific case, we will encounter other situations in which we need to limit an event spatially (preventing the event from being sent to certain elements) or temporally (preventing the event from being sent at certain times).

Altering the journey: the event object

We have already seen one situation in which **event bubbling** can cause problems. To show a case in which `.hover()` does not help our cause, we'll alter the collapsing behavior we implemented earlier.

Suppose we wish to expand the clickable area that triggers the collapsing or expanding of the style switcher. One way to do this is to move the event handler from the label, `<h3>`, to its containing `<div>` element:

```
// Unfinished code
$(document).ready(function() {
  $('#switcher').click(function() {
    $('#switcher button').toggleClass('hidden');
  });
});
```

Listing 3.12

This alteration makes the entire area of the style switcher clickable to toggle its visibility. The downside is that clicking on a button also collapses the style switcher after the style on the content has been altered. This is due to event bubbling; the event is first handled by the buttons, then passed up through the DOM tree until it reaches the `<div id="switcher">`, where our new handler is activated and hides the buttons.

To solve this problem, we need access to the **event object**. This is a DOM construct that is passed to each element's event handler when it is invoked. It provides information about the event, such as where the mouse cursor was at the time of the event. It also provides some methods that can be used to affect the progress of the event through the DOM.

Event object reference

For detailed information about jQuery's implementation of the event object and its properties, see `http://api.jquery.com/category/events/event-object/`

To use the event object in our handlers, we only need to add a parameter to the function, as follows:

```
$(document).ready(function() {
  $('#switcher').click(function(event) {
    $('#switcher button').toggleClass('hidden');
  });
});
```

Note that we have named this parameter `event` because it is descriptive, not because we need to. Naming it `flapjacks` or anything else for that matter would work just as well.

Event targets

Now we have the event object available to us as the variable `event` within our handler. The property `event.target` can be helpful in controlling where an event takes effect. This property is a part of the DOM API, but is not implemented in all browsers; jQuery extends the event object as necessary to provide the property in every browser. With `.target`, we can determine which element in the DOM was the first to receive the event—that is, in the case of a `click` event, the actual item clicked on. Remembering that `this` gives us the DOM element handling the event, we can write the following code:

```
// Unfinished code
$(document).ready(function() {
  $('#switcher').click(function(event) {
    if (event.target == this) {
      $('#switcher button').toggleClass('hidden');
    }
  });
});
```

Listing 3.13

This code ensures that the item clicked on was `<div id="switcher">`, not one of its sub-elements. Now clicking on buttons will not collapse the style switcher, and clicking on the switcher's background will. However, clicking on the label, `<h3>`, now does nothing, because it too is a sub-element. Instead of placing this check here, we can modify the behavior of the buttons to achieve our goals.

Stopping event propagation

The event object provides the `.stopPropagation()` method, which can halt the bubbling process completely for the event. Like `.target`, this method is a plain JavaScript feature, but cannot be safely used across all browsers. As long as we register all of our event handlers using jQuery, though, we can use it with impunity.

We'll remove the `event.target == this` check we just added, and instead add some code in our buttons' `click` handlers, as shown in the following code snippet:

```
$(document).ready(function() {
  $('#switcher').click(function(event) {
    $('#switcher button').toggleClass('hidden');
  });
});

$(document).ready(function() {
  $('#switcher-default').addClass('selected');

  $('#switcher button').click(function(event) {
    var bodyClass = this.id.split('-')[1];

    $('body').removeClass().addClass(bodyClass);

    $('#switcher button').removeClass('selected');
    $(this).addClass('selected');
    event.stopPropagation();
  });
});
```

Listing 3.14

As before, we need to add a parameter to the function we're using as the `click` handler, so we have access to the event object. Then we simply call `event.stopPropagation()` to prevent any other DOM element from responding to the event. Now our click is handled by the buttons, and only the buttons; clicks anywhere else on the style switcher will collapse or expand it.

Default actions

Were our `click` event handler registered on a link element (`<a>`) rather than a generic `<button>` outside of a form, we would face another problem. When a user clicks on a link, the browser loads a new page. This behavior is not an **event handler** in the same sense as the ones we have been discussing; instead, this is the **default action** for a click on a link element. Similarly, when the *Enter* key is pressed while the user is editing a form, the `submit` event is triggered on the form, but then the form submission actually occurs after this.

If these default actions are undesired, then calling `.stopPropagation()` on the event will not help. These actions occur nowhere in the normal flow of event propagation. Instead, the `.preventDefault()` method will serve to stop the event in its tracks before the default action is triggered.

> Calling `.preventDefault()` is often useful after we have done some tests on the environment of the event. For example, during a form submission we might wish to check that required fields are filled in, and prevent the default action only if they are not.

Event propagation and default actions are independent mechanisms; either can be stopped while the other still occurs. If we wish to halt both, then we can return `false` at the end of our event handler, which is a shortcut for calling both `.stopPropagation()` and `.preventDefault()` on the event.

Event delegation

Event bubbling isn't always a hindrance; we can often use it to great benefit. One great technique that exploits bubbling is called **event delegation**. With it, we can use an event handler on a single element to do the work of many.

In our example, there are just three `<button>` elements that have attached `click` handlers. However, what if there were many? This is more common than one might think. Consider, for example, a large table of information in which each row has an interactive item requiring a `click` handler. Implicit iteration makes assigning all of these `click` handlers easy, but performance can suffer because of the looping being done internally to jQuery, and because of the memory footprint of maintaining all the handlers.

Instead, we can assign a single `click` handler to an ancestor element in the DOM. An uninterrupted `click` event will eventually reach the ancestor due to event bubbling, and we can do our work there.

As an example, let's apply this technique to our style switcher (even though the number of items does not demand the approach). As seen in the preceding Listing 3.13, we can use the `event.target` property to check what element is under the mouse cursor when the click occurs:

```
$(document).ready(function() {
    $('#switcher').click(function(event) {
        if ($(event.target).is('button')) {
            var bodyClass = event.target.id.split('-')[1];

            $('body').removeClass().addClass(bodyClass);

            $('#switcher button').removeClass('selected');
            $(event.target).addClass('selected');
            event.stopPropagation();
        }
    });
});
```

Listing 3.15

We've used a new method here, called `.is()`. This method accepts the selector expressions we investigated in the previous chapter, and tests the current jQuery object against the selector. If at least one element in the set is matched by the selector, then `.is()` returns `true`. In this case, `$(event.target).is('button')` asks whether the element clicked is a `<button>`. If so, then we proceed with the code from before, with one significant alteration: the keyword `this` now refers to `<div id="switcher">`, so every time we are interested in the clicked button we must now refer to it with `event.target`.

.is() and .hasClass()

We can test for the presence of a class on an element with `.hasClass()`. The `.is()` method is more flexible, however, and can test any selector expression.

We have an unintentional side-effect from this code, however. When a button is clicked now, the switcher collapses, as it did before we added the call to `.stopPropagation()`. The handler for the switcher visibility toggle is now bound to the same element as the handler for the buttons, so halting the event bubbling does not stop the toggle from being triggered. To sidestep this issue, we can remove the `.stopPropagation()` call and instead add another `.is()` test.

Furthermore, as we're making the entire switcher `<div>` clickable, we ought to toggle the class while the user's mouse is over any part of it, as shown in the following code snippet:

```
$(document).ready(function() {
  $('#switcher').hover(function() {
    $(this).addClass('hover');
  }, function() {
    $(this).removeClass('hover');
  });
});

$(document).ready(function() {
  $('#switcher').click(function(event) {
    if (!$(event.target).is('button')) {
      $('#switcher button').toggleClass('hidden');
    }
  });
});

$(document).ready(function() {
  $('#switcher-default').addClass('selected');

  $('#switcher').click(function(event) {
    if ($(event.target).is('button')) {
      var bodyClass = event.target.id.split('-')[1];

      $('body').removeClass().addClass(bodyClass);

      $('#switcher button').removeClass('selected');
      $(event.target).addClass('selected');
    }
  });
});
```

Listing 3.16

This example is a bit overcomplicated for its size, but as the number of elements with event handlers increases, so does event delegation's benefit. Additionally, we can avoid some of the code repetition by combining the two `click` handlers and using a single if-else statement for the `.is()` test, as follows:

```
$(document).ready(function() {
  $('#switcher-default').addClass('selected');
```

```
$('#switcher').click(function(event) {
  if ($(event.target).is('button')) {
    var bodyClass = event.target.id.split('-')[1];

    $('body').removeClass().addClass(bodyClass);

    $('#switcher button').removeClass('selected');
    $(event.target).addClass('selected');
  } else {
    $('#switcher button').toggleClass('hidden');
  }
});
});
```

Listing 3.17

While our code could still use some fine tuning, it is approaching a state at which we can feel comfortable using it for what we set out to do. Nevertheless, for the sake of learning more about jQuery's event handling, we'll back up to Listing 3.16 and continue to modify that version of the code.

 Event delegation is also useful in other situations we'll see later, such as when new elements are added by **DOM manipulation** methods (*Chapter 5, Manipulating the DOM*) or **Ajax** routines (*Chapter 6, Sending Data with Ajax*).

Methods for event delegation

As event delegation can be helpful in so many situations, jQuery includes a set of methods specifically for using this technique. We'll fully examine these methods—.live(), .die(), .delegate(), and .undelegate()—in *Chapter 10, Advanced Events*. It's worth mentioning now, however, that .live() can be used as a drop-in replacement for .bind() while providing much of the benefit of event delegation. For example, to bind a live click handler to the style-switcher buttons, we can write the following code snippet:

```
$('#switcher button').live('click', function() {
  var bodyClass = event.target.id.split('-')[1];

  $('body').removeClass().addClass(bodyClass);

  $('#switcher button').removeClass('selected');
  $(this).addClass('selected');
});
```

Behind the scenes, jQuery actually binds the `click` handler to the `document` object and uses `event.target` to check if it (or any of its ancestors) matches the selector expression, in this case, `'#switcher button'`. If it does, then jQuery maps the `this` keyword to the matched element. So, while it doesn't provide the potential benefit of avoiding the selection of many elements, it does avoid binding to all of them. Furthermore, because the `document` object itself is available, even when the script is referenced in the `<head>`, `.live()` events can always be bound outside of `$(document).ready()`.

Removing an event handler

There are times when we will be done with an event handler we previously registered. Perhaps the state of the page has changed such that the action no longer makes sense. It is typically possible to handle this situation with conditional statements inside our event handlers, but it may be more elegant to **unbind** the handler entirely.

Suppose that we want our collapsible style switcher to remain expanded whenever the page is not using the normal style. While the **Narrow Column** or **Large Print** button is selected, clicking the background of the style switcher should do nothing. We can accomplish this by calling the `.unbind()` method to remove the collapsing handler when one of the non-default style switcher buttons is clicked:

```
$(document).ready(function() {
  $('#switcher').click(function(event) {
    if (!$(event.target).is('button')) {
      $('#switcher button').toggleClass('hidden');
    }
  });

  $('#switcher-narrow, #switcher-large').click(function() {
    $('#switcher').unbind('click');
  });
});
```

Listing 3.18

Now when a button such as **Narrow Column** is clicked, the click handler on the style switcher `<div>` is removed, and clicking the background of the box no longer collapses it. However, the buttons don't work anymore! They are affected by the `click` event of the style switcher `<div>` as well, because we rewrote the button-handling code to use event delegation. This means that when we call `$('#switcher').unbind('click')`, both behaviors are removed.

Event namespacing

We need to make our `.unbind()` call more specific, so that it does not remove both of the click handlers we have registered. One way of doing this is to use **event namespacing**. We can introduce additional information when an event is bound that allows us to identify that particular handler later. To use namespacing, we need to return to the non-shorthand method of binding event handlers, the `.bind()` method itself.

The first parameter we pass to `.bind()` is the name of the event we want to watch for. We can use a special syntax here, though, that allows us to subcategorize the event, as shown in the following code snippet:

```
$(document).ready(function() {
  $('#switcher').bind('click.collapse', function(event) {
    if (!$(event.target).is('button')) {
      $('#switcher button').toggleClass('hidden');
    }
  });

  $('#switcher-narrow, #switcher-large').click(function() {
    $('#switcher').unbind('click.collapse');
  });
});
```

Listing 3.19

The `.collapse` suffix is invisible to the event handling system; `click` events are handled by this function, just as if we wrote `.bind('click')`. However, the addition of the namespace means that we can unbind just this handler, without affecting the separate `click` handler we wrote for the buttons.

> There are other ways of making our `.unbind()` call more specific, as we will see in a moment. However, event namespacing is a useful tool in our arsenal. It is especially handy in the creation of plugins, as we'll see in later chapters.

Rebinding events

Now clicking the **Narrow Column** or **Large Print** button causes the style switcher collapsing functionality to be disabled. However, we want the behavior to return when the **Default** button is pressed. To do this, we will need to **rebind** the handler whenever **Default** is clicked.

First, we should give our handler function a name so that we can use it more than once without repeating ourselves:

```
$(document).ready(function() {
  var toggleSwitcher = function(event) {
    if (!$(event.target).is('button')) {
      $('#switcher button').toggleClass('hidden');
    }
  };

  $('#switcher').bind('click.collapse', toggleSwitcher);
});
```

Listing 3.20

Note here, that we are using a new syntax for defining a function. Rather than use a **function declaration** (defining the function by leading with the `function` keyword and naming it), we use an **anonymous function expression**, assigning a no-name function to a **local variable**. Aside from a couple of subtle differences that don't apply in this case, the two syntaxes are functionally equivalent. Here, our use of the function expression is a stylistic choice to make our event handlers and other function definitions resemble each other more closely.

Also, recall that `.bind()` takes a **function reference** as its second argument. It is important to remember when using a named function here to omit parentheses after the function name; parentheses would cause the function to be called, rather than referenced.

Now that the function can be referenced, we can bind it again later without repeating the function definition, as shown in the following code snippet:

```
// Unfinished code
$(document).ready(function() {
  var toggleSwitcher = function(event) {
    if (!$(event.target).is('button')) {
      $('#switcher button').toggleClass('hidden');
    }
  };

  $('#switcher').bind('click.collapse', toggleSwitcher);

  $('#switcher-narrow, #switcher-large').click(function() {
    $('#switcher').unbind('click.collapse');
  });
});
```

```
$('#switcher-default').click(function() {
  $('#switcher')
    .bind('click.collapse', toggleSwitcher);
});
});
```

Listing 3.21

Now the toggle behavior is bound when the document is loaded, unbound when **Narrow Column** or **Large Print** is clicked, and rebound when **Normal** is clicked after that.

As we have named the function, we no longer need to use namespacing. The .unbind() method can take a function as a second argument; in this case, it unbinds only that specific handler. However, we have run into another problem. Remember that when a handler is bound to an event in jQuery, previous handlers remain in effect. In this case, each time **Normal** is clicked, another copy of the toggleSwitcher handler is bound to the style switcher. In other words, the function is called an extra time for each additional click until the user clicks **Narrow** or **Large Print**, which unbinds all of toggleSwitcher handlers at once.

When an even number of toggleSwitcher handlers are bound, clicks on the style switcher (but not on a button), appear to have no effect. In fact, the hidden class is being toggled multiple times, ending up in the same state it was when it began. To remedy this problem, we can unbind the handler when a user clicks on any button, and rebind only after ensuring that the clicked button's ID is switcher-default.

```
$(document).ready(function() {
  var toggleSwitcher = function(event) {
    if (!$(event.target).is('button')) {
      $('#switcher button').toggleClass('hidden');
    }
  };

  $('#switcher').bind('click', toggleSwitcher);

  $('#switcher button').click(function() {
    $('#switcher').unbind('click', toggleSwitcher);

    if (this.id == 'switcher-default') {
      $('#switcher').bind('click', toggleSwitcher);
    }
  });
});
```

Listing 3.22

A shortcut is also available for the situation in which we want to unbind an event handler immediately after the first time it is triggered. This shortcut, called .one(), is used as follows:

```
$('#switcher').one('click', toggleSwitcher);
```

This would cause the toggle action to occur only once.

Simulating user interaction

At times, it is convenient to execute code that we have bound to an event, even if the normal circumstances of the event are not occurring. For example, suppose we wanted our style switcher to begin in its collapsed state. We could accomplish this by hiding buttons from within the stylesheet, or by adding our hidden class or calling the .hide() method from a $(document).ready() handler. Another way would be to simulate a click on the style switcher so that the toggling mechanism we've already established is triggered.

The .trigger() method allows us to do just this:

```
$(document).ready(function() {
  $('#switcher').trigger('click');
});
```

Listing 3.23

Now when the page loads, the switcher is collapsed, just as if it had been clicked, as shown in the following screenshot:

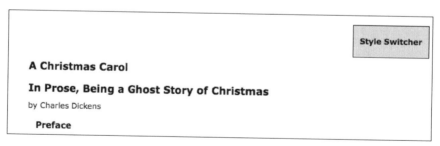

If we were hiding content that we wanted people without JavaScript enabled to see, then this would be a reasonable way to implement **graceful degradation**.

The `.trigger()` method provides the same set of shortcuts that `.bind()` does. When these shortcuts are used with no arguments, the behavior is to trigger the action rather than bind it, as follows:

```
$(document).ready(function() {
  $('#switcher').click();
});
```

Listing 3.24

Keyboard events

As another example, we can add keyboard shortcuts to our style switcher. When the user types the first letter of one of the display styles, we will have the page behave as if the corresponding button were clicked. To implement this feature, we will need to explore **keyboard events**, which behave a bit differently from **mouse events**.

There are two types of keyboard events: those that react to the keyboard directly (`keyup` and `keydown`) and those that react to text input (`keypress`). A single character entry event could correspond to several keys: for example, the *Shift* key in combination with the *X* key creates the capital letter **X**. While the specifics of implementation differ from one browser to the next (unsurprisingly), a safe rule of thumb is as follows: if you want to know what key the user pushed, then you should observe the `keyup` or `keydown` event; if you want to know what character ended up on the screen as a result, then you should observe the `keypress` event. For this feature, we just want to know when the user presses the *D*, *N*, or *L* key, so we will use `keyup`.

Next, we need to determine which element should watch for the event. This is a little less obvious than with mouse events, where we have an obvious mouse cursor to tell us about the event's target. Instead, the target of a keyboard event is the element that currently has the **keyboard focus**. The element with focus can be changed in several ways, including mouse clicks and presses of the *Tab* key. Not every element can get the focus either; only items that have default keyboard-driven behaviors such as form fields, links, and elements with a `.tabIndex` property are candidates.

In this case, we don't really care what element has the focus; we want our switcher to work whenever the user presses one of the keys. Event bubbling will once again come in handy, as we can bind our `keyup` event to the `document` element and have assurance that eventually any key event will bubble up to us.

Finally, we will need to know which key was pressed when our `keyup` handler gets triggered. We can inspect the `event` object for this. The `.keyCode` property of the event contains an identifier for the key that was pressed, and for alphabetic keys, this identifier is the ASCII value of the uppercase letter. So we can create a **map**, or **object literal**, of letters and their corresponding buttons to click. When the user presses a key, we'll see if its identifier is in the map, and if so, trigger the click, as follows:

```
$(document).ready(function() {
  var triggers = {
    D: 'default',
    N: 'narrow',
    L: 'large'
  };

  $(document).keyup(function(event) {
    var key = String.fromCharCode(event.keyCode);
    if (key in triggers) {
      $('#switcher-' + triggers[key]).click();
    }
  });
});
```

Listing 3.25

Presses of these three keys now simulate mouse clicks on the buttons—provided that the key event is not interrupted by features such as Firefox's "search for text when I start typing."

As an alternative to using `.trigger()` to simulate this click, let's explore how to factor out code into a function so that more than one handler can call it—in this case, both `click` and `keyup`. While not necessary in this case, this technique can be useful in eliminating code redundancy:

```
$(document).ready(function() {
  // Enable hover effect on the style switcher
  $('#switcher').hover(function() {
    $(this).addClass('hover');
  }, function() {
    $(this).removeClass('hover');
  });

  // Allow the style switcher to expand and collapse
  var toggleSwitcher = function(event) {
```

```
    if (!$(event.target).is('button')) {
      $('#switcher button').toggleClass('hidden');
    }
};
$('#switcher').bind('click', toggleSwitcher);

// Simulate a click so we start in a collapsed state
$('#switcher').click();

// The setBodyClass() function changes the page style
// The style switcher state is also updated
var setBodyClass = function(className) {
  $('body').removeClass().addClass(className);

  $('#switcher button').removeClass('selected');
  $('#switcher-' + className).addClass('selected');

  $('#switcher').unbind('click', toggleSwitcher);

  if (className == 'default') {
    $('#switcher').bind('click', toggleSwitcher);
  }
};

// Begin with the switcher-default button "selected"
$('#switcher-default').addClass('selected');

// Map key codes to their corresponding buttons to click
var triggers = {
  D: 'default',
  N: 'narrow',
  L: 'large'
};

// Call setBodyClass() when a button is clicked
$('#switcher').click(function(event) {
  if ($(event.target).is('button')) {
    var bodyClass = event.target.id.split('-')[1];
    setBodyClass(bodyClass);
  }
});

// Call setBodyClass() when a key is pressed
```

```
$(document).keyup(function(event) {
  var key = String.fromCharCode(event.keyCode);
  if (key in triggers) {
    setBodyClass(triggers[key]);
  }
});
});
```

Listing 3.26

Summary

The abilities we've discussed in this chapter allow us to:

- Use the .ready() method to let multiple JavaScript libraries coexist on a single page with .noConflict()

- React to a user's click on a page element with **mouse event handlers** and the .bind() and .click() methods

- Observe **event context** to perform different actions depending on the element clicked, even when the handler is bound to several elements

- Alternately expand and collapse a page element by using .toggle()

- Highlight elements under the mouse cursor by using .hover()

- Influence **event propagation** and **default actions** to determine which elements get to respond to an event by using .stopPropagation() and .preventDefault()

- Implement **event delegation** to reduce the number of bound event handlers necessary on a page

- Call .unbind() to remove an event handler we're finished with

- Segregate related event handlers with **event namespacing** so they can be acted on as a group

- Cause bound event handlers to execute with .trigger()

- Use **keyboard event handlers** to react to a user's key press with .keyup()

We can use these capabilities to build quite interactive pages. In the next chapter, we'll learn how to provide visual feedback to the user during these interactions.

Further reading

The topic of event handling will be explored in more detail in *Chapter 10*. A complete list of jQuery's event methods is available in *Appendix C* of this book, in *jQuery Reference Guide,* or in the official jQuery documentation at `http://api.jquery.com/`.

Exercises

To complete these exercises, you will need the `index.html` file for this chapter, as well as the finished JavaScript code as found in `complete.js`. These files can be downloaded from the Packt Publishing website at `http://www.packtpub.com/support`.

Challenge exercises may require use of the official jQuery documentation at `http://api.jquery.com/`.

1. When **Charles Dickens** is clicked, apply the `selected` style to it.

2. When a chapter title (`<h3 class="chapter-title">`) is double-clicked, toggle the visibility of the chapter text.

3. When the user presses the right arrow key, cycle to the next body class. The key code for the right arrow key is `39`.

4. **Challenge**: Use the `console.log()` function to log the coordinates of the mouse as it moves across any paragraph. (Note: `console.log()` displays its results via the Firebug extension for Firefox, Safari's Web Inspector, or the Developer Tools in Chrome).

5. **Challenge**: Use `.mousedown()` and `.mouseup()` to track mouse events anywhere on the page. If the mouse button is released above where it was pressed, then add the `hidden` class to all paragraphs. If it is released below where it was pressed, then remove the `hidden` class from all paragraphs.

4
Styling and Animating

If actions speak louder than words, then in the JavaScript world, effects make actions speak louder still. With jQuery, we can easily add impact to our actions through a set of simple visual **effects**, and even craft our own, more sophisticated **animations**.

The effects offered by jQuery supply simple visual flourishes that grant a sense of movement and modernity to any page. However, apart from being mere decoration, they can also provide important usability enhancements that help orient the user when there is some change on a page (especially common in Ajax applications). In this chapter, we will explore a number of these effects and combine them in interesting ways.

Inline CSS modification

Before we jump into the nifty jQuery effects, a quick look at CSS is in order. In earlier chapters, we have been modifying a document's appearance by defining styles for classes in a separate stylesheet and then adding or removing those classes with jQuery. Typically, this is the preferred process for injecting CSS into HTML because it respects the stylesheet's role in dealing with the presentation of a page. However, there may be times when we need to apply styles that haven't been, or can't easily be, defined in a stylesheet. Fortunately, jQuery offers the `.css()` method for such occasions.

This method acts as both a **getter** and a **setter**. To get the value of a style property, we simply pass the name of the property as a string, like `.css('backgroundColor')`. Multi-word properties such as this one can be interpreted by jQuery when in hyphenated CSS notation (`background-color`), or camel-cased DOM notation (`backgroundColor`). For setting-style properties, the `.css()` method comes in two flavors—one that takes a single style property and its value, and one that takes a **map** of property-value pairs, as shown in the following code snippet:

```
// Single property and its value
.css('property', 'value')
```

```
// Map of property-value pairs
.css({
  property1: 'value1',
  'property-2': 'value2'
})
```

Experienced JavaScript developers will recognize these jQuery maps as JavaScript **object literals**.

> **Object literal notation**
>
> In a property value, strings are enclosed in quotes as usual, but other data types such as numbers do not require them. Since property names are strings, they typically would be contained in quotes. However, quotation marks are not required for property names if they are valid JavaScript identifiers, such as when they are written in camel-cased DOM notation.

We use the `.css()` method the same way we've been using `.addClass()`: we apply it to a jQuery object, which in turn points to a collection of DOM elements. To demonstrate this, we'll play with a style switcher similar to the one from *Chapter 3, Handling Events*:

```html
<div id="switcher">
  <div class="label">Text Size</div>
  <button id="switcher-default">Default</button>
  <button id="switcher-large">Bigger</button>
  <button id="switcher-small">Smaller</button>
</div>
<div class="speech">
  <p>Fourscore and seven years ago our fathers brought forth
    on this continent a new nation, conceived in liberty,
    and dedicated to the proposition that all men are created
    equal.
  </p>
</div>
```

By linking to a stylesheet with a few basic style rules, the page will initially look like the following screenshot:

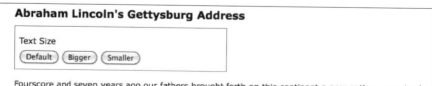

Once we're done with our code, clicking on the **Bigger** and **Smaller** buttons will increase or decrease , respectively, the text size of `<div class="speech">`, while clicking on the **Default** button will reset `<div class="speech">` to its original text size.

If all we wanted were to change the font size a single time to a predetermined value, then we could still use the `.addClass()` method. However, let's suppose that now we want the text to continue increasing or decreasing incrementally each time the respective button is clicked. Although it might be possible to define a separate class for each click and iterate through them, a more straightforward approach would be to compute the new text size each time by getting the current size and increasing it by a set factor (for example, 40%).

Our code will start with the `$(document).ready()` and `$('#switcher-large').click()` event handlers, as follows:

```
$(document).ready(function() {
  $('#switcher-large').click(function() {
  });
});
```

Listing 4.1

Next, the font size can be easily discovered by using the `.css()` method: `$('div.speech').css('fontSize')`. However, the returned value is a string, containing both the numeric font size value and the units of that value (px). We'll need to strip the unit label off in order to perform calculations with the numeric value. Also, when we plan to use a jQuery object more than once, it's generally a good idea to **cache** the selector by storing the resulting jQuery object in a variable. We'll take care of these needs with the introduction of a couple of local variables:

```
$(document).ready(function() {
  var $speech = $('div.speech');
  $('#switcher-large').click(function() {
    var num = parseFloat($speech.css('fontSize'));
  });
});
```

Listing 4.2

The first line inside `$(document).ready()` now creates a variable containing a jQuery object pointing to `<div class="speech">`. Notice the use of a $ in the variable name, $speech. As $ is a legal character in JavaScript identifiers, we can use it as a reminder that the variable is storing a jQuery object.

Inside the `.click()` handler, we use `parseFloat()` to get the font size property's numeric value only. The `parseFloat()` function looks at a string from left to right until it encounters a non-numeric character. The string of digits is converted into a floating-point (decimal) number. For example, it would convert the string `'12'` to the number `12`. In addition, it strips non-numeric trailing characters from the string, so `'12px'` becomes `12` as well. If the string begins with a non-numeric character, `parseFloat()` returns `NaN`, which stands for **Not a Number**.

All that's left to do is to modify the parsed numeric value and to reset the font size based on the new value. For our example, we'll increase the font size by 40% each time the button is clicked. To achieve this, we'll multiply `num` by `1.4` and then set the font size by concatenating `num` and `'px'`, as shown in the following code snippet:

```
$(document).ready(function() {
  var $speech = $('div.speech');
  $('#switcher-large').click(function() {
    var num = parseFloat($speech.css('fontSize'));
    num *= 1.4;
    $speech.css('fontSize', num + 'px');
  });
});
```

Listing 4.3

Shorthand operators

The equation `num *= 1.4` is shorthand for `num = num * 1.4`. We can use the same type of shorthand for the other basic mathematical operations, as well: addition (a += b), subtraction (a -= b), division (a /= b), and modulus/remainder (a %= b).

Now when a user clicks on the **Bigger** button, the text becomes larger. Another click and the text becomes even larger, as shown in the following screenshot:

Abraham Lincoln's Gettysburg Address

Text Size

Fourscore and seven years ago our fathers brought forth on this continent a new nation, conceived in liberty, and dedicated to the proposition that all men are created equal.

To get the **Smaller** button to decrease the font size, we will divide rather than multiply—num /= 1.4. Better still, we'll combine the two into a single .click() handler on all <button> elements within <div id="switcher">. Then, after finding the numeric value, we can either multiply or divide depending on the ID of the button that was clicked. The following code snippet, Listing 4.4, illustrates this:

```
$(document).ready(function() {
  var $speech = $('div.speech');
  $('#switcher button').click(function() {
    var num = parseFloat($speech.css('fontSize'));
    if (this.id == 'switcher-large') {
      num *= 1.4;
    } else if (this.id == 'switcher-small') {
      num /= 1.4;
    }
    $speech.css('fontSize', num + 'px');
  });
});
```

Listing 4.4

Recall from *Chapter 3* that we can access the id property of the DOM element referred to by this, which appears here inside the if and else if statements. Here, it is more efficient to use this than to create a jQuery object just to test the value of a property.

It would also be nice to have a way to return the font size to its initial value. To allow the user to do so, we can simply store the font size in a variable immediately when the DOM is ready. We can then restore this value whenever the **Default** button is clicked. To handle this click, we could add another else if statement. A switch statement may be more appropriate, as shown in the following code snippet:

```
$(document).ready(function() {
  var $speech = $('div.speech');
  var defaultSize = $speech.css('fontSize');
  $('#switcher button').click(function() {
    var num = parseFloat($speech.css('fontSize'));
    switch (this.id) {
      case 'switcher-large':
        num *= 1.4;
        break;
      case 'switcher-small':
        num /= 1.4;
        break;
      default:
```

```
        num = parseFloat(defaultSize);
    }
    $speech.css('fontSize', num + 'px');
  });
});
```

Listing 4.5

Here we're still checking the value of `this.id` and changing the font size based on it, but if its value is neither `'switcher-large'` nor `'switcher-small'` it will default to the initial font size.

Basic hide and show

The basic `.hide()` and `.show()` methods, without any parameters, can be thought of as smart shorthand methods for `.css('display', 'string')`, where `'string'` is the appropriate display value. The effect, as might be expected, is that the matched set of elements will be immediately hidden or shown, with no animation.

The `.hide()` method sets the **inline style attribute** of the matched set of elements to `display: none`. The smart part here is that it remembers the value of the `display` property—typically `block` or `inline`—before it was changed to `none`. Conversely, the `.show()` method restores display properties of the matched set of elements to whatever they initially were before `display: none` was applied.

The display property

For more information about the `display` property and how its values are visually represented in a web page, visit the Mozilla Developer Center at `https://developer.mozilla.org/en/CSS/display/` and view examples at `https://developer.mozilla.org/samples/cssref/display.html`.

This feature of `.show()` and `.hide()` is especially helpful when hiding elements whose default `display` property is overridden in a stylesheet. For example, the `<li>` element has the property `display: block` by default, but we might want to change it to `display: inline` for a horizontal menu. Fortunately, using the `.show()` method on a hidden element such as one of these `<li>` tags would not merely reset it to its default `display: block`, because that would put the `<li>` on its own line. Instead, the element is restored to its previous `display: inline` state, thus preserving the horizontal design.

We can set up a quick demonstration of these two methods by working with a second paragraph and a **read more** link after the first paragraph in the example HTML, as follows:

```
<div class="speech">
  <p>Fourscore and seven years ago our fathers brought forth
    on this continent a new nation, conceived in liberty,
    and dedicated to the proposition that all men are
    created equal.
  </p>
  <p>Now we are engaged in a great civil war, testing whether
    that nation, or any nation so conceived and so dedicated,
    can long endure. We are met on a great battlefield of
    that war. We have come to dedicate a portion of that
    field as a final resting-place for those who here gave
    their lives that the nation might live. It is altogether
    fitting and proper that we should do this. But, in a
    larger sense, we cannot dedicate, we cannot consecrate,
    we cannot hallow, this ground.
  </p>
  <a href="#" class="more">read more</a>
</div>
```

When the DOM is ready, we select an element and call `.hide()` on it:

```
$(document).ready(function() {
  $('p').eq(1).hide();
});
```

Listing 4.6

The `.eq()` method is similar to the `:eq()` pseudo-class discussed in *Chapter 2, Selecting Elements*. It returns a jQuery object pointing to a single element at the provided zero-based index. In this case, the method selects the second paragraph and hides it, resulting in the following:

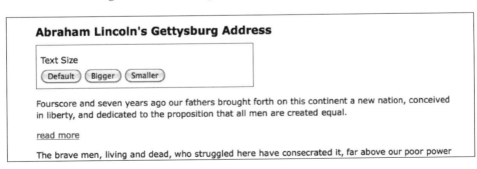

Then, when the user clicks on **read more** at the end of the first paragraph, that link is hidden and the second paragraph is shown:

```
$(document).ready(function() {
  $('p').eq(1).hide();
  $('a.more').click(function() {
    $('p').eq(1).show();
    $(this).hide();
    return false;
  });
});
```

Listing 4.7

Note the use of `return false` to keep the link from activating its default action. Now the speech looks similar to the following screenshot:

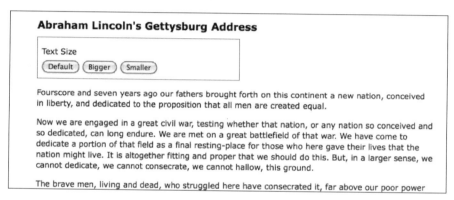

The `.hide()` and `.show()` methods are quick and useful, but they aren't very flashy. To add some flair, we can give them a speed, which is explained in the following section.

Effects and speed

When we include a **speed** (or, more precisely, a **duration**) with `.show()` or `.hide()`, it becomes animated—occurring over a specified period of time. The `.hide('speed')` method, for example, decreases an element's height, width, and opacity simultaneously until all three reach zero, at which point the CSS rule `display: none` is applied. The `.show('speed')` method will increase the element's height from top to bottom, width from left to right, and opacity from 0 to 1 until its contents are completely visible.

Speeding in

With any jQuery effect, we can use one of three preset speeds: `'slow'`, `'normal'`, and `'fast'`. Using `.show('slow')` makes the show effect complete in .6 seconds, `.show('normal')` in .4 seconds, and `.show('fast')` in .2 seconds. For even greater precision, we can specify a number of milliseconds, for example `.show(850)`. Note that in this case we are specifying a numeric value, so we do not use quotation marks.

Let's include a speed in our example when showing the second paragraph of Lincoln's Gettysburg Address:

```
$(document).ready(function() {
  $('p').eq(1).hide();
  $('a.more').click(function() {
    $('p').eq(1).show('slow');
    $(this).hide();
    return false;
  });
});
```

Listing 4.8

When we capture the paragraph's appearance at roughly halfway through the effect, we see something similar to the following screenshot:

Abraham Lincoln's Gettysburg Address

Text Size

Fourscore and seven years ago our fathers brought forth on this continent a new nation, conceived in liberty, and dedicated to the proposition that all men are created equal.

Now we are engaged in a great civil war, testing whether that nation, or any nation so conceived and so dedicated, can long endure. We are met on a great battlefield of that

The brave men, living and dead, who struggled here have consecrated it, far above our poor power to add or detract. The world will little note, nor long remember, what we say here, but it can never forget what they did here. It is for us the living, rather, to be dedicated here to the unfinished work which they who fought here have thus far so nobly advanced.

It is rather for us to be here dedicated to the great task remaining before us—that from these

Fading in and fading out

While the animated `.show()` and `.hide()` methods are certainly flashy, in practice they animate more properties than are useful. Fortunately, jQuery offers a couple of other pre-built animations for a more subtle effect. For example, to have the whole paragraph appear just by gradually increasing the opacity, we can use `.fadeIn('slow')` instead:

```
$(document).ready(function() {
  $('p').eq(1).hide();
  $('a.more').click(function() {
    $('p').eq(1).fadeIn('slow');
    $(this).hide();
    return false;
  });
});
```

Listing 4.9

Now when we look at the paragraph during the effect, it looks similar to the following screenshot:

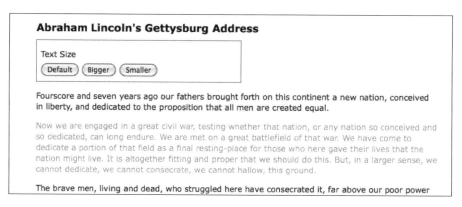

The difference here is that the `.fadeIn()` effect starts by setting the dimensions of the paragraph so that the contents can simply fade into it. To gradually decrease the opacity we can use `.fadeOut()`.

Sliding up and sliding down

The fading animations are very useful for items that are outside the flow of the document. For example, these are typical effects to apply to "lightbox" elements that are overlaid on the page. However, when an element is part of the document flow, calling `.fadeIn()` on it causes the document to "jump" to provide the real estate needed for the new element, which is not very aesthetically pleasing.

In these cases, jQuery's `.slideDown()` and `.slideUp()` methods are often the right choice. These effects animate only the height of the selected elements. To have our paragraph appear using a vertical slide effect, we can call `.slideDown('slow')`, as follows:

```
$(document).ready(function() {
  $('p').eq(1).hide();
  $('a.more').click(function() {
    $('p').eq(1).slideDown('slow');
    $(this).hide();
    return false;
  });
});
```

Listing 4.10

This time when we examine the paragraph at the animation's midpoint, it looks similar to the following screenshot:

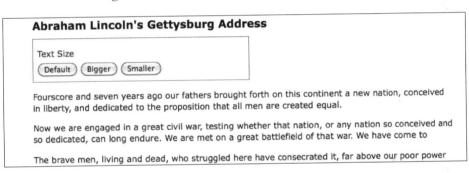

To reverse the effect, we would instead call `.slideUp()`.

Compound effects

Sometimes, we have a need to toggle the visibility of elements, rather than displaying them once as we have done in the preceding examples. This toggling can be achieved by first checking the visibility of the matched elements and then calling the appropriate method. Using the fade effects again, we can modify the example script to look similar to the following code snippet:

```
$(document).ready(function() {
  var $firstPara = $('p').eq(1);
  $firstPara.hide();
  $('a.more').click(function() {
    if ($firstPara.is(':hidden')) {
```

```
        $firstPara.fadeIn('slow');
        $(this).text('read less');
      } else {
        $firstPara.fadeOut('slow');
        $(this).text('read more');
      }
      return false;
    });
  });
```

Listing 4.11

As we did earlier in the chapter, we're caching our selector here to avoid repeated DOM traversal. Notice, too, that we're no longer hiding the clicked link; instead, we're changing its text.

 To examine the text contained by an element and to change that text, we're using the .text() method. This method will be more fully explored in *Chapter 5, Manipulating the DOM.*

Using an if/else statement is a perfectly reasonable way to toggle elements' visibility. However, with jQuery's **compound effects** we can remove some conditional logic from our code. jQuery provides a .toggle() method, which acts like .show() and .hide(), and like them, can be used with a speed argument or without. Other compound methods include .fadeToggle() and .slideToggle(), which show or hide elements using the corresponding effects. The following code snippet is what the script looks like when we use the .slideToggle() method:

```
$(document).ready(function() {
  var $firstPara = $('p').eq(1);
  $firstPara.hide();
  $('a.more').click(function() {
    $firstPara.slideToggle('slow');
    var $link = $(this);
    if ($link.text() == 'read more') {
      $link.text('read less');
    } else {
      $link.text('read more');
    }
    return false;
  });
});
```

Listing 4.12

To reduce repetition of `$(this)`, we're storing the result in the `$link` variable for performance and readability. Also, the conditional statement checks for the text of the link rather than the visibility of the second paragraph, as we're only using it to change the text.

Creating custom animations

In addition to the pre-built effect methods, jQuery provides a powerful `.animate()` method that allows us to create our own custom animations with fine-grained control. The `.animate()` method comes in two forms. The first takes up to four arguments, which are as follows:

1. A **map** of style properties and values—similar to the `.css()` map discussed earlier in this chapter

2. An optional **speed**—which can be one of the preset strings or a number of milliseconds

3. An optional **easing type**—an advanced option discussed in *Chapter 11, Advanced Effects*

4. An optional **callback function**—which will be discussed later in this chapter

All together, the four arguments look similar to the following code snippet:

```
.animate({property1: 'value1', property2: 'value2'},
  speed, easing, function() {
    alert('The animation is finished.');
  }
);
```

The second form takes two arguments: a map of `properties` and a map of `options`:

```
.animate({properties}, {options})
```

In effect, the second argument wraps up the second through fourth arguments of the first form into another map, and adds some more advanced options to the mix. When we adjust the line breaks for readability, the second form looks similar to the following code snippet:

```
.animate({
  property1: 'value1',
  property2: 'value2'
}, {
  duration: 'value',
  easing: 'value',
  specialEasing: {
```

```
    property1: 'easing1',
    property2: 'easing2'
  },
  complete: function() {
    alert('The animation is finished.');
  },
  queue: true,
  step: callback
});
```

For now, we'll use the first form of the `.animate()` method, but we'll return to the second form later in the chapter when we discuss queuing effects.

Building effects by hand

We have already seen several pre-packaged effects for showing and hiding elements. To begin our discussion of the `.animate()` method, it will be useful to see how we could achieve the same results as calling `.slideToggle()` using this lower-level interface. Replacing the `.slideToggle()` line of the preceding example with our custom animation turns out to be quite simple, as shown in the following code snippet:

```
$(document).ready(function() {
  var $firstPara = $('p').eq(1);
  $firstPara.hide();
  $('a.more').click(function() {
    $firstPara.animate({height: 'toggle'}, 'slow');
    var $link = $(this);
    if ($link.text() == 'read more') {
      $link.text('read less');
    } else {
      $link.text('read more');
    }
    return false;
  });
});
```

Listing 4.13

 This is not a perfect replacement for `.slideToggle()`; the actual implementation also animates the margin and padding of elements.

As the example illustrates, the `.animate()` method provides convenient shorthand values for CSS properties — `'show'`, `'hide'`, and `'toggle'` — to ease the way when we want to emulate the behavior of pre-packaged effect methods such as `.slideToggle()`.

Animating multiple properties at once

With the `.animate()` method, we can modify any combination of properties simultaneously. For example, to create a simultaneous sliding and fading effect when toggling the second paragraph, we simply add the `opacity` property-value pair to `.animate()`'s properties map, as follows:

```
$(document).ready(function() {
  var $firstPara = $('p').eq(1);
  $firstPara.hide();
  $('a.more').click(function() {
    $firstPara.animate({
      opacity: 'toggle',
      height: 'toggle'
    }, 'slow');
    var $link = $(this);
    if ($link.text() == 'read more') {
      $link.text('read less');
    } else {
      $link.text('read more');
    }
    return false;
  });
});
```

Listing 4.14

Additionally, we have not only the style properties used for the shorthand effect methods at our disposal, but numeric CSS properties, such as `left`, `top`, `fontSize`, `margin`, `padding`, and `borderWidth`. Recall Listing 4.5, which changed the text size of the speech paragraphs. We could animate the increase or decrease in size by simply substituting the `.animate()` method for the `.css()` method, as shown in the following code snippet:

```
$(document).ready(function() {
  var $speech = $('div.speech');
  var defaultSize = $speech.css('fontSize');
  $('#switcher button').click(function() {
    var num = parseFloat($speech.css('fontSize'));
```

```
    switch (this.id) {
      case 'switcher-large':
        num *= 1.4;
        break;
      case 'switcher-small':
        num /= 1.4;
        break;
      default:
        num = parseFloat(defaultSize);
    }
    $speech.animate({fontSize: num + 'px'}, 'slow');
  });
});
```

Listing 4.15

The extra properties allow us to create much more complex effects, too. We can, for example, move an item from the left side of the page to the right while increasing its height by 20 pixels and changing its border width to 5 pixels. We will illustrate this complicated set of property animations with the `<div id="switcher">` box. The following screenshot is what it looks like before we animate it:

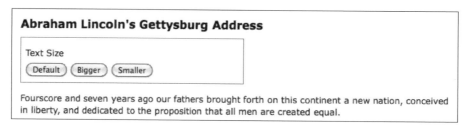

With a flexible-width layout, we need to compute the distance that the box needs to travel before it lines up at the right side of the page. Assuming that the paragraph's width is 100%, we can subtract the **Text Size** box's width from the paragraph's width. We have jQuery's `.outerWidth()` method at our disposal to calculate these widths, including padding and border. We'll use this method to compute the new `left` property of the switcher. For the sake of this example, we'll trigger the animation by clicking on the **Text Size** label, just above the buttons. The following code snippet is what the code should look like:

```
$(document).ready(function() {
  $('div.label').click(function() {
    var paraWidth = $('div.speech p').outerWidth();
    var $switcher = $(this).parent();
    var switcherWidth = $switcher.outerWidth();
```

```
    $switcher.animate({
      borderWidth: '5px',
      left: paraWidth - switcherWidth,
      height: '+=20px'
    }, 'slow');
  });
});
```

Listing 4.16

It is worth examining these animated properties in detail. The `borderWidth` property is straightforward, as we are specifying a constant value with units, just as we would in a stylesheet. The `left` property is a computed numeric value. The unit suffix is optional on these properties; as we omit it here, `px` is assumed. Finally, the `height` property uses a syntax we have not seen before. The `+=` prefix on a property value indicates a relative value. So, instead of animating the height to 20 pixels, the height is animated to 20 pixels greater than the current height. Because of the special characters involved, relative values must be specified as a string, so must be enclosed in quotes.

Although this code successfully increases the height of the `<div>` and widens its border, at the moment the `left` position remains unchanged, as shown in the following screenshot:

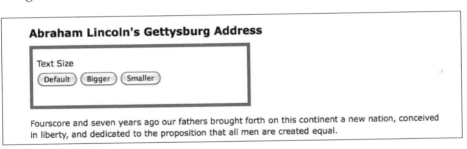

We still need to enable changing this box's position in the CSS.

Positioning with CSS

When working with `.animate()`, it's important to keep in mind the limitations that CSS imposes on the elements that we wish to change. For example, adjusting the `left` property will have no effect on the matching elements unless those elements have their CSS position set to `relative` or `absolute`. The default CSS position for all block-level elements is `static`, which accurately describes how those elements will remain if we try to move them without first changing their `position` value.

For more information on absolute and relative positioning, see Joe Gillespie's article, **Absolutely Relative**, at:
`http://www.wpdfd.com/issues/78/absolutely_relative/`

In our stylesheet, we could set `<div id="switcher">` to be relatively positioned:

```
#switcher {
  position: relative;
}
```

Instead, though, let's practice our jQuery skills by altering this property through JavaScript when needed, as shown in the following code snippet:

```
$(document).ready(function() {
  $('div.label').click(function() {
    var paraWidth = $('div.speech p').outerWidth();
    var $switcher = $(this).parent();
    var switcherWidth = $switcher.outerWidth();
    $switcher.css({
      position: 'relative'
    }).animate({
      borderWidth: '5px',
      left: paraWidth - switcherWidth,
      height: '+=20px'
    }, 'slow');
  });
});
```

Listing 4.17

With the CSS taken into account, the result of clicking on **Text Size**, when the animation has completed, will look similar to the following screenshot:

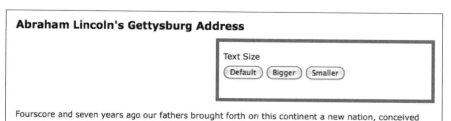

Simultaneous versus queued effects

The `.animate()` method, as we've just discovered, is very useful for creating simultaneous effects affecting a particular set of elements. There may be times, however, when we want to queue our effects, having them occur one after the other.

Working with a single set of elements

When applying multiple effects to the same set of elements, **queuing** is easily achieved by chaining those effects. To demonstrate this queuing, we'll repeat Listing 4.17, by moving the **Text Size** box to the right, increasing its height, and increasing its border width. This time, however, we perform the three effects sequentially, simply by placing each in its own `.animate()` method and chaining the three together:

```
$(document).ready(function() {
  $('div.label').click(function() {
    var paraWidth = $('div.speech p').outerWidth();
    var $switcher = $(this).parent();
    var switcherWidth = $switcher.outerWidth();
    $switcher
      .css({position: 'relative'})
      .animate({left: paraWidth - switcherWidth}, 'slow')
      .animate({height: '+=20px'}, 'slow')
      .animate({borderWidth: '5px'}, 'slow');
  });
});
```

Listing 4.18

Recall that chaining permits us to keep all three `.animate()` methods on the same line, but here we have indented them and put each on its own line for greater readability.

We can queue any of the jQuery effect methods, not just `.animate()`, by chaining them. We could, for example, queue effects on `<div id="switcher">` in the following order:

1. Fade its opacity to .5 with `.fadeTo()`

2. Move it to the right with `.animate()`

3. Fade it back in to full opacity with `.fadeTo()`

4. Hide it with `.slideUp()`

5. Show it once more with `.slideDown()`

All we need to do is chain the effects in the same order in our code, as shown in the following code snippet:

```
$(document).ready(function() {
  $('div.label').click(function() {
    var paraWidth = $('div.speech p').outerWidth();
    var $switcher = $(this).parent();
    var switcherWidth = $switcher.outerWidth();
    $switcher
      .css({position: 'relative'})
      .fadeTo('fast', 0.5)
      .animate({left: paraWidth - switcherWidth}, 'slow')
      .fadeTo('slow', 1.0)
      .slideUp('slow')
      .slideDown('slow');
  });
});
```

Listing 4.19

Bypassing the queue

However, what if we want to move the `<div>` to the right at the same time as it fades to half opacity? If the two animations were occurring at the same speed, then we could simply combine them into a single `.animate()` method. However, in this example, the fade is using the `'fast'` speed, while the move to the right is using the `'slow'` speed. The following code snippet is where the second form of the `.animate()` method comes in handy:

```
$(document).ready(function() {
  $('div.label').click(function() {
    var paraWidth = $('div.speech p').outerWidth();
    var $switcher = $(this).parent();
    var switcherWidth = $switcher.outerWidth();
    $switcher
      .css({position: 'relative'})
      .fadeTo('fast', 0.5)
      .animate({
        left: paraWidth - switcherWidth
      }, {
        duration: 'slow',
        queue: false
      })
      .fadeTo('slow', 1.0)
```

```
      .slideUp('slow')
      .slideDown('slow');
    });
  });
```

Listing 4.20

The second argument, an options map, provides the `queue` option, which when set to `false` makes the animation start simultaneously with the previous one.

Manual queueing

One final observation about queuing effects on a single set of elements is that queuing does not automatically apply to other, non-effect methods such as `.css()`. So let's suppose we wanted to change the background color of `<div id="switcher">` to red after the `.slideUp()` but before the `slideDown()`.

To do this we can use the following code snippet:

```
// Unfinished code
$(document).ready(function() {
  $('div.label').click(function() {
    var paraWidth = $('div.speech p').outerWidth();
    var $switcher = $(this).parent();
    var switcherWidth = $switcher.outerWidth();
    $switcher
      .css({position: 'relative'})
      .fadeTo('fast', 0.5)
      .animate({
        left: paraWidth - switcherWidth
      }, {
        duration: 'slow',
        queue: false
      })
      .fadeTo('slow', 1.0)
      .slideUp('slow')
      .css({backgroundColor: '#f00'})
      .slideDown('slow');
  });
});
```

Listing 4.21

However, even though the background-changing code is placed at the correct position in the chain, it occurs immediately upon the click.

One way we can add non-effect methods to the queue is to use the appropriately-named `.queue()` method, as follows:

```
$(document).ready(function() {
  $('div.label').click(function() {
    var paraWidth = $('div.speech p').outerWidth();
    var $switcher = $(this).parent();
    var switcherWidth = $switcher.outerWidth();
    $switcher
      .css({position: 'relative'})
      .fadeTo('fast', 0.5)
      .animate({
        left: paraWidth - switcherWidth
      }, {
        duration: 'slow',
        queue: false
      })
      .fadeTo('slow', 1.0)
      .slideUp('slow')
      .queue(function(next) {
        $switcher.css({backgroundColor: '#f00'});
        next();
      })
      .slideDown('slow');
  });
});
```

Listing 4.22

When given a callback function, as it is here, the `.queue()` method adds the function to the queue of effects to perform on the matched elements. Within the function, we set the background color to red and then call `next()`, a function that is passed as a parameter to our callback. Including this `next()` function call allows the animation queue to pick up where it left off and complete the chain with the following `.slideDown('slow')` line. If we hadn't called `next()`, the animation would have stopped.

 More information and examples for `.queue()` are available at `http://api.jquery.com/category/effects/`.

We'll discover another way to queue non-effect methods as we examine effects with multiple sets of elements.

Working with multiple sets of elements

Unlike with a single set of elements, when we apply effects to different sets, they occur at virtually the same time. To see these simultaneous effects in action, we'll slide one paragraph down while sliding another paragraph up. We'll be working with paragraphs three and four of our sample document, as follows:

```
<p>Fourscore and seven years ago our fathers brought forth
    on this continent a new nation, conceived in liberty,
    and dedicated to the proposition that all men are
    created equal.</p>
<p>Now we are engaged in a great civil war, testing whether
    that nation, or any nation so conceived and so
    dedicated, can long endure. We are met on a great
    battlefield of that war. We have come to dedicate a
    portion of that field as a final resting-place for those
    who here gave their lives that the nation might live. It
    is altogether fitting and proper that we should do this.
    But, in a larger sense, we cannot dedicate, we cannot
    consecrate, we cannot hallow, this ground.</p>
<a href="#" class="more">read more</a>
<p>The brave men, living and dead, who struggled here have
    consecrated it, far above our poor power to add or
    detract. The world will little note, nor long remember,
    what we say here, but it can never forget what they did
    here. It is for us the living, rather, to be dedicated
    here to the unfinished work which they who fought here
    have thus far so nobly advanced.</p>
<p>It is rather for us to be here dedicated to the great
    task remaining before us&mdash;that from these honored
    dead we take increased devotion to that cause for which
    they gave the last full measure of devotion&mdash;that
    we here highly resolve that these dead shall not have
    died in vain&mdash;that this nation, under God, shall
    have a new birth of freedom and that government of the
    people, by the people, for the people, shall not perish
    from the earth.</p>
```

To help us see what's happening during the effect, we'll give the third paragraph a 1-pixel border and the fourth paragraph a gray background. We'll also hide the fourth paragraph when the DOM is ready, as shown in the following code snippet:

```
$(document).ready(function() {
    $('p').eq(2).css('border', '1px solid #333');
    $('p').eq(3).css('backgroundColor', '#ccc').hide();
});
```

Listing 4.23

Our sample document now displays the opening paragraph, followed by the **read more** link and the bordered paragraph, as shown in the following screenshot:

> Fourscore and seven years ago our fathers brought forth on this continent a new nation, conceived in liberty, and dedicated to the proposition that all men are created equal.
>
> read more
>
> The brave men, living and dead, who struggled here have consecrated it, far above our poor power to add or detract. The world will little note, nor long remember, what we say here, but it can never forget what they did here. It is for us the living, rather, to be dedicated here to the unfinished work which they who fought here have thus far so nobly advanced.

Finally, we'll add the `.click()` method to the third paragraph so that when it is clicked, the third paragraph will slide up (and out of view), while the fourth paragraph slides down (and into view):

```
$(document).ready(function() {
  $('p').eq(2)
    .css('border', '1px solid #333')
    .click(function() {
      $(this).slideUp('slow').next().slideDown('slow');
    });
  $('p').eq(3).css('backgroundColor', '#ccc').hide();
});
```

Listing 4.24

A screenshot of these two effects in mid-slide confirms that they do, indeed, occur simultaneously, as follows:

> Fourscore and seven years ago our fathers brought forth on this continent a new nation, conceived in liberty, and dedicated to the proposition that all men are created equal.
>
> read more
>
> The brave men, living and dead, who struggled here have consecrated it, far above our poor power
>
> It is rather for us to be here dedicated to the great task remaining before us—that from these honored dead we take increased devotion to that cause for which they gave the last full measure of devotion—that we here highly resolve that these dead shall not have died in vain—that this nation,

The third paragraph, which started visible, is halfway through sliding up at the same time as the fourth paragraph, which started hidden, is halfway through sliding down.

Callbacks

In order to allow queuing effects on different elements, jQuery provides a **callback function** for each effect method. As we have seen with event handlers and with the `.queue()` method, callbacks are simply functions passed as method arguments. In the case of effects, they appear as the last argument of the method.

If we use a callback to queue the two slide effects, then we can have the fourth paragraph slide down before the third paragraph slides up. Let's first try moving the `.slideUp()` call into the `.slideDown()` method's completion callback, as shown in the following code snippet:

```
$(document).ready(function() {
  $('p').eq(2)
    .css('border', '1px solid #333')
    .click(function() {
      $(this).next().slideDown('slow', function() {
        $(this).slideUp('slow');
      });
    });
  $('p').eq(3).css('backgroundColor', '#ccc').hide();
});
```

Listing 4.25

We do need to be careful here, however, about what is actually going to slide up. The **context** of the function—the keyword `this`—is different because the callback is inside the `.slideDown()` method. Here, `$(this)` is no longer the third paragraph, as it was directly within the `click` handler; rather, as the `.slideDown()` method is being called on the result of `$(this).next()`, the callback within that method now sees `$(this)` as the next sibling, or the fourth paragraph. Therefore, if we put `$(this).slideUp('slow')` inside the callback, as we have in Listing 4.25, we would end up hiding the same paragraph that we had just made visible.

A simple way to keep the `$(this)` reference stable is to store it in a variable right away within the `click` handler, like `var $clickedItem = $(this)`.

Now `$clickedItem` will refer to the third paragraph, both outside and inside the effect method callback. The following code snippet is what the code looks like using our new variable:

```
$(document).ready(function() {
  $('p').eq(2)
    .css('border', '1px solid #333')
    .click(function() {
      var $clickedItem = $(this);
```

```
    $clickedItem.next().slideDown('slow', function() {
      $clickedItem.slideUp('slow');
    });
  });
  $('p').eq(3).css('backgroundColor', '#ccc').hide();
});
```

Listing 4.26

 Using `$clickedItem` inside the `.slideDown()` callback relies on the properties of **closures**. We'll be discussing this important, yet difficult-to-master, topic in *Appendix A*.

This time, a snapshot halfway through the effects will reveal that both the third and the fourth paragraphs are visible; the fourth has finished sliding down and the third is about to begin sliding up, as shown in the following screenshot:

> Fourscore and seven years ago our fathers brought forth on this continent a new nation, conceived in liberty, and dedicated to the proposition that all men are created equal.
>
> read more
>
> The brave men, living and dead, who struggled here have consecrated it, far above our poor power to add or detract. The world will little note, nor long remember, what we say here, but it can never forget what they did here. It is for us the living, rather, to be dedicated here to the unfinished work which they who fought here have thus far so nobly advanced.
>
> It is rather for us to be here dedicated to the great task remaining before us—that from these honored dead we take increased devotion to that cause for which they gave the last full measure of devotion—that we here highly resolve that these dead shall not have died in vain—that this nation, under God, shall have a new birth of freedom and that government of the people, by the people, for

Now that we've discussed callbacks, we can return to the code from Listing 4.22, in which we queued a background-color change near the end of a series of effects. Instead of using the `.queue()` method, as we did then, we can simply use a callback function, as follows:

```
$(document).ready(function() {
  $('div.label').click(function() {
    var paraWidth = $('div.speech p').outerWidth();
    var $switcher = $(this).parent();
    var switcherWidth = $switcher.outerWidth();
    $switcher
      .css({position: 'relative'})
      .fadeTo('fast', 0.5)
      .animate({
        left: paraWidth - switcherWidth
      }, {
        duration: 'slow',
```

```
        queue: false
      })
      .fadeTo('slow', 1.0)
      .slideUp('slow', function() {
        $switcher.css({backgroundColor: '#f00'});
      })
      .slideDown('slow');
    });
  });
```

Listing 4.27

Here, again, the background color of `<div id="switcher">` changes to red after it slides up, and before it slides back down. Note that when using an effect's completion callback rather than `.queue()`, we don't need to worry about calling `next()` from within the callback.

In a nutshell

With all the variations to consider when applying effects, it can become difficult to remember whether the effects will occur simultaneously or sequentially. A brief outline might help:

1. Effects on a single set of elements are:
   - **simultaneous** when applied as multiple properties in a single `.animate()` method
   - **queued** when applied in a chain of methods, unless the `queue` option is set to `false`
2. Effects on multiple sets of elements are:
   - **simultaneous** by default
   - **queued** when applied within the callback of another effect or within the callback of the `.queue()` method

Summary

By using effect methods that we have explored in this chapter, we should now be able to modify inline style attributes from JavaScript, apply pre-packaged jQuery effects to elements, and create our own custom animations. In particular, we learned to incrementally increase and decrease text size by using either the `.css()` or the `.animate()` method, gradually hide and show page elements by modifying several attributes, and to animate elements, simultaneously or sequentially, in a number of ways.

In the first four chapters of the book, all of our examples have involved manipulating elements that have been hard-coded into the page's HTML. In *Chapter 5*, we will explore ways to manipulate the DOM directly, including using jQuery to create new elements and insert them into the DOM wherever we choose.

Further reading

The topic of animation will be explored in more detail in *Chapter 11*. A complete list of available effect and styling methods is available in *Appendix C* of this book, in *jQuery Reference Guide*, or in the official jQuery documentation at http://api.jquery.com/.

Exercises

To complete these exercises, you will need the index.html file for this chapter, as well as the finished JavaScript code as found in complete.js. These files can be downloaded from the Packt Publishing website at http://www.packtpub.com/support.

The challenge exercise may require use of the official jQuery documentation at http://api.jquery.com/.

1. Alter the stylesheet to hide the contents of the page initially. When the page is loaded, fade in the contents slowly.

2. Give each paragraph a yellow background only when the mouse is over it.

3. Make a click of the title (<h2>) simultaneously make it fade to 25% opacity and get a left margin of 20px, then when this is complete, fade the speech text to 50% opacity.

4. **Challenge**: React to presses of the arrow keys by smoothly moving the switcher box 20 pixels in the corresponding direction. The key codes for the arrow keys are: 37 (left), 38 (up), 39 (right), and 40 (down).

5

Manipulating the DOM

The web experience is a partnership between web servers and web browsers. Traditionally, it has been the domain of the server to produce an HTML document ready for consumption by the browser. The techniques we have seen have shifted this arrangement slightly, by using CSS techniques to alter the appearance of that HTML on the fly. To really flex our JavaScript muscles, though, we'll need to learn to alter the document itself.

With jQuery, we can easily modify the document by using the interface provided by the Document Object Model (DOM). This will allow us to create elements and text in a web page, whenever we need to. We can also make any of these things vanish, or indeed transform them on the fly by adding, removing, or modifying their attributes.

Manipulating attributes

Throughout the first four chapters of this book, we have been using the `.addClass()` and `.removeClass()` methods to demonstrate how we can change the appearance of elements on a page. Effectively, what these two methods are doing is manipulating the `class` attribute (or, in DOM scripting parlance, the `className` property) of the element. The `.addClass()` method creates or adds to the attribute, while `.removeClass()` deletes or shortens it. Add to these the `.toggleClass()` method, which alternates between adding and removing a class, and we have an efficient and robust way of handling classes.

Nevertheless, the `class` attribute is only one of several attributes that we may need to access or change: for example, `id`, `rel`, and `href`. For manipulating these attributes, jQuery provides the `.attr()` and `.removeAttr()` methods. We could even use `.attr()` and `.removeAttr()` to modify the `class` attribute, but the specialized `.addClass()` and `.removeClass()` methods are better in this situation because they correctly handle cases where multiple classes are applied to a single element, such as `<div class="first second">`.

Non-class attributes

Some attributes are not so easily manipulated without the help of jQuery. In addition, jQuery lets us modify more than one attribute at a time, similar to the way we worked with multiple CSS properties using the `.css()` method in *Chapter 4, Styling and Animating*.

For example, we can easily set the `id`, `rel`, and `title` attributes for links, all at once. Let's start with some sample HTML, as follows:

```
<h1 id="f-title">Flatland: A Romance of Many Dimensions</h1>
<div id="f-author">by Edwin A. Abbott</div>
<h2>Part 1, Section 3</h2>
<h3 id="f-subtitle">
  Concerning the Inhabitants of Flatland
</h3>
<div id="excerpt">an excerpt</div>
<div class="chapter">
  <p class="square">Our Professional Men and Gentlemen are
    Squares (to which class I myself belong) and Five-Sided
    Figures or <a
    href="http://en.wikipedia.org/wiki/Pentagon">Pentagons
    </a>.
  </p>
  <p class="nobility hexagon">Next above these come the
    Nobility, of whom there are several degrees, beginning at
    Six-Sided Figures, or <a
    href="http://en.wikipedia.org/wiki/Hexagon">Hexagons</a>,
    and from thence rising in the number of their sides till
    they receive the honourable title of <a
    href="http://en.wikipedia.org/wiki/Polygon">Polygonal</a>,
    or many-Sided. Finally when the number of the sides
    becomes so numerous, and the sides themselves so small,
    that the figure cannot be distinguished from a <a
    href="http://en.wikipedia.org/wiki/Circle">circle</a>, he
    is included in the Circular or Priestly order; and this is
    the highest class of all.
  </p>
  <p><span class="pull-quote">It is a <span class="drop">Law
    of Nature</span> with us that a male child shall have
    <strong>one more side</strong> than his father</span>, so
    that each generation shall rise (as a rule) one step in
```

```
    the scale of development and nobility. Thus the son of a
    Square is a Pentagon; the son of a Pentagon, a Hexagon;
    and so on.
  </p>
<!-- . . . code continues . . . -->
</div>
```

Now we can iterate through each of the links inside `<div class="chapter">` and apply attributes to them one by one. If we need to set a single attribute value for all of the links, then we can do so with a single line of code within our `$(document).ready()` handler, as follows:

```
$(document).ready(function() {
  $('div.chapter a').attr({rel: 'external'});
});
```

Listing 5.1

Much like the `.css()` method, `.attr()` can accept a pair of parameters, the first specifying the attribute name and the second its new value. More typically, though, we supply a **map** of key-value pairs, as we have in Listing 5.1. This syntax allows us to easily expand our example to modify multiple attributes at once, as follows:

```
$(document).ready(function() {
  $('div.chapter a').attr({
    rel: 'external',
    title: 'Learn more at Wikipedia'
  });
});
```

Listing 5.2

Value callbacks

The straightforward technique for passing `.attr()` a map of constants is sufficient when we want the attribute or attributes to have the same value for each matched element. Often, though, the attributes we add or change must have different values each time. One common example is that for any given document, each `id` value must be unique if we want our JavaScript code to behave predictably. To set a unique `id` for each link, we can harness another feature of jQuery methods such as `.css()` and `.each()`: the **value callback**.

A value callback is simply a function that is supplied instead of the value for an argument. This function is then invoked once per element in the matched set. Whatever data is returned from the function is used as the new value for the attribute. For example, we can use this technique to generate a different `id` value for each element, as follows:

```
$(document).ready(function() {
  $('div.chapter a').attr({
    rel: 'external',
    title: 'Learn more at Wikipedia',
    id: function(index, oldValue) {
      return 'wikilink-' + index;
    }
  });
});
```

Listing 5.3

Each time our value callback is fired, it is passed a pair of parameters. The first is an integer indicating the iteration count; we're using it here to give the first link an `id` value of `wikilink-0`, the second `wikilink-1`, and so on. The second parameter, which is unused in Listing 5.3, contains the value of the attribute prior to modification.

We are using the `title` attribute to invite people to learn more about the linked term at Wikipedia. In the HTML we have used so far, all of the links point to Wikipedia. However, to account for other types of links, we should make the selector expression a little more specific, as follows:

```
$(document).ready(function() {
  $('div.chapter a[href*="wikipedia"]').attr({
    rel: 'external',
    title: 'Learn more at Wikipedia',
    id: function(index, oldValue) {
      return 'wikilink-' + index;
    }
  });
});
```

Listing 5.4

To complete our tour of the `.attr()` method, we'll enhance the `title` attribute of these links to be more specific about the link destination. Once again, a value callback is the right tool for the job, as follows:

```
$(document).ready(function() {
  $('div.chapter a[href*="wikipedia"]').attr({
    rel: 'external',
    title: function() {
      return 'Learn more about ' + $(this).text()
        + ' at Wikipedia.';
    },
    id: function(index, oldValue) {
      return 'wikilink-' + index;
    }
  });
});
```

Listing 5.5

This time we've taken advantage of the **context** of value callbacks. Just as with event handlers, the keyword `this` points to the DOM element we're manipulating each time the callback is invoked. Here, we're wrapping the element in a jQuery object so that we can use the `.text()` method (introduced in *Chapter 4*) to retrieve the textual content of the link. This makes our link titles nicely specific:

Flatland: A Romance of Many Dimensions
by Edwin A. Abbott

Part 1, Section 3

Concerning the Inhabitants of Flatland
an excerpt

Our Professional Men and Gentlemen are Squares (to which class I myself belong) and Five-Sided Figures or Pentagons.

Next above these come the Nobility, of who... Learn more about Pentagons at Wikipedia.
degrees, beginning at Six-Sided Figures, or Hexagons, and from thence rising in the number of their sides till they receive the honourable title of Polygonal, or many-Sided. Finally when the number

DOM element properties

As mentioned briefly above, there is a subtle distinction between HTML **attributes** and DOM **properties**. Attributes are the values given in quotation marks in the HTML source for the page, while properties are the values as accessed by JavaScript. We can observe attributes and properties easily in a developer tool like Firebug, as shown in the following screenshot:

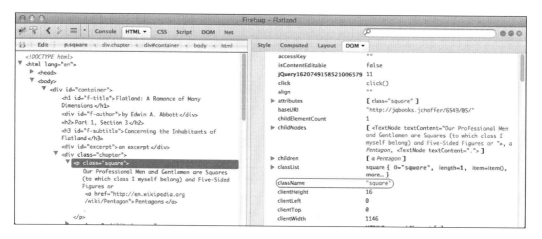

The Firebug inspector shows us that the highlighted `<p>` element has an attribute called `class` with a value of `square`. In the right panel, we can see that this element has a corresponding property called `className` with a value of `square`. This illustrates one of the rare situations in which an attribute and its equivalent property have different names.

In most cases, attributes and properties are functionally interchangeable, and jQuery takes care of the naming inconsistencies for us. However, at times we do need to be mindful of the differences between the two. In particular, data types may differ: the `checked` attribute has a string value, while the `checked` property has a Boolean value. For these **Boolean attributes**, it is best to test and set the *property* rather than the *attribute* to ensure consistent cross-browser behavior.

We can get and set properties from jQuery using the `.prop()` method, as follows:

```
// Get the current value of the "checked" property
var currentlyChecked = $('.my-checkbox').prop('checked');

// Set a new value for the "checked" property
$('.my-checkbox').prop('checked', false);
```

The `.prop()` method has all of the same features as `.attr()`, such as accepting a map of multiple values to set at the same time, and taking value callback functions.

DOM tree manipulation

The `.attr()` and `.prop()` methods are very powerful tools, and with them we can change the document itself. We still haven't seen ways to change the structure of the document, though. To actually manipulate the DOM tree, we'll need to learn a bit more about the function that lies at the very heart of the jQuery library.

The $() function revisited

From the start of this book, we've been using the `$()` function to access elements in a document. As we've seen, this function acts as a factory, producing new jQuery objects that point to the elements described by CSS selectors.

This isn't all that the `$()` function can do, however. It also boasts a feature so powerful that it can change not only the visual appearance but also the actual contents of a page. Simply by passing a snippet of HTML code to the function, we can create an entirely new DOM structure from thin air.

Accessibility reminder

We should keep in mind, once again, the inherent danger in making certain functionality, visual appeal, or textual information available only to those with web browsers capable of (and enabled for) using JavaScript. Important information should be accessible to all, not just people who happen to be using the right software.

Creating new elements

A feature commonly seen on FAQ pages is the **back to top** link that appears after each question-and-answer pair. It could be argued that these links serve no semantic purpose and, therefore, can be legitimately included via JavaScript as an enhancement for a subset of the visitors to a page. For our example, we'll add a **back to top** link after each paragraph, as well as the anchor to which the **back to top** links will take us. To begin, we simply create the new elements, as follows:

```
// Unfinished code
$(document).ready(function() {
  $('<a href="#top">back to top</a>');
  $('<a id="top"></a>');
});
```

Listing 5.6

We've created a **back to top** link in the first line of code, and a target anchor for the link in the second line. However, no **back to top** links appear on the page yet:

> Our Professional Men and Gentlemen are Squares (to which class I myself belong) and Five-Sided Figures or Pentagons.
>
> Next above these come the Nobility, of whom there are several degrees, beginning at Six-Sided Figures, or Hexagons, and from thence rising in the number of their sides till they receive the honourable title of Polygonal, or many-Sided. Finally when the number of the sides becomes so numerous, and the sides themselves so small, that the figure cannot be distinguished from a circle, he is included in the Circular or Priestly order; and this is the highest class of all.
>
> It is a Law of Nature with us that a male child shall have **one more**

While the two lines of code we've written do indeed create the elements, they don't yet add the elements to the page. We need to tell the browser where these new elements should go. To do that, we can use one of the many jQuery **insertion methods**.

Inserting new elements

The jQuery library has a number of methods available for inserting elements into the document. Each one dictates the relationship the new content will have to the existing content. For example, we will want our **back to top** links to appear after each paragraph, so we'll use the appropriately-named `.insertAfter()` method to accomplish this, as follows:

```
// Unfinished code
$(document).ready(function() {
  $('<a href="#top">back to top</a>').insertAfter('div.chapter
    p');
  $('<a id="top"></a>');
});
```

Listing 5.7

So, now that we've actually inserted the links into the page (and into the DOM) after each paragraph that appears within `<div class="chapter">`, the **back to top** links will appear, as illustrated in the following screenshot:

> Our Professional Men and Gentlemen are Squares (to which class I myself belong) and Five-Sided Figures or Pentagons.
>
> back to top
>
> Next above these come the Nobility, of whom there are several degrees, beginning at Six-Sided Figures, or Hexagons, and from thence rising in the number of their sides till they receive the honourable title of Polygonal, or many-Sided. Finally when the number of the sides becomes so numerous, and the sides themselves so small, that the figure cannot be distinguished from a circle, he is included in the Circular or Priestly order; and this is the highest class of all.
>
> back to top
>
> It is a Law of Nature with us that a male child shall have **one more**

Note that the new links appear on their own line, not within the paragraph. This is because the `.insertAfter()` method, and its counterpart `.insertBefore()`, add content outside the specified element.

Unfortunately, the links won't work yet. We still need to insert the anchor with `id="top"`. This time, we'll use one of the methods that insert elements inside of other elements, as follows:

```
$(document).ready(function() {
    $('<a href="#top">back to top</a>').insertAfter('div.chapter
      p');
    $('<a id="top"></a>').prependTo('body');
});
```

Listing 5.8

This additional code inserts the anchor right at the beginning of the `<body>`; in other words, at the top of the page. Now, with the `.insertAfter()` method for the links and the `.prependTo()` method for the anchor, we have a fully functioning set of **back to top** links for the page.

Once we add the corresponding `.appendTo()` method, we now have a complete set of options for inserting new elements before and after other elements:

1. `.insertBefore()` adds content outside of and before existing elements
2. `.prependTo()` adds content inside of and before existing elements
3. `.appendTo()` adds content inside of and after existing elements
4. `.insertAfter()` adds content outside of and after existing elements

Moving elements

When adding the **back to top** links, we created new elements and inserted them on the page. It's also possible to take elements from one place on the page and insert them into another place. A practical application of this type of insertion is the dynamic placement and formatting of footnotes. One footnote already appears in the original Flatland text that we are using for the following example, but we'll also designate a couple of other portions of the text as footnotes for the purpose of this demonstration:

```
<p>How admirable is the Law of Compensation!
  <span class="footnote">
    And how perfect a proof of the natural
    fitness and, I may almost say, the divine origin of the
    aristocratic constitution of the States of Flatland!
  </span>
  By a judicious use of this Law of Nature, the Polygons and
  Circles are almost always able to stifle sedition in its
  very cradle, taking advantage of the irrepressible and
  boundless hopefulness of the human mind.&hellip;
</p>
```

Our HTML document contains three footnotes; this paragraph contains one example. The footnote text is inside the paragraph text, set apart using `<span class="footnote"></span>`. By marking up the HTML in this way, we can preserve the context of the footnote. A CSS rule applied in the stylesheet italicizes the footnotes, so an affected paragraph initially looks like the following screenshot:

How admirable is the Law of Compensation! *And how perfect a proof of the natural fitness and, I may almost say, the divine origin of the aristocratic constitution of the States of Flatland!* By a judicious use of this Law of Nature, the Polygons and Circles are almost always able to stifle sedition in its very cradle, taking advantage of the irrepressible and boundless hopefulness of the human mind....

Now we need to grab the footnotes and move them to the bottom of the document. Specifically, we'll insert them in between `<div class="chapter">` and `<div id="footer">`.

Keep in mind that even in cases of implicit iteration, the order in which elements are processed is precisely defined, starting at the top of the DOM tree and working down. As it's important to maintain the correct order of the footnotes in their new place on the page, we should use `.insertBefore('#footer')`, as shown in the following code snippet. This will place each footnote directly before the `<div id="footer">` so that footnote 1 is placed between `<div class="chapter">` and `<div id="footer">`, footnote 2 is placed between footnote 1 and `<div`

id=`"footer"`>, and so on. Using `.insertAfter('div.chapter')`, on the other hand, would cause the footnotes to appear in reverse order.

So far, our code looks like the following:

```
$(document).ready(function() {
  $('span.footnote').insertBefore('#footer');
});
```

Listing 5.9

The footnotes are in a `<span>` tag, which means they display inline by default, one right after the other with no separation. However, we've anticipated this in the CSS, giving `span.footnote` elements a `display` value of `block` when they are outside of `<div class="chapter">`. So, the footnotes are now beginning to take shape, as follows:

to mutual warfare, and perish by one another's angles. No less than one hundred and twenty rebellions are recorded in our annals, besides minor outbreaks numbered at two hundred and thirty-five; and they have all ended thus.

back to top

"What need of a certificate?" a Spaceland critic may ask: "Is not the procreation of a Square Son a certificate from Nature herself, proving the Equal-sidedness of the Father?" I reply that no Lady of any position will marry an uncertified Triangle. Square offspring has sometimes resulted from a slightly Irregular Triangle; but in almost every such case the Irregularity of the first generation is visited on the third; which either fails to attain the Pentagonal rank, or relapses to the Triangular.

The Equilateral is bound by oath never to permit the child henceforth to enter his former home or so much as to look upon his relations again, for fear lest the freshly developed organism may, by force of unconscious imitation, fall back again into his hereditary level.

And how perfect a proof of the natural fitness and, I may almost say, the divine origin of the aristocratic constitution of the States of Flatland!

The footnotes are in the proper position now, yet there is still a lot of work that can be done to them. A more robust footnote solution should:

1. Number each footnote.
2. Mark the location in the text from which each footnote is pulled, using the number of the footnote.
3. Create a link from the text location to its matching footnote, and from the footnote back to the text location.

Wrapping elements

To number the footnotes, we could explicitly add numbers in the markup, but here we can take advantage of the standard ordered list element that takes care of numbering for us. To do this, we need to create a containing `<ol>` element surrounding all of the footnotes, and an `<li>` element surrounding each one individually. The **wrapping methods** will come to our rescue here.

When wrapping elements in another element, we need to be clear about whether we want each element wrapped in its own container, or all elements wrapped in a single container. For our footnote numbering, we need both types of wrapper, as follows:

```
$(document).ready(function() {
  $('span.footnote')
    .insertBefore('#footer')
    .wrapAll('<ol id="notes"></ol>')
    .wrap('<li></li>');
});
```

Listing 5.10

Once we have inserted the footnotes before the footer, we wrap the entire set inside a single `<ol>` using `.wrapAll()`. We then proceed to wrap each individual footnote inside its own `<li>` using `.wrap()`. We can see in the following screenshot that this has created properly-numbered footnotes:

have all ended thus.

back to top

1. *"What need of a certificate?" a Spaceland critic may ask: "Is not the procreation of a Square Son a certificate from Nature herself, proving the Equal-sidedness of the Father?" I reply that no Lady of any position will marry an uncertified Triangle. Square offspring has sometimes resulted from a slightly Irregular Triangle; but in almost every such case the Irregularity of the first generation is visited on the third; which either fails to attain the Pentagonal rank, or relapses to the Triangular.*

2. *The Equilateral is bound by oath never to permit the child henceforth to enter his former home or so much as to look upon his relations again, for fear lest the freshly developed organism may, by force of unconscious imitation, fall back again into his hereditary level.*

3. *And how perfect a proof of the natural fitness and, I may almost say, the divine origin of the aristocratic constitution of the States of Flatland!*

Now we're ready to mark and number the place from which we're pulling the footnote. To do this in a straightforward manner, though, we need to rewrite our existing code without relying on implicit iteration.

The `.each()` method, which acts as an **explicit iterator**, is very similar to a `for` loop. It can be employed when the code we want to use on each of the matched elements is too complex for the implicit iteration syntax. The method is passed a callback function which will be called once for each element in the matched set, as follows:

```
$(document).ready(function() {
  var $notes = $('<ol id="notes"></ol>').insertBefore('#footer');
  $('span.footnote').each(function(index) {
    $(this).appendTo($notes).wrap('<li></li>');
  });
});
```

Listing 5.11

The motivation for our change here will become clear shortly. First, we need to understand the information that's provided to our `.each()` callback.

As with other callbacks we've seen, such as the value callbacks we worked with earlier in this chapter, the context keyword `this` points to the DOM element in question. In Listing 5.11, we use the context to create a jQuery object pointing to a single footnote `<span>`, append the element to the notes `<ol>`, and finally wrap the footnote inside an `<li>` element.

To mark the locations in the text from which the footnotes were pulled, we can take advantage of the `.each()` callback's parameter. This parameter provides the iteration count, starting at zero and incrementing each time the callback is invoked. Therefore, this counter will always be one less than the number of the footnote. We'll use this fact to produce the appropriate labels in the text, as follows:

```
$(document).ready(function() {
var $notes = $('<ol id="notes"></ol>').insertBefore('#footer');
  $('span.footnote').each(function(index) {
    $('<sup>' + (index + 1) + '</sup>').insertBefore(this);
    $(this).appendTo($notes).wrap('<li></li>');
  });
});
```

Listing 5.12

Now, before each footnote is yanked out of the text to be placed at the bottom of the page, we create a new `<sup>` element containing the footnote's number and insert it into the text. The order of actions is important here; we need to make sure that the marker is inserted before the footnote is moved and we lose track of its initial position. Note also that the expression `(index + 1)` must be in parentheses so that it is interpreted as addition, as + is also used for string concatenation in JavaScript.

Looking at our page again, now we can see footnote markers where the inline footnotes used to be:

> subject of rejoicing in our country for many furlongs round. After a strict examination conducted by the Sanitary and Social Board, the infant, if certified as Regular, is with solemn ceremonial admitted into the class of Equilaterals. He is then immediately taken from his proud yet sorrowing parents and adopted by some childless Equilateral. [2]
>
> back to top
>
> How admirable is the Law of Compensation! [3] By a judicious use of this Law of Nature, the Polygons and Circles are almost always able to stifle sedition in its very cradle, taking advantage of the irrepressible and boundless hopefulness of the human mind....

Inverted insertion methods

In Listing 5.12, we inserted content before an element, and then appended that same element to another place in the document. Typically, when working with elements in jQuery, we can use chaining to perform multiple actions succinctly and efficiently. We weren't able to do that here, though, because `this` is the target of `.insertBefore()`, and the "subject" of `.appendTo()`. The **inverted insertion methods** will help us get around this limitation.

Each of the insertion methods, such as `.insertBefore()` and `.appendTo()`, has a corresponding inverted method. The inverted methods perform exactly the same task as the standard ones, but the "subject" and "target" are reversed. For example:

```
$('<p>Hello</p>').appendTo('#container');
```

is the same as:

```
$('#container').append('<p>Hello</p>');
```

Using `.before()`, the inverted form of `.insertBefore()`, we can now refactor our code to exploit chaining, as follows:

```
$(document).ready(function() {
  var $notes = $('<ol id="notes"></ol>')
    .insertBefore('#footer');
  $('span.footnote').each(function(index) {
    $(this)
      .before('<sup>' + (index + 1) + '</sup>')
      .appendTo($notes)
      .wrap('<li></li>');
  });
});
```

Listing 5.13

Insertion method callbacks

The inverted insertion methods can accept a function as an argument, much as `.attr()` and `.css()` can. This function is invoked once per target element, and should return the HTML string to be inserted. We could use this technique here, but as we will encounter several such situations for each footnote, the single `.each()` call will end up being the cleaner solution.

We're now ready to take care of the final step in our checklist: create a link from the text location to its matching footnote and from the footnote back to the text location. We'll need four pieces of markup per footnote to achieve this: two links, one in the text and one after the footnote, and two `id` attributes in those same locations. Because the argument to the `.before()` method is about to get complex, this is a good time to introduce a new notation for string creation.

In Listing 5.13, we prepare our footnote marker by using the + operator to concatenate strings. This is a very useful technique, but for joining a large number of strings it can start to look cluttered. Instead, we can use the array method `.join()` to construct the larger string. The following statements have the same effect:

```
var str = 'a' + 'b' + 'c';
var str = ['a', 'b', 'c'].join('');
```

While it requires a few more characters to type in this example, the `.join()` method can add clarity in cases where addition mixed with string concatenation would become confusing. Let's look at our code again, this time using `.join()` to create the string, as follows:

```
$(document).ready(function() {
  var $notes = $('<ol id="notes"></ol>')
    .insertBefore('#footer');
  $('span.footnote').each(function(index) {
    $(this)
      .before([
        '<sup>',
        index + 1,
        '</sup>'
      ].join(''))
      .appendTo($notes)
      .wrap('<li></li>');
  });
});
```

Listing 5.14

Notice that as each array entry is computed separately, we don't need parentheses around `index + 1` anymore.

Using this technique, we can augment the footnote marker with a link to the bottom of the page as well as a unique `id` value. While we're at it, we'll also add an `id` for the `<li>` element, so the link has a destination to point at:

```
$(document).ready(function() {
  var $notes = $('<ol id="notes"></ol>')
    .insertBefore('#footer');
  $('span.footnote').each(function(index) {
    $(this)
      .before([
        '<a href="#footnote-',
        index + 1,
        '" id="context-',
        index + 1,
        '" class="context">',
        '<sup>',
        index + 1,
        '</sup></a>'
      ].join(''))
      .appendTo($notes)
      .wrap('<li id="footnote-' + (index + 1) + '"></li>');
  });
});
```

Listing 5.15

With the additional markup in place, each footnote marker now links down to the corresponding footnote at the bottom of the document. All that remains is to create a link back from the footnote to its context. For this, we can employ the inverse of the `.appendTo()` method, `.append()`, as follows:

```
$(document).ready(function() {
  var $notes = $('<ol id="notes"></ol>')
    .insertBefore('#footer');
  $('span.footnote').each(function(index) {
    $(this)
      .before([
        '<a href="#footnote-',
        index + 1,
        '" id="context-',
        index + 1,
```

```
            '" class="context">',
            '<sup>',
            index + 1,
            '</sup></a>'
        ].join(''))
        .appendTo($notes)
        .append([
            ' (<a href="#context-',
            index + 1,
            '">context</a>)'
        ].join(''))
        .wrap('<li id="footnote-' + (index + 1) + '"></li>');
    });
});
```

Listing 5.16

Notice that the `href` points back to the `id` of the corresponding marker. In the following screenshot you can see the footnotes again, this time with the new link appended to each:

have all ended thus.

back to top

1. *"What need of a certificate?" a Spaceland critic may ask: "Is not the procreation of a Square Son a certificate from Nature herself, proving the Equal-sidedness of the Father?" I reply that no Lady of any position will marry an uncertified Triangle. Square offspring has sometimes resulted from a slightly Irregular Triangle; but in almost every such case the Irregularity of the first generation is visited on the third; which either fails to attain the Pentagonal rank, or relapses to the Triangular. (context)*

2. *The Equilateral is bound by oath never to permit the child henceforth to enter his former home or so much as to look upon his relations again, for fear lest the freshly developed organism may, by force of unconscious imitation, fall back again into his hereditary level. (context)*

3. *And how perfect a proof of the natural fitness and, I may almost say, the divine origin of the aristocratic constitution of the States of Flatland! (context)*

Copying elements

So far in this chapter we have inserted newly created elements, moved elements from one location in the document to another, and wrapped new elements around existing ones. Sometimes, though, we may want to copy elements. For example, a navigation menu that appears in the page's header could be copied and placed in the footer as well. Whenever elements can be copied to enhance a page visually, we have an opportunity to use jQuery. After all, why write something twice and double our chance of error when we can write it once and let jQuery do the heavy lifting?

For copying elements, jQuery's `.clone()` method is just what we need; it takes any set of matched elements and creates a copy of them for later use. As with the `$()` function's element creation process we explored earlier in this chapter, the copied elements will not appear in the document until we apply one of the insertion methods.

For example, the following line creates a copy of the first paragraph inside `<div class="chapter">`:

```
$('div.chapter p:eq(0)').clone();
```

This alone is not enough to change the content of the page. We can make the cloned paragraph appear before `<div class="chapter">` with an insertion method, as follows:

```
$('div.chapter p:eq(0)').clone().insertBefore('div.chapter');
```

This will cause the first paragraph to appear twice. So, to use a familiar analogy, `.clone()` is to the insertion methods as copy is to paste.

> **Clone with events**
>
> The `.clone()` method, by default, does not copy any events that are bound to the matching element or any of its descendants. However, it can take a single Boolean parameter that, when set to true, clones events as well: `.clone(true)`. This convenient event cloning allows us to avoid having to deal with manually rebinding events, as was discussed in *Chapter 3*.

Cloning for pull quotes

Many websites, like their print counterparts, use pull quotes to emphasize small portions of text and attract the reader's eye. A pull quote is simply an excerpt from the main document that is presented with a special graphical treatment alongside the text. We can easily accomplish this embellishment with the `.clone()` method. First, let's take another look at the third paragraph of our example text, as follows:

```
<p>
  <span class="pull-quote">
    It is a Law of Nature
    <span class="drop">
      with us
    </span>
    that a male child shall have
    <strong>
      one more side
    </strong>
```

```
    than his father
  </span>,
  so that each generation shall rise (as a rule) one step in
  the scale of development and nobility. Thus the son of a
  Square is a Pentagon; the son of a Pentagon, a Hexagon; and
  so on.
</p>
```

Notice that the paragraph begins with `<span class="pull-quote">`. This is the class we will be targeting for cloning. Once the copied text inside that `<span>` is pasted into another place, we need to modify its style properties to set it apart from the rest of the text.

To accomplish this type of styling, we'll add a `pulled` class to the copied `<span>`. In our stylesheet, that class receives the following style rule:

```css
.pulled {
  background: #e5e5e5;
  position: absolute;
  width: 145px;
  top: -20px;
  right: -180px;
  padding: 12px 5px 12px 10px;
  font: italic 1.4em "Times New Roman", Times, serif;
}
```

An element with this class gets a light gray background, some padding, and a different font. Most importantly, it's absolutely positioned, 20 pixels above and 20 pixels to the right of the nearest (`absolute` or `relative`) positioned ancestor in the DOM. If no ancestor has positioning (other than `static`) applied, the pull quote will be positioned relative to the document `<body>`. Because of this, we need to make sure in the jQuery code that the cloned pull quote's parent element has `position: relative` set.

CSS position calculation

While the top positioning is fairly intuitive, it may not be clear at first how the pull quote box will be located 20 pixels to the right of its positioned parent. We derive the number first from the total width of the pull-quote box, which is the value of the `width` property plus the left and right padding, or 145px + 5px + 10px = 160px. We then set the `right` property of the pull quote. A value of 0 would align the pull quote's right side with that of its parent. Therefore, to place its left side 20 pixels to the right of the parent, we need to move it in a negative direction 20 pixels more than its total width, or -180px.

Now we can consider the jQuery code needed to apply this style. We'll start with a selector expression to find all of the `<span class="pull-quote">` elements, and apply the `position: relative` style to each parent element as we just discussed, as follows:

```
$(document).ready(function() {
  $('span.pull-quote').each(function(index) {
    var $parentParagraph = $(this).parent('p');
    $parentParagraph.css('position', 'relative');
  });
});
```

Listing 5.17

We'll be referring to the parent paragraph again later, so the `$parentParagraph` variable will improve performance and readability.

Next we need to create the pull quote itself, taking advantage of the CSS we've prepared. We need to clone each `<span>`, add the `pulled` class to the copy, and insert it into the beginning of its parent paragraph, as follows:

```
$(document).ready(function() {
  $('span.pull-quote').each(function(index) {
    var $parentParagraph = $(this).parent('p');
    $parentParagraph.css('position', 'relative');

    var $clonedCopy = $(this).clone();
    $clonedCopy
      .addClass('pulled')
      .prependTo($parentParagraph);
  });
});
```

Listing 5.18

Once again, we're introducing a variable here (`$clonedCopy`) that will be useful later.

Because we're using absolute positioning for the pull quote, the placement of it within the paragraph is irrelevant. As long as it remains inside the paragraph, it will be positioned in relation to the top and right of the paragraph, based on our CSS rules.

The pull quote now appears alongside its originating paragraph, as intended:

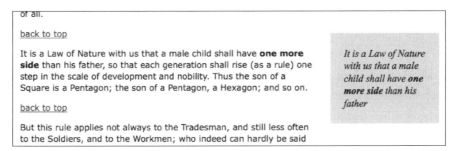

This is a good start. For our next enhancements, we'll clean up the content of the pull quotes a bit.

Content getter and setter methods

It would be nice to be able to modify the pull quote a bit, dropping some words, and replacing them with ellipses to keep the content brief. To demonstrate this, we have wrapped a few words of the example text in a `<span class="drop">` tag.

The easiest way to accomplish this replacement is to directly specify the new HTML that is to replace the old. The `.html()` method is perfect for our needs, as shown in the following code snippet:

```
$(document).ready(function() {
  $('span.pull-quote').each(function(index) {
    var $parentParagraph = $(this).parent('p');
    $parentParagraph.css('position', 'relative');

    var $clonedCopy = $(this).clone();
    $clonedCopy
      .addClass('pulled')
      .find('span.drop')
        .html('&hellip;')
      .end()
      .prependTo($parentParagraph);
  });
});
```

Listing 5.19

The new lines in Listing 5.19 rely on the DOM traversal techniques we learned in *Chapter 2*. We use `.find()` to search inside the pull quote for any `<span class="drop">` elements, operate on them, and then return to the pull quote itself by calling `.end()`. In between these methods, we invoke `.html()` to change the content into an ellipsis (using the appropriate HTML entity).

When called without arguments, `.html()` returns a string representation of the HTML inside the matched element. With an argument, the contents of the element are replaced by the supplied HTML. Take care to only specify valid HTML, escaping special characters properly, when using this technique.

The specified words have now been replaced by an ellipsis, as shown in the following screenshot:

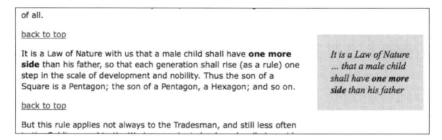

Pull quotes typically do not retain their original font formatting, such as the boldfaced **one more side** text in this example. What we really want to display is the text of `<span class="pull-quote">`, stripped of any `<strong>`, `<em>`, `<a href>` or other inline tags. To replace all of the pull-quote HTML with a stripped, text-only version, we can employ `.html()`'s companion method, `.text()`.

Like `.html()`, the `.text()` method can either retrieve the content of the matched element, or replace its content with a new string. Unlike `.html()`, however, `.text()` always gets or sets a plain text string. When `.text()` retrieves content, all of the included tags are ignored and HTML entities translated into plain characters. When it sets content, special characters such as `<` are translated into their HTML entity equivalents:

```
$(document).ready(function() {
  $('span.pull-quote').each(function(index) {
    var $parentParagraph = $(this).parent('p');
    $parentParagraph.css('position', 'relative');

    var $clonedCopy = $(this).clone();
    $clonedCopy
      .addClass('pulled')
```

```
    .find('span.drop')
      .html('&hellip;')
    .end()
    .text($clonedCopy.text())
    .prependTo($parentParagraph);
  });
});
```

Listing 5.20

When this sneaky bit of code fetches the content of the pull quote with `$clonedCopy.text()`, we get a plain string containing the text without tags. Therefore, when that text is fed right back into `.text()`, the markup is removed, and the bold text in our example is no more:

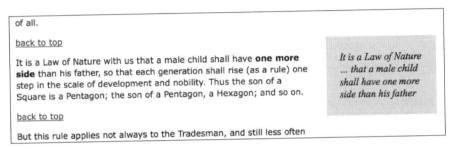

Further style adjustments

To complete our example, we'll grant some extra visual appeal to our pull quotes, adding rounded corners and drop shadows. In modern browsers, there are some CSS advances that can apply such effects simply. For maximum browser compatibility in our case, we will rely on an old-fashioned background image technique. The variable height of the pull-quote boxes requires us to apply two background images to achieve this.

Two background images imply at least two elements to apply them to (and maintain cross-browser parity). Therefore, we need to add another `<div>` around the pull quote content, as follows:

```
$(document).ready(function() {
  $('span.pull-quote').each(function(index) {
    var $parentParagraph = $(this).parent('p');
    $parentParagraph.css('position', 'relative');

    var $clonedCopy = $(this).clone();
    $clonedCopy
```

```
      .addClass('pulled')
      .find('span.drop')
        .html('&hellip;')
      .end()
      .text($clonedCopy.text())
      .prependTo($parentParagraph)
      .addClass('rounded-top')
      .wrapInner('<div class="rounded-bottom"></div>');
  });
});
```

Listing 5.21

We're using `.wrapInner()` here, another variant on the wrapping methods we examined earlier. This method adds the new element inside the element it's applied to, but surrounding all of the inner content. This new `<div>` supplies one of our needed classes, and we apply the other with a simple `.addClass()` call. We could combine this with the existing `.addClass()`, but we've kept it separate here to better group the related code.

The rules in our CSS apply appropriate background images to elements with the `rounded-top` and `rounded-bottom` classes, yielding quite nice results, as shown in the following screenshot:

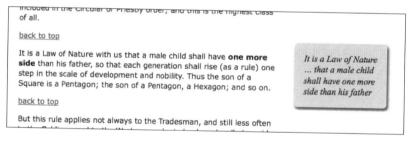

DOM manipulation methods in a nutshell

The extensive DOM manipulation methods that jQuery provides vary according to their task and their target location. We haven't covered them all here, but most are analogous to the ones we've seen, and more will be discussed in *Chapter 12*. The following outline can serve as a reminder of which method we can use to accomplish which task:

1. To create new elements from HTML, use the `$()` function.
2. To insert new element(s) inside every matched element, use:
    - `.append()`
    - `.appendTo()`

- ○ `.prepend()`
- ○ `.prependTo()`

3. To insert new element(s) adjacent *to* every matched element, use:
   - ○ `.after()`
   - ○ `.insertAfter()`
   - ○ `.before()`
   - ○ `.insertBefore()`

4. To insert new element(s) around every matched element, use:
   - ○ `.wrap()`
   - ○ `.wrapAll()`
   - ○ `.wrapInner()`

5. To replace every matched element with new element(s) or text, use:
   - ○ `.html()`
   - ○ `.text()`
   - ○ `.replaceAll()`
   - ○ `.replaceWith()`

6. To remove element(s) inside every matched element, use:
   - ○ `.empty()`

7. To remove every matched element and descendants from the document without actually deleting them, use:
   - ○ `.remove()`
   - ○ `.detach()`

Summary

In this chapter we have created, copied, reassembled, and embellished content using jQuery's DOM modification methods. We've applied these methods to a single web page, transforming a handful of generic paragraphs to a footnoted, pull-quoted, linked, and stylized literary excerpt.

Next up, we'll take a round-trip journey to the server via jQuery's Ajax methods.

Further reading

The topic of DOM manipulation will be explored in more detail in *Chapter 12*. A complete list of available DOM manipulation methods is available in *Appendix C* of this book, in *jQuery Reference Guide*, or in the official jQuery documentation at `http://api.jquery.com/`.

Exercises

To complete these exercises, you will need the `index.html` file for this chapter, as well as the finished JavaScript code as found in `complete.js`. These files can be downloaded from the Packt Publishing website at `http://www.packtpub.com/support`.

The challenge exercises may require use of the official jQuery documentation at `http://api.jquery.com/`.

1. Alter the code that introduces the **back to top** links so that the links only appear beginning after the fourth paragraph.

2. When a **back to top** link is clicked, add a new paragraph after the link, containing the message **You were here**. Ensure that the link still works.

3. When the author's name is clicked, turn it bold (by adding a tag, rather than manipulating classes or CSS attributes).

4. **Challenge**: On a subsequent click of the bolded author's name, remove the `<b>` element that was added (thereby toggling between bold and normal text).

5. **Challenge**: Add a class of `inhabitants` to each of the chapter's paragraphs, without calling `.addClass()`. Make sure to preserve any existing classes.

6
Sending Data with Ajax

The term **Ajax** was coined by Jesse James Garrett in 2005 as an acronym standing for **Asynchronous JavaScript and XML**. Since then it has come to represent many different things, as the term encompasses a group of related capabilities and techniques. At its most basic level, an Ajax solution includes the following technologies:

- JavaScript, to capture interactions with the user or other browser-related events
- The `XMLHttpRequest` object, which allows requests to be made to the server without interrupting other browser tasks
- A file on the server, presenting text in a data format such as XML, HTML, or JSON
- More JavaScript, to interpret the data from the server and present it on the page

Ajax has been hailed as the savior of the web landscape, transforming static web pages into interactive web applications. Many frameworks have sprung up to assist developers in taming it, because of the inconsistencies in the browsers' implementations of the `XMLHttpRequest` object; jQuery is no exception.

Let us see if Ajax can truly perform miracles.

Loading data on demand

Underneath all the hype and trappings, Ajax is just a means of loading data from the server to the web browser, or client, without a visible page refresh. This data can take many forms, and we have many options for what to do with it when it arrives. We'll see this by performing the same basic task in many ways.

We are going to build a page that displays entries from a dictionary, grouped by the starting letter of the dictionary entry. The HTML defining the content area of the page will look like the following code snippet:

```
<div id="dictionary">
</div>
```

Yes, really! Our page will have no content to begin with. We are going to use jQuery's various Ajax methods to populate this <div> with dictionary entries.

We're going to need a way to trigger the loading process, so we'll add some links for our event handlers to latch onto, as follows:

```
<div class="letters">
  <div class="letter" id="letter-a">
    <h3><a href="#">A</a></h3>
  </div>
  <div class="letter" id="letter-b">
    <h3><a href="#">B</a></h3>
  </div>
  <div class="letter" id="letter-c">
    <h3><a href="#">C</a></h3>
  </div>
  <div class="letter" id="letter-d">
    <h3><a href="#">D</a></h3>
  </div>
  <!-- and so on -->
</div>
```

 As always, a real-world implementation should use **progressive enhancement** to make the page function without requiring JavaScript. Here, to simplify our example, the links do nothing until we add behaviors to them with jQuery.

Adding a few CSS rules, we get a page that looks like the following screenshot:

The Devil's Dictionary

by Ambrose Bierce

A

B

C

D

Now we can focus on getting content onto the page.

Appending HTML

Ajax applications are often no more than a request for a chunk of HTML. This technique, sometimes referred to as **AHAH (Asynchronous HTTP and HTML)**, is almost trivial to implement with jQuery. First we need some HTML to insert, which we'll place in a file called a.html alongside our main document. This secondary HTML file begins as follows:

```
<div class="entry">
  <h3 class="term">ABDICATION</h3>
  <div class="part">n.</div>
  <div class="definition">
    An act whereby a sovereign attests his sense of the high
      temperature of the throne.
    <div class="quote">
      <div class="quote-line">Poor Isabella's Dead, whose
        abdication</div>
      <div class="quote-line">Set all tongues wagging in the
        Spanish nation.</div>
      <div class="quote-line">For that performance 'twere
        unfair to scold her:</div>
      <div class="quote-line">She wisely left a throne too
        hot to hold her.</div>
      <div class="quote-line">To History she'll be no royal
        riddle &mdash;</div>
      <div class="quote-line">Merely a plain parched pea that
        jumped the griddle.</div>
      <div class="quote-author">G.J.</div>
    </div>
  </div>
</div>

<div class="entry">
  <h3 class="term">ABSOLUTE</h3>
  <div class="part">adj.</div>
  <div class="definition">
    Independent, irresponsible. An absolute monarchy is one
    in which the sovereign does as he pleases so long as he
    pleases the assassins.  Not many absolute monarchies are
    left, most of them having been replaced by limited
    monarchies, where the sovereign's power for evil (and for
```

```
    good)  is  greatly  curtailed,  and  by  republics,  which  are
    governed  by  chance.
  </div>
</div>
```

The page continues with more entries in this HTML structure. Rendered on its own, this page is quite plain:

ABDICATION

n.
An act whereby a sovereign attests his sense of the high temperature of the throne.
Poor Isabella's Dead, whose abdication
Set all tongues wagging in the Spanish nation.
For that performance 'twere unfair to scold her:
She wisely left a throne too hot to hold her.
To History she'll be no royal riddle —
Merely a plain parched pea that jumped the griddle.
G.J.

ABSOLUTE

adj.
Independent, irresponsible. An absolute monarchy is one in which the sovereign does as he pleases so long as he pleases the assassins. Not many absolute monarchies are left, most of them having been replaced by limited monarchies, where the sovereign's power for evil (and for good) is greatly curtailed, and by republics, which are governed by chance.

ACKNOWLEDGE

Note that a.html is not a true HTML document; it contains no <html>, <head>, or <body>, all of which are normally required. We usually call such a file a **snippet** or **fragment**; its only purpose is to be inserted into another HTML document, which we'll accomplish as follows:

```
$(document).ready(function() {
  $('#letter-a a').click(function() {
    $('#dictionary').load('a.html');
    return false;
  });
});
```

Listing 6.1

The .load() method does all our heavy lifting for us! We specify the target location for the HTML snippet by using a normal jQuery selector, and then pass the URL of the file to be loaded as a parameter to the method. Now, when the first link is clicked, the file is loaded and placed inside <div id="dictionary">. The browser will render the new HTML as soon as it is inserted, as shown in the following screenshot:

Note that the HTML is now styled, whereas before it was plain. This is due to the CSS rules in the main document; as soon as the new HTML snippet is inserted, the rules apply to its elements as well.

When testing this example, the dictionary definitions will probably appear instantaneously when the button is clicked. This is a hazard of working on our applications locally; it is hard to account for delays or interruptions in transferring documents across the network. Suppose we added an alert box to display after the definitions are loaded, as shown in the following code snippet:

```
$(document).ready(function() {
  $('#letter-a a').click(function() {
    $('#dictionary').load('a.html');
    alert('Loaded!');
    return false;
  });
});
```

<div style="text-align:center">Listing 6.2</div>

We might assume from the structure of this code that the alert can only be displayed after the load has been performed. JavaScript execution is usually **synchronous**, working on one task after another in strict sequence.

However, when this particular code is tested on a production web server, the alert will quite possibly have come and gone before the load has completed, due to network lag. This happens because all Ajax calls are by default **asynchronous**. Otherwise, we'd have to call it "Sjax", which hardly has the same ring to it!

Asynchronous loading means that once the HTTP request to retrieve the HTML snippet is issued, script execution immediately resumes without waiting. Sometime later, the browser receives the response from the server and handles it. This is generally desired behavior; it is unfriendly to lock up the whole web browser while waiting for data to be retrieved.

If actions must be delayed until the load has been completed, jQuery provides a **callback** for this. We've already used callbacks in *Chapter 4, Styling and Animating*, using them to execute actions after an effect has completed. Ajax callbacks perform a similar function, executing after data arrives from the server. An example will be provided below.

Working with JavaScript objects

Pulling in fully-formed HTML on demand is very convenient, but it means having to transfer a lot of information about the HTML structure along with the actual content. There are times when we would rather transfer as little data as possible and process it after it arrives. In this case, we need to retrieve the data in a structure that we can traverse with JavaScript.

With jQuery's selectors, we could traverse the HTML we get back and manipulate it, but a more native JavaScript data format typically involves less data to transfer and less code to process it.

Retrieving JSON

As we have often seen, **JavaScript objects** are just sets of **key-value pairs**, and can be defined succinctly using curly brackets ({ }). JavaScript **arrays**, on the other hand, are defined on the fly with square brackets ([ ]) and have implicit keys, which are incrementing integers. Combining these two concepts, we can easily express some very complex and rich data structures.

The term **JavaScript Object Notation (JSON)** was coined by Douglas Crockford to capitalize on this simple syntax. This notation can offer a concise alternative to the sometimes-bulky XML format, as shown in the following code snippet:

```
{
  "key": "value",
  "key 2": [
    "array",
    "of",
    "items"
  ]
}
```

While based on JavaScript **object literals** and **array literals**, JSON is more prescriptive about its syntax requirements and more restrictive about the values it allows. For example, JSON specifies that all object keys, as well as all string values, must be enclosed in double quotes. Furthermore, functions are not valid JSON values. Because of its strictness, developers should avoid hand-editing JSON and instead rely on a server-side language to format it properly.

For information on JSON's syntax requirements, some of its potential advantages, and its implementations in many programming languages, visit http://json.org/.

We can encode our data using this format in many ways. We'll place some dictionary entries in a JSON file and we'll call it b.json:

```
[
  {
    "term": "BACCHUS",
    "part": "n.",
    "definition": "A convenient deity invented by the...",
    "quote": [
      "Is public worship, then, a sin,",
      "That for devotions paid to Bacchus",
      "The lictors dare to run us in,",
      "And resolutely thump and whack us?"
    ],
    "author": "Jorace"
  },
  {
    "term": "BACKBITE",
    "part": "v.t.",
    "definition": "To speak of a man as you find him when..."
  },
  {
    "term": "BEARD",
    "part": "n.",
    "definition": "The hair that is commonly cut off by..."
  },
  ... file continues ...
```

In order to retrieve this data, we'll use the $.getJSON() method, which fetches the file and processes it. When the data arrives from the server, it is simply a text string in JSON format. The $.getJSON() method **parses** this string and provides the calling code with the resulting JavaScript object.

Global jQuery functions

To this point, all jQuery methods that we've used have been attached to a jQuery object that we've built with the $() function. The selectors have allowed us to specify a set of DOM nodes to work with, and the methods have operated on them in some way. This $.getJSON() function, however, is different. There is no logical DOM element to which it could apply; the resulting object has to be provided to the script, not injected into the page. For this reason, getJSON() is defined as a method of the **global jQuery object** (a single object called jQuery or $ defined once by the jQuery library), rather than of an individual **jQuery object instance** (the object returned by the $() function).

If JavaScript had classes like other object-oriented languages, then we'd call $.getJSON() a class method. For our purposes, we'll refer to this type of method as a **global function**; in effect, they are functions that use the jQuery **namespace** so as not to conflict with other function names.

To use this function, we pass it the filename as before, as shown in the following code snippet:

```
// Unfinished code
$(document).ready(function() {
  $('#letter-b a').click(function() {
    $.getJSON('b.json');
    return false;
  });
});
```

Listing 6.3

This code has no apparent effect when we click the link. The function call loads the file, but we have not instructed JavaScript what to do with the resulting data. For this, we need to use a **callback function**.

The $.getJSON() function takes a second argument, which is a function to be called when the load is complete. As mentioned earlier, Ajax calls are **asynchronous**, and the callback provides a way to wait for the data to be transmitted rather than executing code right away. The callback function also takes an argument, which is filled with the resulting data. So, we can write the following code snippet:

```
// Unfinished code
$(document).ready(function() {
  $('#letter-b a').click(function() {
    $.getJSON('b.json', function(data) {
    });
```

```
      return false;
    });
  });
```

Listing 6.4

Here we are using an **anonymous function expression** as our callback, as has been common in our jQuery code for brevity. A reference to a **function declaration** could equally be provided as the callback.

Inside this function, we can use the `data` variable to traverse the JSON structure as necessary. We'll need to iterate over the top-level array, building the HTML for each item. We could do this with a standard for loop, but instead we'll introduce another of jQuery's useful global functions, `$.each()`. We saw its counterpart, the `.each()` method, in *Chapter 5, Manipulating the DOM*. Instead of operating on a jQuery collection of DOM elements, this function takes an array or map as its first parameter and a callback function as its second. Each time through the loop, the current **iteration index** and the current item in the array or map are passed as two parameters to the callback function, as shown in the following code snippet:

```
$(document).ready(function() {
  $('#letter-b a').click(function() {
    $.getJSON('b.json', function(data) {
      var html = '';
      $.each(data, function(entryIndex, entry) {
        html += '<div class="entry">';
        html += '<h3 class="term">' + entry.term + '</h3>';
        html += '<div class="part">' + entry.part + '</div>';
        html += '<div class="definition">';
        html += entry.definition;
        html += '</div>';
        html += '</div>';
      });
      $('#dictionary').html(html);
    });
    return false;
  });
});
```

Listing 6.5

We use `$.each()` to examine each item in turn, building an HTML structure using the contents of the entry map. Once the entire HTML has been built for each entry, insert it into `<div id="dictionary">` with `.html()`, replacing anything that may have already been there.

Safe HTML

This approach presumes that the data is safe for HTML consumption; it should not contain any stray < characters, for example.

All that's left is to handle the entries with quotations, which takes another `$.each()` loop:

```
$(document).ready(function() {
  $('#letter-b a').click(function() {
    $.getJSON('b.json', function(data) {
      var html = '';
      $.each(data, function(entryIndex, entry) {
        html += '<div class="entry">';
        html += '<h3 class="term">' + entry.term + '</h3>';
        html += '<div class="part">' + entry.part + '</div>';
        html += '<div class="definition">';
        html += entry.definition;
        if (entry.quote) {
          html += '<div class="quote">';
          $.each(entry.quote, function(lineIndex, line) {
            html += '<div class="quote-line">' + line + '</div>';
          });
          if (entry.author) {
            html += '<div class="quote-author">' + entry.author +
              '</div>';
          }
          html += '</div>';
        }
        html += '</div>';
        html += '</div>';
      });
      $('#dictionary').html(html);
    });
    return false;
  });
});
```

Listing 6.6

With this code in place, we can click the **B** link and confirm our results, as shown in the following screenshot:

The Devil's Dictionary

by Ambrose Bierce

A

B

C

D

BACCHUS *n.*

A convenient deity invented by the ancients as an excuse for getting drunk.

Is public worship, then, a sin,
That for devotions paid to Bacchus
The lictors dare to run us in,
And resolutely thump and whack us?

Jorace

The JSON format is concise, but not forgiving. Every bracket, brace, quote, and comma must be present and accounted for, or the file will not load. In some cases, we won't even get an error message; the script will just silently fail.

Executing a script

Occasionally, we don't want to retrieve all the JavaScript we will need when the page is first loaded. We might not know what scripts will be necessary until some user interaction occurs. We could introduce `<script>` tags on the fly when they are needed, but a more elegant way to inject additional code is to have jQuery load the `.js` file directly.

Pulling in a script is about as simple as loading an HTML fragment. In this case we use the `$.getScript()` function, which, like its siblings, accepts a URL locating the script file, as shown in the following code snippet:

```
$(document).ready(function() {
  $('#letter-c a').click(function() {
    $.getScript('c.js');
    return false;
  });
});
```

Listing 6.7

In our last example, we then needed to process the result data so that we could do something useful with the loaded file. With a script file, though, the processing is automatic; the script is simply run.

Scripts fetched in this way are run in the **global context** of the current page. This means they have access to all globally-defined functions and variables, notably including jQuery itself. We can, therefore, mimic the JSON example to prepare and insert HTML on the page when the script is executed, and place this code in c.js, as follows:

```
var entries = [
  {
    "term": "CALAMITY",
    "part": "n.",
    "definition": "A more than commonly plain and..."
  },
  {
    "term": "CANNIBAL",
    "part": "n.",
    "definition": "A gastronome of the old school who..."
  },
  {
    "term": "CHILDHOOD",
    "part": "n.",
    "definition": "The period of human life intermediate..."
  }
  // and so on
];

var html = '';

$.each(entries, function() {
  html += '<div class="entry">';
  html += '<h3 class="term">' + this.term + '</h3>';
  html += '<div class="part">' + this.part + '</div>';
  html += '<div class="definition">' + this.definition + '</div>';
  html += '</div>';
});

$('#dictionary').html(html);
```

Now clicking on the **C** link has the expected result, showing the appropriate dictionary entries.

Loading an XML document

XML is part of the acronym Ajax, but we haven't actually loaded any XML yet. Doing so is straightforward, and mirrors the JSON technique fairly closely. First we'll need an XML file, `d.xml`, containing some data we wish to display:

```xml
<?xml version="1.0" encoding="UTF-8"?>
<entries>
  <entry term="DEFAME" part="v.t.">
    <definition>
      To lie about another.  To tell the truth about another.
    </definition>
  </entry>
  <entry term="DEFENCELESS" part="adj.">
    <definition>
      Unable to attack.
    </definition>
  </entry>
  <entry term="DELUSION" part="n.">
    <definition>
      The father of a most respectable family, comprising
      Enthusiasm, Affection, Self-denial, Faith, Hope,
      Charity and many other goodly sons and daughters.
    </definition>
    <quote author="Mumfrey Mappel">
      <line>All hail, Delusion!  Were it not for thee</line>
      <line>The world turned topsy-turvy we should see;
        </line>
      <line>For Vice, respectable with cleanly fancies,
        </line>
      <line>Would fly abandoned Virtue's gross advances.
        </line>
    </quote>
  </entry>
</entries>
```

This data could be expressed in many ways, of course, and some would more closely mimic the structure we established for the HTML or JSON used earlier. Here, however, we're illustrating some of the features of XML designed to make it more readable to humans, such as the use of **attributes** for `term` and `part` rather than **tags**.

We'll start off our function in a familiar manner, as follows:

```
// Unfinished code
$(document).ready(function() {
  $('#letter-d a').click(function() {
    $.get('d.xml', function(data) {

    });
    return false;
  });
});
```

Listing 6.8

This time it's the $.get() function that does our work. In general, this function simply fetches the file at the supplied URL and provides the plain text to the callback. However, if the response is known to be XML because of its server-supplied **MIME type**, the callback will be handed the XML DOM tree.

Fortunately, as we have already seen, jQuery has substantial DOM traversing capabilities. We can use the normal .find(), .filter(), and other traversal methods on the XML document just as we would on HTML, as shown in the following code snippet:

```
$(document).ready(function() {
  $('#letter-d a').click(function() {
    $.get('d.xml', function(data) {
      $('#dictionary').empty();
      $(data).find('entry').each(function() {
        var $entry = $(this);
        var html = '<div class="entry">';
        html += '<h3 class="term">' + $entry.attr('term');
          html += '</h3>';
        html += '<div class="part">' + $entry.attr('part');
          html += '</div>';
        html += '<div class="definition">';
        html += $entry.find('definition').text();
        var $quote = $entry.find('quote');
        if ($quote.length) {
          html += '<div class="quote">';
          $quote.find('line').each(function() {
            html += '<div class="quote-line">';
              html += $(this).text() + '</div>';
          });
```

```
        if ($quote.attr('author')) {
          html += '<div class="quote-author">';
            html += $quote.attr('author') + '</div>';
        }
        html += '</div>';
      }
      html += '</div>';
      html += '</div>';
      $('#dictionary').append($(html));
    });
  });
  return false;
  });
});
```

Listing 6.9

This has the expected effect when the **D** link is clicked, as shown in the following screenshot:

The Devil's Dictionary

by Ambrose Bierce

A

B

C

D

DANCE *v.i.*

To leap about to the sound of tittering music, preferably with arms about your neighbor's wife or daughter. There are many kinds of dances, but all those requiring the participation of the two sexes have two characteristics in common: they are conspicuously innocent, and warmly loved by the vicious.

DAY

This is a new use for the DOM traversal methods we already know, shedding some light on the flexibility of jQuery's CSS selector support. CSS syntax is typically used to help beautify HTML pages, and thus selectors in standard .css files use HTML tag names such as div and body to locate content. However, jQuery can use arbitrary XML tag names, such as entry and definition here, just as readily as the standard HTML ones.

The advanced selector engine inside jQuery facilitates finding parts of the XML document in much more complicated situations, as well. For example, suppose we wanted to limit the displayed entries to those that have quotes that in turn have attributed authors. To do this, we can limit the entries to those with nested <quote> elements by changing entry to entry:has(quote). Then we can further restrict the entries to those with author attributes on the <quote> elements by writing entry:has(quote[author]).

The line in Listing 6.9 with the initial selector now reads as follows:

```
$(data).find('entry:has(quote[author])').each(function() {
```

This new selector expression restricts the returned entries correspondingly:

```
The Devil's Dictionary
by Ambrose Bierce


A          DEBT   n.

B          An ingenious substitute for the chain and whip of the slave-driver.

C              As, pent in an aquarium, the troutlet
               Swims round and round his tank to find an outlet,
               Pressing his nose against the glass that holds him,
D              Nor ever sees the prison that enfolds him;
               So the poor debtor, seeing naught around him,
               Yet feels the narrow limits that impound him,
               Grieves at his debt and studies to evade it,
               And finds at last he might as well have paid it.
                                                   Barlow
                                                   S. Vode
```

Choosing a data format

We have looked at four formats for our external data, each of which is handled by jQuery's Ajax functions. We have also verified that all four can handle the task at hand, loading information onto an existing page when the user requests it and not before. How, then, do we decide which one to use in our applications?

HTML snippets require very little work to implement. The external data can be loaded and inserted into the page with one simple method, which does not even require a callback function. No traversal of the data is necessary for the straightforward task of adding the new HTML into the existing page. On the other hand, the data is not necessarily structured in a way that makes it reusable for other applications. The external file is tightly coupled with its intended container.

JSON files are structured for simple reuse. They are compact and easy to read. The data structure must be traversed to pull out the information and present it on the page, but this can be done with standard JavaScript techniques. As modern browsers parse the files natively with a single call to `JSON.parse()`, reading in a JSON file is extremely fast. Errors in the JSON file can cause silent failure or even side effects on the page, so the data must be crafted carefully by a trusted party.

JavaScript files offer the ultimate in flexibility, but are not really a data storage mechanism. As the files are language-specific, they cannot be used to provide the same information to disparate systems. Instead, the ability to load a JavaScript file means that behaviors that are rarely needed can be factored out into external files, reducing code size unless and until it is needed.

While **XML** has fallen out of favor in the JavaScript community, with most developers preferring JSON, it is still so common that providing data in this format makes it very likely the data can be reused elsewhere. Indeed, many popular social websites export XML representations of their data, which has allowed many interesting **mashups** of their data to arise. The XML format is somewhat bulky, though, and can be a bit slower to parse and manipulate than other options.

With these characteristics in mind, it is typically easiest to provide external data as HTML snippets, as long as the data is not needed in other applications as well. In cases where the data will be reused but the other applications can also be influenced, JSON is often a good choice due to its performance and size. When the remote application is not known, XML may provide the greatest assurance that interoperability will be possible.

More than any other consideration, we should determine if the data is already available. If it is, then chances are it's in one of these formats to begin with, so our decision may be made for us.

Passing data to the server

Our examples to this point have focused on the task of retrieving **static** data files from the web server. However, the Ajax technique really comes into its own only when the server can **dynamically** shape the data based on input from the browser. We're helped along by jQuery in this task as well; all of the methods we've covered so far can be modified so that data transfer becomes a two-way street.

Interacting with server-side code

As demonstrating these techniques requires interaction with the web server, we'll need to use server-side code for the first time here. The examples given will use the PHP scripting language, which is very widely used, as well as freely available. We will not cover how to set up a web server with PHP here; help on this can be found on the websites of Apache (`http://apache.org/`) or PHP (`http://php.net/`), or from your site's hosting company.

Performing a GET request

To illustrate the communication between client and server, we'll write a script that only sends one dictionary entry to the browser on each request. The entry chosen will depend on a parameter sent from the browser. Our script will pull its data from an internal data structure like the following code snippet:

```php
<?php
$entries = array(
  'EAVESDROP' => array(
    'part' => 'v.i.',
    'definition' => 'Secretly to overhear a catalogue of the
      crimes and vices of another or yourself.',
    'quote' => array(
      'A lady with one of her ears applied',
      'To an open keyhole heard, inside,',
      'Two female gossips in converse free &mdash;',
      'The subject engaging them was she.',
      '"I think," said one, "and my husband thinks',
      'That she\'s a prying, inquisitive minx!"',
      'As soon as no more of it she could hear',
      'The lady, indignant, removed her ear.',
      '"I will not stay," she said, with a pout,',
      '"To hear my character lied about!"',
    ),
    'author' => 'Gopete Sherany',
  ),
  'EDIBLE' => array(
    'part' => 'adj.',
    'definition' => 'Good to eat, and wholesome to digest, as
      a worm to a toad, a toad to a snake, a snake to a pig,
      a pig to a man, and a man to a worm.',
  ),
  // and so on
);
?>
```

In a production version of this example, the data would probably be stored in a database and loaded on demand. As the data is a part of the script here, the code to retrieve it is quite straightforward. We examine the data that has been posted and call a function that returns the HTML snippet to display, as follows:

```php
<?php
if (isset($entries[strtoupper($_REQUEST['term'])])) {
  $term = strtoupper($_REQUEST['term']);
```

```php
    $entry = $entries[$term];
    echo build_entry($term, $entry);
  } else {
    echo '<div>Sorry, your term was not found.</div>';
  }
}

function build_entry($term, $entry) {
  $html = '<div class="entry">';
  $html .= '<h3 class="term">';
  $html .= $term;
  $html .= '</h3>';

  $html .= '<div class="part">';
  $html .= $entry['part'];
  $html .= '</div>';

  $html .= '<div class="definition">';
  $html .= $entry['definition'];
  if (isset($entry['quote'])) {
    foreach ($entry['quote'] as $line) {
      $html .= '<div class="quote-line">'. $line .'</div>';
    }
    if (isset($entry['author'])) {
      $html .= '<div class="quote-author">'.
         $entry['author'] .'</div>';
    }
  }
  $html .= '</div>';

  $html .= '</div>';
  return $html;
}
?>
```

Now requests to this script, which we'll call `e.php`, will return the HTML snippet corresponding to the term that was sent in the **GET** parameters. For example, when accessing the script with `e.php?term=eavesdrop`, we get back something similar to the following screenshot:

Once again, we note the lack of formatting we saw with earlier HTML snippets, because CSS rules have not been applied.

As we're showing how data is passed to the server, we will use a different method to request entries than the solitary buttons we've been relying on so far. Instead, we'll present a list of links for each term, and cause a click on any of them to load the corresponding definition. The HTML we'll add for this looks similar to the following code snippet:

```
<div class="letter" id="letter-e">
  <h3>E</h3>
  <ul>
    <li><a href="e.php?term=Eavesdrop">Eavesdrop</a></li>
    <li><a href="e.php?term=Edible">Edible</a></li>
    <li><a href="e.php?term=Education">Education</a></li>
    <li><a href="e.php?term=Eloquence">Eloquence</a></li>
    <li><a href="e.php?term=Elysium">Elysium</a></li>
    <li><a href="e.php?term=Emancipation">Emancipation</a>
      </li>
    <li><a href="e.php?term=Emotion">Emotion</a></li>
    <li><a href="e.php?term=Envelope">Envelope</a></li>
    <li><a href="e.php?term=Envy">Envy</a></li>
    <li><a href="e.php?term=Epitaph">Epitaph</a></li>
    <li><a href="e.php?term=Evangelist">Evangelist</a></li>
  </ul>
</div>
```

Now we need to get our JavaScript code to call the PHP script with the right parameters. We could do this with the normal `.load()` mechanism, appending the query string right to the URL and fetching data with addresses like `e.php?term=eavesdrop` directly. Instead, though, we can have jQuery construct the query string based on a map we provide to the `$.get()` function, as follows:

```
$(document).ready(function() {
  $('#letter-e a').click(function() {
    var requestData = {term: $(this).text()};
    $.get('e.php', requestData, function(data) {
      $('#dictionary').html(data);
    });
    return false;
  });
});
```

Listing 6.10

Now that we have seen other Ajax interfaces that jQuery provides, the operation of this function seems familiar. The only difference is the second parameter, which allows us to supply a map of keys and values that become part of the query string. In this case, the key is always `term` but the value is taken from the text of each link. Now, clicking on the first link in the list causes its definition to appear, as follows:

All the links here have addresses given, even though we are not using them in the code. This provides an alternative method of navigating the information for users who have JavaScript turned off or unavailable (a form of **progressive enhancement**). To prevent the links from being followed normally when clicked, the event handler returns `false`.

Performing a POST request

HTTP requests using the **POST** method are almost identical to those using GET. One of the most visible differences is that GET places its arguments in the query string portion of the URL, whereas POST requests do not. However, in Ajax calls, even this distinction is invisible to the average user. Generally, the only reason to choose one method over the other is to conform to the norms of the server-side code, or to provide for large amounts of transmitted data; GET has a more stringent limit. We have coded our PHP example to cope equally well with either method, so we can change from GET to POST simply by changing the jQuery function we call:

```
$(document).ready(function() {
  $('#letter-e a').click(function() {
    var requestData = {term: $(this).text()};
    $.post('e.php', requestData, function(data) {
      $('#dictionary').html(data);
    });
    return false;
  });
});
```

Listing 6.11

The arguments are the same, and the request will now be made via POST. We can further simplify the code by using the `.load()` method, which uses POST by default when it is supplied with a map of arguments:

```
$(document).ready(function() {
  $('#letter-e a').click(function() {
    var requestData = {term: $(this).text()};
    $('#dictionary').load('e.php', requestData);
    return false;
  });
});
```

Listing 6.12

This cut-down version functions the same way when a link is clicked, as shown in the following screenshot:

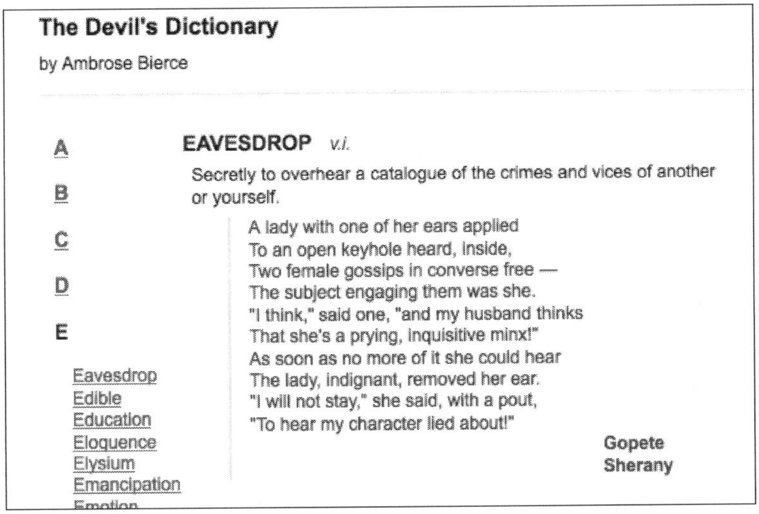

Serializing a form

Sending data to the server often involves the user filling out forms. Rather than relying on the normal form submission mechanism, which will load the response in the entire browser window, we can use jQuery's Ajax toolkit to submit the form asynchronously and place the response inside the current page.

To try this out, we'll need to construct a simple form, as follows:

```
<div class="letter" id="letter-f">
  <h3>F</h3>
  <form action="f.php">
    <input type="text" name="term" value="" id="term" />
    <input type="submit" name="search" value="search"
      id="search" />
  </form>
</div>
```

This time we'll return a set of entries from the server by using PHP to search for the supplied search term as a substring of a dictionary term. We'll use our `build_entry()` function from `e.php` to return the data in the same format as before, but we'll modify the logic somewhat in `f.php`:

```
<?php
$output = array();
foreach ($entries as $term => $entry) {
```

```php
    if (strpos($term, strtoupper($_REQUEST['term'])) !== FALSE) {
        $output[] = build_entry($term, $entry);
    }
}

if (!empty($output)) {
    echo implode("\n", $output);
} else {
    echo '<div class="entry">Sorry, no entries found for ';
    echo '<strong>' . $_REQUEST['term'] . '</strong>.';
    echo '</div>';
}
?>
```

The call to `strpos()` scans the word for the supplied search string. Now we can react to a form submission and craft the proper query parameters by traversing the DOM tree, as follows:

```javascript
$(document).ready(function() {
    $('#letter-f form').submit(function(event) {
        event.preventDefault();
        $.get('f.php', {'term': $('input[name="term"]').val()},
            function(data) {
                $('#dictionary').html(data);
            });
    });
});
```

Listing 6.13

Return false or prevent default?

In Listing 6.13, we have chosen to pass the `event` object into the `submit` handler and use `event.preventDefault()` rather than ending the handler with `return false`. This practice is recommended when the default action would otherwise reload the page or load another page. If our `submit` handler, for example, contains a JavaScript error, then preventing default on the handler's first line ensures that the form will not be submitted and our browser's error console will properly report the error. Remember from *Chapter 3, Handling Events*, however, that `return false` calls both `event.preventDefault()` and `event.stopPropagation()`. In order to stop the event from bubbling, we would need to call the latter as well.

This code has the intended effect, but searching for input fields by name and appending them to a map one by one is cumbersome. In particular, this approach does not scale well as the form becomes more complex. Fortunately, jQuery offers a shortcut for this often-used idiom. The `.serialize()` method acts on a jQuery object and translates the matched DOM elements into a query string that can be passed along with an Ajax request. We can generalize our submission handler as follows:

```
$(document).ready(function() {
  $('#letter-f form').submit(function(event) {
    event.preventDefault();
    var formValues = $(this).serialize();
    $.get('f.php', formValues, function(data) {
      $('#dictionary').html(data);
    });
  });
});
```

Listing 6.14

Now the same script will work to submit the form, even as the number of fields increases. When we perform a search for "**fid**," for example, the terms containing that substring are displayed, as shown in the following screenshot:

Delivering different content for Ajax requests

When returning HTML data, we have shown how the document fragments appear unstyled if we actually let the browser go to the page rather than use JavaScript. To provide a better experience to users without JavaScript, however, we can conditionally load a complete document with `<html>`, `<head>`, and `<body>` elements and all that they contain. To do so, we can take advantage of a request header that jQuery sends along with every Ajax request. In our server-side code (PHP, in this case): we just need to look for the `X-Requested-With` header. If it is set and has a value of `XMLHttpRequest`, then we only deliver the fragment; otherwise, we deliver the full document. A basic implementation in PHP might look like the following code snippet:

```php
<?php
$ajax = isset($_SERVER['HTTP_X_REQUESTED_WITH']) &&
    $_SERVER['HTTP_X_REQUESTED_WITH'] == 'XMLHttpRequest';

if (!$ajax):
// Show <head> and start of <body> for non-Ajax
?>
  <!DOCTYPE HTML>
  <html lang="en">
  <head>
    <!-- title, meta, link elements -->
  </head>
  <body>
  <!-- page heading, form, etc. -->
<?php
endif;

// show entry information for both Ajax and non-Ajax


if (!$ajax):
// Close open <div>s, <body>, and <html> for non-Ajax
?>

</body>
</html>

<?php endif; ?>
```

Now we have a true example of **progressive enhancement** in which those without JavaScript have a usable form with styled results and those with JavaScript have an enhanced experience.

This kind of setup in a server script allows for even more dramatic differences in the data that is returned. For example, we could return JSON data for Ajax requests and HTML for others:

```php
<?php
$ajax = isset($_SERVER['HTTP_X_REQUESTED_WITH']) &&
    $_SERVER['HTTP_X_REQUESTED_WITH'] == 'XMLHttpRequest';

// Set the $entries array

if ($ajax) {
header('Content-type: application/json');
  echo json_encode($entries);
}
else {
  // Print the full HTML document
}
```

This means less data to transfer, but requires building the HTML once the data is received, as we did in Listing 6.9.

Keeping an eye on the request

So far, it has been sufficient for us to make a call to an Ajax method and patiently await the response. At times, though, it is handy to know a bit more about the HTTP request as it progresses. If such a need arises, then jQuery offers a suite of functions that can be used to register **callbacks** when various Ajax-related events occur.

The `.ajaxStart()` and `.ajaxStop()` methods are two examples of these observer functions, and can be attached to any `jQuery` object. When an Ajax call begins with no other transfer in progress, the `.ajaxStart()` callback is fired. Conversely, when the last active request ends, the callback attached with `.ajaxStop()` will be executed. All of the observers are **global**, in that they are called when any Ajax communication occurs, regardless of what code initiates it.

We can use these methods to provide some feedback to the user in the case of a slow network connection. The HTML for the page can have a suitable loading message appended, as follows:

```html
<div id="loading">
  Loading...
</div>
```

This message is just a piece of arbitrary HTML; it could include an animated GIF image as a loading indicator, for instance. In this case, we'll add a few simple styles to the CSS file, so that when the message is displayed, the page looks like the following screenshot:

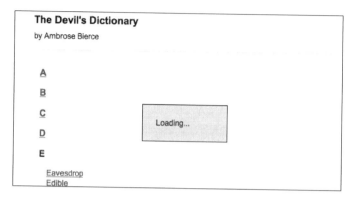

In keeping with the spirit of progressive enhancement, however, we won't put this HTML markup directly on the page. It's only relevant for us when JavaScript is available, so we will insert it using jQuery, as follows:

```
$(document).ready(function() {
  $('<div id="loading">Loading...</div>')
    .insertBefore('#dictionary')
});
```

Our CSS file will give this `<div>` a `display: none;` style declaration so that the message is initially hidden. To display it at the right time, we just register it as an observer with `.ajaxStart()`:

```
$(document).ready(function() {
  $('<div id="loading">Loading...</div>')
    .insertBefore('#dictionary')
    .ajaxStart(function() {
      $(this).show();
    });
});
```

We can **chain** the hiding behavior right onto this:

```
$(document).ready(function() {
  $('<div id="loading">Loading...</div>')
    .insertBefore('#dictionary')
```

```
    .ajaxStart(function() {
      $(this).show();
    }).ajaxStop(function() {
      $(this).hide();
    });
  });
```

Listing 6.15

Voilà! We have our loading feedback.

Once again, note that these methods have no association with the particular ways in which the Ajax communications begin. The `.load()` attached to the **A** link and the `.getJSON()` attached to the **B** link both cause these actions to occur.

In this case, this global behavior is desirable. If we need to get more specific, though, then we have a few options at our disposal. Some of the observer methods, like `.ajaxError()`, send their callback a reference to the `XMLHttpRequest` object. This can be used to differentiate one request from another, and provide different behaviors. Other more specific handling can be achieved by using the low-level `$.ajax()` function, which we'll discuss a bit later.

The most common way of interacting with the request, though, is the `success` callback, which we have already covered. We have used this in several of our examples to interpret the data coming back from the server and to populate the page with the results. It can be used for other feedback too, of course. Consider once again our `.load()` example from Listing 6.1, as follows:

```
$(document).ready(function() {
  $('#letter-a a').click(function() {
    $('#dictionary').load('a.html');
    return false;
  });
});
```

We can create a small enhancement here by making the loaded content fade into view rather than appear suddenly. The `.load()` can take a callback to be fired on completion, as follows:

```
$(document).ready(function() {
  $('#letter-a a').click(function() {
    $('#dictionary').hide().load('a.html', function() {
      $(this).fadeIn();
    });
```

```
        return false;
    });
});
```

Listing 6.16

First, we hide the target element, and then initiate the load. When the load is complete, we use the callback to show the newly-populated element by fading it in.

Error handling

So far we have only dealt with successful responses to Ajax requests, loading the page with new content when everything goes as planned. Responsible developers, however, should account for the possibility of network or data errors and report them appropriately. Developing Ajax applications in a local environment can lull developers into a sense of complacency since, aside from a possible mistyped URL, Ajax errors just don't happen locally. Unfortunately, the Ajax convenience methods such as `$.get()` and `.load()` do not provide an error callback argument themselves, so the global `.ajaxError()` method has been, at least in early versions of jQuery, the only way to handle errors with these methods. However, with the overhaul of jQuery's Ajax component in version 1.5, we now can chain `success()`, `complete()`, and `error()` callbacks to any Ajax function except `.load()`. For example, we can take the code from Listing 6.16 and change the URL to one that doesn't exist, we can test the `error()` callback, as shown in the following code snippet:

```
$(document).ready(function() {
    $('#letter-e a').click(function() {
        var requestData = {term: $(this).text()};
        $.get('z.php', requestData, function(data) {
            $('#dictionary').html(data);
        }).error(function(jqXHR) {
            $('#dictionary')
            .html('An error occurred: ' + jqXHR.status)
            .append(jqXHR.responseText);
        });
        return false;
    });
});
```

(handwritten annotation: doesn't act on a CSS selector)

Listing 6.17

Now, clicking on any of the links for terms beginning with **E** will produce an error message, as shown in the following screenshot. The exact content of `jqXHR.responseText` will vary depending on the server configuration:

The `.status` property contains a numeric code provided by the server. These codes are defined in the HTTP specification, and when an `.error()` handler is triggered, will represent an error condition such as:

Response code	Description
400	Bad request
401	Unauthorized
403	Forbidden
404	Not found
500	Internal server error

A complete list of response codes can be found on the W3C's site: `http://www.w3.org/Protocols/rfc2616/rfc2616-sec10.html`

We will examine error handling more closely in *Chapter 13, Advanced Ajax*.

Ajax and events

Suppose we wanted to allow each dictionary term name to control the display of the definition that follows; clicking on the term name would show or hide the associated definition. With the techniques we have seen so far, this should be pretty straightforward:

```
// Unfinished code
$(document).ready(function() {
```

```
  $('h3.term').click(function() {
    $(this).siblings('.definition').slideToggle();
  });
});
```

Listing 6.18

When a term is clicked, this code finds siblings of the element that have a class of definition, and slides them up or down as appropriate.

All seems in order, but a click does nothing with this code. Unfortunately, the terms have not yet been added to the document when we attach the click handlers. Even if we managed to attach click handlers to these items, once we clicked on a different letter the handlers would no longer be attached.

This is a common problem with areas of a page populated by Ajax. A popular solution is to **rebind** handlers each time the page area is refreshed. This can be cumbersome; however, as the event binding code needs to be called each time anything causes the DOM structure of the page to change.

An often superior alternative was introduced in *Chapter 3*: We can implement **event delegation**, actually binding the event to an ancestor element that never changes. In this case, we'll attach the click handler to the document using .live() and catch our clicks that way:

```
$(document).ready(function() {
  $('h3.term').live('click', function() {
    $(this).siblings('.definition').slideToggle();
  });
});
```

Listing 6.19

The .live() method tells the browser to observe all clicks anywhere in the document. If (and only if) the clicked element matches the h3.term selector, then the handler is executed. Now the toggling behavior will take place on any term, even if it is added by a later Ajax transaction.

Security limitations

For all its utility in crafting dynamic web applications, XMLHttpRequest (the underlying browser technology behind jQuery's Ajax implementation) is subject to strict boundaries. To prevent various **cross-site scripting attacks**, it is not generally possible to request a document from a server other than the one that hosts the original page.

This is typically a positive situation. For example, some cite the implementation of JSON parsing by using `eval()` as insecure. If malicious code is present in the data file, then it could be run by the `eval()` call. However, as the data file must reside on the same server as the web page itself, the ability to inject code in the data file is largely equivalent to the ability to inject code in the page directly. This means that, for the case of loading trusted JSON files, `eval()` is not a significant security concern.

 When jQuery parses JSON, it avoids the use of `eval()` altogether. It first attempts to use the browser's native `JSON.parse()` method. If the browser does not support this method, then it uses the `Function` constructor to evaluate the data, returning the result of `(new Function("return " + data))()`. This feature-testing parse operation is abstracted into the `jQuery.parseJSON()` function.

There are many cases, though, in which it would be beneficial to load data from a third-party source. There are several ways to work around the security limitations and allow this to happen.

One method is to rely on the server to load the remote data, and then provide it when requested by the client. This is a very powerful approach as the server can perform pre-processing on the data as needed. For example, we could load XML files containing RSS news feeds from several sources, aggregate them into a single feed on the server, and publish this new file for the client when it is requested.

To load data from a remote location without server involvement, we have to get a bit sneakier. A popular approach for the case of loading foreign JavaScript files is injecting `<script>` tags on demand. As jQuery can help us insert new DOM elements, it is simple to do this, as follows:

```
$(document.createElement('script'))
    .attr('src', 'http://example.com/example.js')
    .appendTo('head');
```

In fact, the `$.getScript()` method will automatically adapt to this technique if it detects a remote host in its URL argument, so even this is handled for us.

The browser will execute the loaded script, but there is no mechanism to retrieve results from the script. For this reason, the technique requires cooperation from the remote host. The loaded script must take some action, such as setting a global variable that has an effect on the local environment. Services that publish scripts that are executable in this way will also provide an API with which to interact with the remote script.

Another option is to use the `<iframe>` HTML tag to load remote data. This element allows any URL to be used as the source for its data fetching, even if it does not match the host page's server. The data can be loaded and easily displayed on the current page. Manipulating the data, however, typically requires the same cooperation needed for the `<script>` tag approach; scripts inside the `<iframe>` need to explicitly provide the data to objects in the parent document.

Cross-origin resource sharing

A more recent technique that has been drafted into a W3C specification is **Cross-Origin Resource Sharing (CORS)**. This technique requires sending a custom HTTP header from one domain that the other domain expects. The receiving domain must send back an `Access-Control-Allow-Origin` response header to the requester saying that the domain is accepted. For more information about CORS, visit `http://www.w3.org/TR/cors/`.

Using JSONP for remote data

The idea of using `<script>` tags to fetch JavaScript files from a remote source can be adapted to pull in JSON files from another server as well. To do this, we need to slightly modify the JSON file on the server, however. There are several mechanisms for doing this, one of which is directly supported by jQuery: **JSON with Padding**, or **JSONP**.

The JSONP file format consists of a standard JSON file that has been wrapped in parentheses and prepended with an arbitrary text string. This string, the "padding", is determined by the client requesting the data. Because of the parentheses, the client can either cause a function to be called or a variable to be set depending on what is sent as the padding string.

A PHP implementation of the JSONP technique is quite simple, as follows:

```php
<?php
  print($_GET['callback'] .'('. $data .')');
?>
```

Here, `$data` is a variable containing a string representation of a JSON file. When this script is called, the `callback` query string parameter is prepended to the resulting file that gets returned to the client.

To demonstrate this technique, we need only slightly modify our earlier JSON example in Listing 6.6 to call this remote data source instead. The $.getJSON() function makes use of a special placeholder character, ?, to achieve this, as shown in the following code snippet:

```
$(document).ready(function() {
  var url = 'http://examples.learningjquery.com/jsonp/g.php';
  $('#letter-g a').click(function() {
    $.getJSON(url + '?callback=?', function(data) {
      var html = '';
      $.each(data, function(entryIndex, entry) {
        html += '<div class="entry">';
        html += '<h3 class="term">' + entry.term + '</h3>';
        html += '<div class="part">' + entry.part + '</div>';
        html += '<div class="definition">';
        html += entry.definition;
        if (entry.quote) {
          html += '<div class="quote">';
          $.each(entry.quote, function(lineIndex, line) {
            html += '<div class="quote-line">' + line +
                '</div>';
          });
          if (entry.author) {
            html += '<div class="quote-author">' +
                entry.author + '</div>';
          }
          html += '</div>';
        }
        html += '</div>';
        html += '</div>';
      });
      $('#dictionary').html(html);
    });
    return false;
  });
});
```

Listing 6.20

We normally would not be allowed to fetch JSON from a remote server (examples. learningjquery.com in this case). However, as this file is set up to provide its data in the JSONP format, we can obtain the data by appending a query string to our URL, using ? as a placeholder for the value of the callback argument. When the request is made, jQuery replaces the ? for us, parses the result, and passes it to the success function as data just as if this were a local JSON request.

Note that the same security cautions hold here as before; whatever the server decides to return to the browser will execute on the user's computer. The JSONP technique should only be used with data coming from a trusted source.

Additional options

The Ajax toolbox provided by jQuery is well-stocked. We've covered several of the available options, but we've just scratched the surface. While there are too many variants to cover here, we will give an overview of some of the more prominent ways to customize Ajax communications.

The low-level Ajax method

We have seen several methods that all initiate Ajax transactions. Internally, jQuery maps each of these methods onto variants of the `$.ajax()` global function. Rather than presuming one particular type of Ajax activity, this function takes a map of options that can be used to customize its behavior.

Our first example, Listing 6.1, loaded an HTML snippet using `$('#dictionary').`
`load('a.html')`. This action could instead be accomplished with `$.ajax()` as follows:

```
$.ajax({
  url: 'a.html',
  success: function(data) {
    $('#dictionary').html(data);
  }
});
```

Listing 6.21

Rather than take separate arguments for URL, data, and a success callback, `$.ajax()` takes a single map of over 30 settings, offering a great deal of flexibility. A few of the special capabilities that come with using a low-level `$.ajax()` call includes:

- Preventing the browser from caching responses from the server. This can be useful if the server produces its data dynamically.
- Registering separate callback functions for when the request completes successfully, with an error, or in all cases.
- Suppressing the global handlers (such as ones registered with `$.ajaxStart()`) that are normally triggered by all Ajax interactions.
- Providing a user name and password for authentication with the remote host.

For details on using these, and other options, consult *Appendix C, jQuery Reference Guide* or see the API reference online (`http://api.jquery.com/jQuery.ajax`).

Modifying default options

The `$.ajaxSetup()` function allows us to specify default values for each of the options used when Ajax methods are called. It takes a map of options identical to the ones available to `$.ajax()` itself, and causes these values to be used on all subsequent Ajax requests unless overridden, as shown in the following code snippet:

```
$.ajaxSetup({
  url: 'a.html',
  type: 'POST',
  dataType: 'html'
});

$.ajax({
  type: 'GET',
  success: function(data) {
    $('#dictionary').html(data);
  }
});
```

Listing 6.22

This sequence of operations behaves the same as our preceding `$.ajax()` example. Note that the URL of the request is specified as a default value by the `$.ajaxSetup()` call, so it does not have to be provided when `$.ajax()` is invoked. In contrast, the `type` parameter is given a default value of POST, but this can still be overridden in the `$.ajax()` call to GET.

Loading parts of an HTML page

The first and simplest Ajax technique we discussed was fetching an HTML snippet and placing it on a page. Sometimes, though, the server already provides the HTML we need, but it is surrounded by an HTML page we do not want. We already saw how the server can be set up to deliver different content for Ajax requests. When it is inconvenient to make the server provide the data in the format we desire, jQuery can help us on the client end.

Consider a case like our first example, but in which the document containing the dictionary definitions is a complete HTML page, called `h.html`:

```html
<html lang="en">
  <head>
    <meta charset="utf-8"/>
    <title>The Devil's Dictionary: H</title>

    <link rel="stylesheet" href="dictionary.css"
      media="screen" />
  </head>
  <body>
    <div id="container">
      <div id="header">
        <h2>The Devil's Dictionary: H</h2>
        <div class="author">by Ambrose Bierce</div>
      </div>

      <div id="dictionary">
        <div class="entry">
          <h3 class="term">HABEAS CORPUS</h3>
          <div class="part">n.</div>
          <div class="definition">
            A writ by which a man may be taken out of jail
            when confined for the wrong crime.
          </div>
        </div>

        <div class="entry">
          <h3 class="term">HABIT</h3>
          <div class="part">n.</div>
          <div class="definition">
            A shackle for the free.
          </div>
        </div>
      </div>

    </div>
  </body>
</html>
```

We can load the whole document into our page using the code we wrote earlier, as follows:

```
// Unfinished code
$(document).ready(function() {
  $('#letter-h a').click(function() {
    $('#dictionary').load('h.html');
    return false;
  });
});
```

Listing 6.23

This produces a strange effect, though, due to the pieces of the HTML page we don't want to include:

To remove these extraneous bits, we can use another feature of the `.load()` method. When specifying the URL of the document to load, we can also provide a jQuery selector expression. If present, then this expression is used to locate a portion of the loaded document. Only the matched part of the document is inserted into the page. In this case, we can use this technique to pull only the dictionary entries from the document and insert them, as follows:

```
$(document).ready(function() {
  $('#letter-h a').click(function() {
    $('#dictionary').load('h.html .entry');
    return false;
  });
});
```

Listing 6.24

Now the irrelevant portions of the document are excluded from the page, as shown in the following screenshot:

Summary

We have learned that the Ajax methods provided by jQuery can help us to load data in several different formats from the server without a page refresh. We can execute scripts from the server on demand, and send data back to the server.

We've also learned how to deal with common challenges of asynchronous loading techniques, such as keeping handlers bound after a load has occurred and loading data from a third-party server.

This concludes our tour of the basic components of the jQuery library. Next, we'll look at how these features can be expanded upon easily, using jQuery plugins.

Further reading

The topic of Ajax will be explored in more detail in *Chapter 13*. A complete list of available Ajax methods is available in *Appendix C* of this book, in *jQuery Reference Guide*, or in the official jQuery documentation at http://api.jquery.com/.

Exercises

To complete these exercises, you will need the `index.html` file for this chapter, as well as the finished JavaScript code as found in `complete.js`. These files can be downloaded from the Packt Publishing website at `http://www.packtpub.com/support`.

The challenge exercise may require use of the official jQuery documentation at `http://api.jquery.com/`.

1. When the page loads, pull the body content of `exercises-content.html` into the content area of the page. ✓

2. Rather than displaying that whole document at once, create "tooltips" for the letters in the left column by loading just the appropriate letter's content from `exercises-content.html` when the user's mouse is over the letter.

3. Add error handling for this page load, displaying the error message in the content area. Test this error handling code by changing the script to request `does-not-exist.html` rather than `exercises-content.html`. *p. 168*

4. **Challenge**: When the page loads, send a JSONP request to Twitter and retrieve a user's last five messages. Insert the messages into the content area of the page. The URL to retrieve the last five messages of user `kswedberg` is: ~~`http://twitter.com/status/user_timeline/kswedberg.json?count=5.`~~

   http://itunes.apple.com/us/rss/topsongs/limit=1/json

7
Using Plugins

Throughout the first six chapters of the book, we have examined jQuery's core components. Doing this has illustrated many of the ways in which the jQuery library can be used to accomplish a wide variety of tasks. Yet as powerful as the library is at its core, its elegant **plugin architecture** has allowed developers to extend jQuery, making it an even more feature-rich library.

The growing jQuery community has created hundreds of plugins—from small selector helpers to full-scale user-interface widgets. In this chapter, we'll look at what a plugin is, how to find plugins developed by others, and how to incorporate them into our web pages. Then, in the following chapter, we'll explore how to create our own contributions to the jQuery plugin ecosystem.

Finding plugins and help

The jQuery website provides a large repository of available plugins at `http://plugins.jquery.com/`, with features such as user ratings, versioning, and bug reporting. Many of the plugins listed in this **Plugin Repository** have links to demos, example code, and tutorials to help us get started. Many more plugins can be found in the general code repositories such as GitHub (`http://github.com/`) and on plugin developers' personal sites. On GitHub we can often get a sense of the quality, or at least the popularity, of a plugin by examining its commit history and by noting how many developers are "watching" it and how many have "forked" it.

If we can't find the answers to all of our questions in the Plugin Repository, GitHub, the author's website, or the plugin's comments, then we can always turn to the jQuery community for assistance. The jQuery forums include a dedicated area for discussion of using plugins at `http://forum.jquery.com/using-jquery-plugins`. Many of the plugin authors are frequent contributors to the forums, and are eager to help with any problems that new users might face.

How to use a plugin

Using a jQuery plugin is very straightforward. We need to simply obtain the plugin code, reference the plugin from our HTML, and invoke the new capabilities from our own scripts. To illustrate this, we need a plugin to examine.

The jQuery **Cycle** plugin will serve our needs well. This plugin, by Mike Alsup, allows us to quickly transform a static set of page elements into an interactive slideshow. Like many popular plugins, it can be very simple to use, but is highly configurable for advanced use cases.

used for slideshows

Downloading and referencing the Cycle plugin

We can find the Cycle plugin using the jQuery Plugin Repository, or on the plugin's home page at `http://www.malsup.com/jquery/cycle/`. This page directs us to download instructions, which yield an archive containing both raw and compressed versions of the plugin code. For our purposes here, we'll use the file called `jquery.cycle.js`.

Once we have the plugin in our site's directory, we need to reference it from the `<head>` of the document, making sure that it appears after the main jQuery source file and before our scripts that need to use the plugin:

```
<head>
  <meta charset="utf-8">
  <title>jQuery Book Browser</title>
  <link rel="stylesheet" href="07.css" type="text/css" />
  <script src="jquery.js"></script>
  <script src="jquery.cycle.js"></script>
  <script src="07.js"></script>
</head>
```

We have now installed our first plugin. As we can see, this is no more complicated that setting up jQuery itself. The plugin's capabilities are now ours to use in our scripts.

Simple plugin use

The Cycle plugin operates on any set of sibling elements on a page. To show it in action, we'll set up some simple HTML containing text and images in a list, as follows:

```
<ul id="books">
  <li>
```

```
    <img src="images/0042.jpg"
      alt="jQuery 1.4 Reference Guide" />
    <div class="title">jQuery 1.4 Reference Guide</div>
    <div class="author">Karl Swedberg</div>
    <div class="author">Jonathan Chaffer</div>
  </li>
  <li>
    <img src="images/2244.jpg"
      alt="jQuery Plugin Development" />
    <div class="title">jQuery Plugin Development</div>
    <div class="author">Giulio Bai</div>
  </li>
  ...
</ul>
```

Some light styling in our CSS file presents these images one after another:

The Cycle plugin will work its magic on this list, transforming it into an attractive animated slideshow. This transformation can be invoked by calling the `.cycle()` method on the appropriate container in the DOM:

```
$(document).ready(function() {
  $('#books').cycle();
});
```

Listing 7.1

This syntax could hardly be simpler. As we would with any built-in jQuery method, we apply `.cycle()` to a jQuery object instance, which in turn points to the DOM elements we want to manipulate. Even without providing any arguments to it, `.cycle()` does a lot of work for us. The styles on the page are altered to present only one list item at a time, and a new item is shown using a cross-fading transition every four seconds:

This simplicity is typical of well-written jQuery plugins. A straightforward method call is all it takes to achieve professional, useful results. However, again like many other plugins, Cycle offers a large number of options for customizing and fine-tuning its behavior.

Specifying plugin method parameters

Passing parameters to plugin methods is no different than doing so with native jQuery methods. In many cases, parameters are passed as a single map of key-value pairs (as we saw with `$.ajax()` in the previous chapter). The choices of options to provide can be quite daunting; `.cycle()` alone has over fifty potential configuration options. The documentation for each plugin details the effect of each option, often with detailed examples.

The Cycle plugin allows us to alter the speed and style of the animation between slides, affect how and when slide transitions are triggered, and react to completed animations using callbacks. To demonstrate some of these capabilities, we'll provide three simple options to the method:

```
$(document).ready(function() {
  $('#books').cycle({
    timeout: 2000,
```

```
    speed: 200,
    pause: true
  });
});
```

Listing 7.2

The `timeout` option specifies the number of milliseconds to wait between each slide transition. In contrast, `speed` determines the number of milliseconds the transitions themselves will take. When set to `true`, the `pause` option causes the slideshow to suspend itself when the mouse is inside the cycling region, which is especially useful when the cycling items are clickable.

Parameter defaults

The Cycle plugin is able to do an impressive task even with no supplied arguments. To accomplish this, it needs a sensible set of **defaults** to use when options are not supplied.

A common pattern, and the one followed by Cycle, is to gather all of the defaults in a single object. In the case of Cycle, the `$.fn.cycle.defaults` object contains all of the default options. When a plugin collects its defaults in a publicly-visible location like this, we can alter the defaults to make our code more convenient when calling the plugin multiple times, as follows:

```
$.fn.cycle.defaults.timeout = 10000;
$.fn.cycle.defaults.random = true;

$(document).ready(function() {
  $('#books').cycle({
    timeout: 2000,
    speed: 200,
    pause: true
  });
});
```

Listing 7.3

Here we've set two defaults—`timeout` and `random`—prior to invoking `.cycle()`. As we declare a value for `timeout` in our `.cycle()` call, the default will be ignored. On the other hand, the new value for `random` does take effect, causing the slides to transition in a random order.

Other types of plugins

Plugins need not be limited to providing additional jQuery methods. They can extend the library in many ways, and even alter the functionality of existing features. Plugins can change the way other parts of the jQuery library operate. Some offer new **easing styles** for animations, for instance, or trigger additional jQuery **events** in response to user actions. The Cycle plugin offers such an enhancement by adding a new **custom selector**.

Custom selectors

Cycle's slideshows can be paused and resumed by calling `.cycle('pause')` and `.cycle('resume')`, respectively. We can easily add buttons that control the slideshow in this way:

```
$(document).ready(function() {
  $('<div id="books-controls"></div>').insertAfter('#books');
  $('<button>Pause</button>').click(function() {
    $('#books').cycle('pause');
    return false;
  }).appendTo('#books-controls');
  $('<button>Resume</button>').click(function() {
    $('#books').cycle('resume');
    return false;
  }).appendTo('#books-controls');
});
```

Listing 7.4

Suppose now that we want our **Resume** button to resume any paused cycle slideshow on the page, in the case there were more than one. We want to find all the `<ul>` elements on the page that are paused slideshows, and resume them all. Cycle's custom `:paused` selector allows us to do this easily, as follows:

```
$(document).ready(function() {
  $('<button>Resume</button>').click(function() {
    $('ul:paused').cycle('resume');
    return false;
  }).appendTo('#books-controls');
});
```

Listing 7.5

With Cycle loaded, `$('ul:paused')` will create a jQuery object referencing all of the paused slideshows on the page, so that we can interact with them at will. Selector extensions such as this that are provided by plugins can be freely combined with any of the standard jQuery selectors. We can easily see that, with the choice of the appropriate plugins, jQuery can be molded into the shape that best suits us.

Global function plugins

Many popular plugins provide new global functions within the `jQuery` namespace. This pattern is common when plugins supply features that are not related to DOM elements on the page, so are not good candidates for standard jQuery methods. For example, the Cookie plugin (`https://github.com/carhartl/jquery-cookie`) offers an interface for reading and writing cookie values on a page. This functionality is provided through the `$.cookie()` function, which can get or set individual cookies.

Let's say, for example, that we want to remember when users click our slideshow's **Pause** button so we can keep it paused if they leave the page and return to it later. After loading the Cookie plugin, reading a cookie is as simple as using the cookie's name as the sole argument.

```
if ( $.cookie('cyclePaused') ) {
  $('#books').cycle('pause');
}
```

Listing 7.6

Here, we look for the existence of a `cyclePaused` cookie; it doesn't matter what the value is for our purpose. If the cookie exists, then the cycle will pause. When we insert this conditional pause immediately after the call to `.cycle()`, the slideshow keeps the first image visible until the user at some point clicks on the **Resume** button.

Of course, because we haven't set the cookie yet, the slideshow is still cycling through the images. Setting a cookie is as simple as getting its value; we just supply a string for the second argument, as shown in the following code snippet:

```
$('<div id="books-controls"></div>').insertAfter('#books');
$('<button>Pause</button>').click(function() {
  $('#books').cycle('pause');
  $.cookie('cyclePaused', 'y');
  return false;
}).appendTo('#books-controls');
$('<button>Resume</button>').click(function() {
  $('ul:paused').cycle('resume');
```

```
    $.cookie('cyclePaused', null);
    return false;
}).appendTo('#books-controls');
```

Listing 7.7

The cookie is set to y when the **Pause** button is clicked and deleted—by passing null—when the **Resume** button is clicked. By default, the cookie remains for the session, which in general means until the browser tab is closed. Furthermore, by default, the cookie is associated with the page on which it was set. To change these default settings we can supply an options map for the function's third argument. In this way, the Cookie plugin is quite similar to other plugins and even jQuery's core functions.

For example, to make the cookie available throughout the site and have it expire after seven days, we can call the function with $.cookie('cyclePaused', 'y', {path: '/', expires: 7}). For information on these, and other options available when calling $.cookie(), we can refer to the documentation for the plugin.

The jQuery UI plugin library

While most plugins, such as Cycle and Cookie, focus on a single task, jQuery UI tackles a wide variety of challenges. In fact, while jQuery UI may be packaged as a single plugin, it is actually a comprehensive suite of related plugins.

The jQuery UI team has created a number of core interaction components and full-fledged widgets to help make the web experience more like that of a desktop application. **Interaction components** include methods for dragging, dropping, sorting, selecting, and resizing items. The current stable of **widgets** includes buttons, accordions, date pickers, dialogs, sliders, progress bars, and tabs, with more on the way. Additionally, jQuery UI provides an extensive set of advanced **effects** to supplement the core jQuery animations.

The full UI library is too extensive to adequately cover within this chapter; indeed, there are entire books devoted to the subject. Fortunately, a major focus of the project is consistency among its features, so exploring a couple of pieces in detail will serve to get us started in using the rest of them as needed.

Downloads, documentation, and demos of all jQuery UI modules are available at http://jqueryui.com/. The download page offers a combined download with all the features baked in, or a customizable download that can contain just the pieces we need.

Effects

The **effects** module of jQuery UI consists of a core and a set of independent effect components. The core file provides animations for colors and classes, as well as advanced easing.

Color animations

With jQuery UI's core effects component linked into the document, the `.animate()` method is extended to accept additional style properties, such as `borderTopColor`, `backgroundColor`, and `color`. For example, we can now gradually change an element from white text on a black background to black text on a light gray background, as follows:

```
$(document).ready(function() {
  $('#books').hover(function() {
    $('#books .title').animate({
      backgroundColor: '#eee',
      color: '#000'
    }, 1000);
  }, function() {
    $('#books .title').animate({
      backgroundColor: '#000',
      color: '#fff'
    }, 1000);
  });
});
```

Listing 7.8

Now when the mouse cursor enters the book slideshow region of the page, the book title's text color and background color both smoothly animate over a period of one second (1000 ms):

Class animations

The three class methods that we have worked with in previous chapters—
.addClass(), .removeClass(), and .toggleClass()—are extended by jQuery UI
to take an optional second argument for the animation duration. When this duration
is specified, the page behaves as if we had called .animate() and directly specified
all of the style attributes that change as a result of applying the class to the element:

```
$(document).ready(function() {
  $('h1').click(function() {
    $(this).toggleClass('highlighted', 'slow');
  });
});
```

Listing 7.9

By adding the code in Listing 7.9, we've caused a click on the page header to add
or remove the highlighted class. As we specified a slow speed, though, the
resulting color, border, and margin changes animate into place rather than
immediately taking effect:

Advanced easing

When we instruct jQuery to perform an animation over a specified duration, it does
not do so at a constant rate. If, for example, we call $('#my-div').slideUp(1000),
we know it will take a full second for the height of the element to reach zero;
however, at the beginning and end of that second the height will be changing slowly,
and in the middle it will be changing quickly. This rate alteration, called **easing**,
helps the animation to appear smooth and natural.

Advanced easing functions vary this acceleration and deceleration curve to provide
distinctive results. For example, the easeInExpo function grows exponentially,
ending an animation at many times the speed at which it started. We can specify a
custom easing function in any of the core jQuery animation methods or jQuery UI
effect methods. This can be done by either adding an argument or adding an option
to an options map, depending on the syntax being used.

To see this in action, we can provide `easeInExpo` as the easing style for the `.toggleClass()` method we just introduced in Listing 7.9:

```
$(document).ready(function() {
  $('h1').click(function() {
    $(this).toggleClass('highlighted', 'slow', 'easeInExpo');
  });
});
```

Listing 7.10

Now whenever the header is clicked, the class attributes begin appearing very gradually, then accelerate and complete the transition abruptly.

View easing functions in action

Demonstrations of the full set of easing functions are available at `http://jqueryui.com/demos/effect/#easing`.

Additional effects

The individual effect files included in jQuery UI add various transitions, some of which can be quite a bit more complex than the simple sliding and fading animations offered by jQuery itself. These effects are invoked by calling the `.effect()` method, which is added by jQuery. Effects that cause an element to be hidden or shown can instead be invoked using `.show()`, `.hide()`, and `.toggle()`, if desired.

The effects supplied by jQuery UI can serve a number of purposes. Some, like `transfer` and `size`, are useful when elements are to change shape and position. Others, such as `explode` and `puff`, offer attractive hiding animations. Still others, including `pulsate` and `shake`, call attention to an element.

View effects in action

All of the jQuery UI effects are showcased at `http://jqueryui.com/demos/effect/#default`.

The `shake` behavior is particularly nice for reinforcing the action that is not currently applicable. We could make use of this effect on our page when the **Resume** button would have no effect, for instance:

```
$(document).ready(function() {
  $('<button>Resume</button>').click(function() {
```

```
    var $paused = $('ul:paused');
    if ($paused.length) {
      $paused.cycle('resume');
      $.cookie('cyclePaused', null);
    }
    else {
      $(this).effect('shake', {
        distance: 10,
        duration: 80
      });
    }
    return false;
  }).appendTo('#books-controls');
});
```

Listing 7.11

Our new code checks the length of $('ul:paused') to determine if there are any paused slideshows to resume. If so, then it calls Cycle's resume action as before. Otherwise, the shake effect is performed. We see here that shake, as with the other effects, has a number of options available to fine-tune its appearance. Here we set the distance and duration of the effect to smaller numbers than the default, to make the button rapidly shake back and forth when clicked, like someone's head shaking "no."

Interaction components

The next piece of the jQuery UI puzzle is its **interaction components**, which are a set of behaviors that can be combined with custom code to produce complex interactive applications. One such component, for example, is Resizable, which can allow the user to change the size of any element with natural dragging movements.

Applying an interaction to an element is as simple as calling the method that bears its name. For instance, we can make the book titles resizable with a call to .resizable(), as follows:

```
$(document).ready(function() {
  $('#books .title').resizable();
});
```

Listing 7.12

This will add a resizing handle to the bottom-right corner of the title box. Dragging this box alters the region's width and height, as shown in the following screenshot:

As by now we might expect, these methods can be customized with a host of options. If, say, we wish to constrain the resizing to only happen vertically, then we can accomplish that by specifying which drag handle should be added:

```
$(document).ready(function() {
  $('#books .title').resizable({
    handles: 's'
  });
});
```

Listing 7.13

With a drag handle only on the south (bottom) side of the region, only the height of the region can be altered, as shown in the following screenshot:

Other interaction components

The other interactions are similarly highly configurable. A list of them including their options is at http://jqueryui.com/demos/.

Widgets

In addition to these building block interaction components, jQuery UI includes a handful of robust user interface **widgets** that appear and function out of the box like the full-fledged elements we are accustomed to seeing in desktop applications. Some of these are quite simple: the Button widget, for example, enhances buttons and links on the page with attractive styling and rollover states.

Granting this appearance and behavior to all button elements on the page is extremely simple:

```
$(document).ready(function() {
  $('button').button();
});
```

Listing 7.14

When the stylesheet for the jQuery UI Smoothness theme is referenced, the buttons take on a glossy, beveled appearance, as shown in the following screenshot:

As with other UI widgets and interactions, Button accepts several options. We may wish to provide appropriate icons for our two buttons, for example; the Button widget comes with a large number of predefined icons that we can employ. To do so, we could separate our .button() call into two, and specify an icon for each, as follows:

```
$(document).ready(function() {
  $('<button>Pause</button>').click(function() {
    // ...
  }).button({
    icons: {primary: 'ui-icon-pause'}
  }).appendTo('#books-controls');
  $('<button>Resume</button>').click(function() {
    // ...
  }).button({
    icons: {primary: 'ui-icon-play'}
  }).appendTo('#books-controls');
});
```

Listing 7.15

The `primary` icons that we specified correspond to standard class names in jQuery UI's theme framework. By default, `primary` icons are displayed to the left of the button text while `secondary` icons are displayed to the right, as illustrated in the following screenshot:

Other widgets are much more sophisticated, on the other hand. The Slider widget introduces a brand new form element, similar to an HTML5 range element but cross-compatible with all popular browsers. This requires a greater degree of customization and sophistication:

```
$(document).ready(function() {
  $('<div id="slider"></div>').slider({
    min: 0,
    max: $('#books li').length - 1
  }).appendTo('#books-controls');
});
```

Listing 7.16

A call to `.slider()` transforms a simple `<div>` element into a slider widget. The widget can be controlled by dragging or by the keyboard's arrows, to aid in accessibility:

In Listing 7.16 we've specified a minimum value of 0 for the slider, up to the index of the last book in our slideshow. We can use this as a manual control for the slideshow, by sending messages back and forth between the slideshow and slider when their respective states change.

To react to the slider's value changing, we can bind a handler to a **custom event** that is triggered by sliders. This event, `slide`, is not a native JavaScript event, but acts like one in our jQuery code. However, observing these events is so common that instead of calling `.bind()` explicitly, we can just add our event handler to the `.slider()` call itself, as follows:

```
$(document).ready(function() {
  $('<div id="slider"></div>').slider({
    min: 0,
    max: $('#books li').length - 1,
```

```
  slide: function(event, ui) {
    $('#books').cycle(ui.value);
  }
}).appendTo('#books-controls');
});
```

Listing 7.17

Whenever the `slide` callback is invoked, its `ui` parameter is populated with information about the widget, including its current value. By passing this value along to the Cycle plugin, we can manipulate the current slide being shown.

To communicate in the opposite direction we can use Cycle's `before` callback, which is triggered before each slide transition:

```
$(document).ready(function() {
  $('#books').cycle({
    timeout: 2000,
    speed: 200,
    pause: true,
    before: function() {
      $('#slider')
        .slider('value', $('#books li').index(this));
    }
  });
});
```

Listing 7.18

Inside the `before` callback, we call the `.slider()` method again. This time, we call it with `'value'` as its first parameter to set the new slider value. In jQuery UI parlance, we call `value` a **method** of Slider, even though it is invoked by calling the `.slider()` method, not by its own dedicated method name.

Other widgets

Each of the jQuery UI widgets has several associated options, events, and methods. For a full list, visit `http://jqueryui.com/demos/`.

jQuery UI ThemeRoller

One of the most exciting features of the jQuery UI library is the ThemeRoller, a web-based interactive theme engine for UI widgets. The ThemeRoller makes creating highly customized, professional-looking elements quick and easy. The buttons and slider that we just created have the default theme applied to them; this theme will be output from the ThemeRoller if no custom settings are supplied:

Generating a completely different set of styles is a simple matter of visiting `http://ui.jquery.com/themeroller/`, modifying the various options as desired, and clicking the **Download Theme** button. A `.zip` file of stylesheets and images can then be unpacked into your site directory. For example, by choosing a few different colors and textures, we can within minutes create a new, coordinated look for our buttons, icons, and slider, as follows:

Summary

In this chapter we have examined ways in which we can incorporate third-party plugins into our web pages. We've looked closely at the Cycle plugin, the Cookie plugin, and jQuery UI, and in the process have learned the patterns that we will encounter time and again in other plugins. In the next chapter, we'll take advantage of jQuery's plugin architecture to develop a few different types of plugins of our own.

Exercises

To complete these exercises, you will need the `index.html` file for this chapter, as well as the finished JavaScript code as found in `complete.js`. These files can be downloaded from the Packt Publishing website at `http://www.packtpub.com/support`.

1. Increase the cycle transition duration to half a second, and change the animation such that each slide fades out before the next one fades in. Refer to the Cycle documentation to find the appropriate option to enable this.

2. Set the `cyclePaused` cookie to persist for 30 days.

3. Constrain the title box to resize only in ten pixel increments.

4. Make the slider animate smoothly from one position to the next as the slideshow advances.

5. Instead of letting the slideshow loop forever, cause it to stop after the last slide is shown. Disable the buttons and slider when this happens.

6. Create a new jQuery UI theme that has a light blue widget background and dark blue text, and apply the theme to our sample document.

8
Developing Plugins

The available third-party plugins provide a bevy of options for enhancing our coding experience, but sometimes we need to reach a bit farther. When we write code that could be reused by others, or even just ourselves, we may want to package it up as a new plugin. Fortunately, the process of developing a plugin is not much more involved than writing the code that uses it.

In this chapter, we cover how to create many different kinds of plugins, from the simple to the complex. We'll start with plugins that simply make new global functions available, and move on to cover jQuery object methods of various types. We will also cover jQuery UI's widget factory, a powerful way to create sophisticated plugins without much work.

Use of the $ alias in plugins

When we write jQuery plugins we, of course, must assume that the jQuery library is loaded. We cannot assume, however, that the $ alias is available. Recall that the `$.noConflict()` method can relinquish control of this shortcut. To account for this, our plugins should always call jQuery methods using the full `jQuery` name or internally define $ themselves.

Especially in longer plugins, many developers find that the lack of the $ shortcut makes code more difficult to read. To combat this, the shortcut can be locally defined for the scope of the plugin by defining a function and immediately invoking it. This syntax for defining and invoking a function at once, often referred to as an **Immediately Invoked Function Expression (IIFE)**, looks like the following code snippet:

```
(function($) {
  // Code goes here
})(jQuery);
```

The wrapping function takes a single parameter, to which we pass the global `jQuery` object. The parameter is named `$`, so within the function we can use the `$` alias with no conflicts.

Adding new global functions

Some of the built-in capabilities of jQuery are provided via what we have been calling **global functions**. As we've seen, these are actually **methods** of the `jQuery` object, but practically speaking, they are functions within a `jQuery` **namespace**.

A prime example of this technique is the `$.ajax()` function. Everything that `$.ajax()` does could be accomplished with a regular global function called simply `ajax()`, but this approach would leave us open for function name conflicts. By placing the function within the `jQuery` namespace, we only have to worry about conflicts with other jQuery methods.

Many of the global functions provided by the core jQuery library are **utility methods**; that is, they provide shortcuts for tasks that are frequently needed, but not difficult to do by hand. The array-handling functions `$.each()`, `$.map()`, and `$.grep()` are good examples of these. To illustrate the creation of such utility methods, we'll add two trivial functions to their number.

To add a function to the `jQuery` namespace, we can just assign the new function as a **property** of the `jQuery` object, as follows:

```
(function($) {
  $.sum = function(array) {
    // Code goes here
  };
})(jQuery);
```

Listing 8.1

Now in any code which uses this plugin, we can write the following:

```
$.sum();
```

This will work just like a basic function call, and the code inside the function will be executed.

This sum method will accept an array, add the values in the array together, and return the result. The code for our plugin is quite brief, as follows:

```
(function($) {
  $.sum = function(array) {
    var total = 0;
```

```
        $.each(array, function(index, value) {
          value = $.trim(value);
          value = parseFloat(value) || 0;

          total += value;
        });
        return total;
      };
    })(jQuery);
```

Listing 8.2

Note that here, we have used the `$.each()` method to iterate over the array's values. We could certainly use a simple `for()` loop here, but as we can be assured that the jQuery library has been loaded before our plugin, we can use the syntax we've grown comfortable with. Also, a nice feature of `$.each()` is that its first parameter can also accept an object.

To test our plugins, we'll build a simple table with an inventory of groceries, as follows:

```
<table id="inventory">
  <thead>
    <tr class="one">
      <th>Product</th>        <th>Quantity</th> <th>Price</th>
    </tr>
  </thead>
  <tfoot>
    <tr id="sum" class="two">
      <td>Total</td>          <td></td>          <td></td>
    </tr>
    <tr id="average">
      <td>Average</td>        <td></td>          <td></td>
    </tr>
  </tfoot>
  <tbody>
    <tr>
      <td>Spam</td>           <td>4</td>          <td>2.50</td>
    </tr>
    <tr>
      <td>Egg</td>            <td>12</td>         <td>4.32</td>
    </tr>
```

```
    <tr>
      <td>Gourmet Spam</td> <td>14</td>          <td>7.89</td>
    </tr>
  </tbody>
</table>
```

Now we'll write a short script that populates the appropriate table footer cell with the sum of all quantities, as follows:

```
$(document).ready(function() {
  var $inventory = $('#inventory tbody');
  var quantities = $inventory.find('td:nth-child(2)')
    .map(function(index, qty) {
      return $(qty).text();
    }).get();
  var sum = $.sum(quantities);
  $('#sum').find('td:nth-child(2)').text(sum);
});
```

Listing 8.3

A look at the rendered HTML page verifies that our plugin is working correctly:

Adding multiple functions

If our plugin needs to provide more than one global function, then we could declare them independently. We'll add a plugin to compute the average of an array of numbers:

```
(function($) {
  $.average = function(array) {
    if ($.isArray(array)) {
      return $.sum(array) / array.length;
```

```
    }
    return '';
  };
})(jQuery);
```

Listing 8.4

For convenience and brevity, we're using the `$.sum()` plugin to assist us in returning the value for `$.average()`. To decrease the chance of errors, we also check the argument to make sure it is an array before computing the average.

Now that a second method is defined, we can call it in the same fashion, as follows:

```
$(document).ready(function() {
  var $inventory = $('#inventory tbody');
  var prices = $inventory.find('td:nth-child(3)')
    .map(function(index, qty) {
      return $(qty).text();
    }).get();

  var average = $.average(prices);
  $('#average').find('td:nth-child(3)')
    .text(average.toFixed(2));
});
```

Listing 8.5

The average now appears in the third column, as shown in the following screenshot:

Inventory

Product	Quantity	Price
Spam	4	2.50
Egg	12	4.32
Gourmet Spam	14	7.89
Total	**30**	
Average		*4.90*

We can also employ an alternate syntax in defining our functions, using the `$.extend()` function:

```
(function($) {
  $.extend({
    sum: function(array) {
      var total = 0;
```

```
        $.each(array, function(index, value) {
          value = $.trim(value);
          value = parseFloat(value) || 0;

          total += value;
        });
        return total;
      },
      average: function(array) {
        if ($.isArray(array)) {
          return $.sum(array) / array.length;
        }
        return '';
      }
    });
  })(jQuery);
```

Listing 8.6

This produces the same results.

We risk a different kind of namespace pollution here, though. Even though we are shielded from most JavaScript function and variable names by using the jQuery namespace, we could still have a conflict with function names defined in other jQuery plugins. To avoid this, it is best to encapsulate all of the global functions for a given plugin into a single object, as follows:

```
(function($) {
  $.mathUtils = {
    sum: function(array) {
      var total = 0;

      $.each(array, function(index, value) {
        value = $.trim(value);
        value = parseFloat(value) || 0;

        total += value;
      });
      return total;
    },
    average: function(array) {
      if ($.isArray(array)) {
        return $.mathUtils.sum(array) / array.length;
```

```
    }
    return '';
    }
  };
})(jQuery);
```

This pattern essentially creates another namespace for our global functions, called `jQuery.mathUtils`. Though we will still informally call these functions global, they are now methods of the `mathUtils` object, itself a property of the global `jQuery` object. We, therefore, have to include the plugin name in our function calls, as follows:

```
$.mathUtils.sum(sum);
$.mathUtils.average(average);
```

With this technique (and a sufficiently unique plugin name), we are protected from namespace collisions in our global functions. We now have the basics of plugin development in our bag of tricks. After saving our functions in a file called `jquery.mathutils.js`, we can include this script and use the functions from other scripts on the page.

Choosing a namespace

For functions that are solely for personal use, it often makes more sense to place them within our own project's global namespace. So, instead of using `jQuery`, we may instead choose to expose one global object of our own. We could, for example, have a global object called `ljQ` and define `ljQ.mathUtils.sum()` and `ljQ.mathUtils.average()` methods instead of `$.mathUtils.sum()` and `$.mathUtils.average()`. This way we completely remove the chance of namespace collisions with third-party plugins that we choose to include.

So we've now seen the namespace protection and guaranteed library availability that jQuery plugins grant. These are just organizational benefits, though. To really tap into the power of jQuery plugins, we need to learn how to create new **methods** on individual jQuery object instances.

Adding jQuery object methods

Most of jQuery's built-in functionality is provided through its object instance methods, and this is where plugins shine as well. Whenever we would write a function that acts on part of the DOM, it is probably appropriate instead to create an object method.

We have seen that adding global functions requires extending the jQuery object with new methods. Adding instance methods is similar, but we instead extend the jQuery.fn object:

```
jQuery.fn.myMethod = function() {
  alert('Nothing happens.');
};
```

 The jQuery.fn object is an alias to jQuery.prototype, provided for conciseness.

We can then call this new method from our code after using any selector expression.

```
$('div').myMethod();
```

Our alert is displayed (once for each `<div>` in the document) when we invoke the method. We might as well have written a global function, though, as we haven't used the matched DOM nodes in any way. A reasonable method implementation acts on its **context**.

Object method context

Within any plugin method, the keyword `this` is set to the current jQuery object. Therefore, we can call any built-in jQuery method on `this`, or extract its DOM nodes and work on them. To examine what we can do with object context, we'll write a small plugin to manipulate the classes on the matched elements.

Our new method will take two class names, and swap which class is applied to each element with every invocation. While jQuery UI has a robust .switchClass() method that even permits animating the class change, we'll provide a simple implementation for demonstration purposes, as follows:

```
// Unfinished code
(function($) {
  $.fn.swapClass = function(class1, class2) {
    if (this.hasClass(class1)) {
      this.removeClass(class1).addClass(class2);
    }
    else if (this.hasClass(class2)) {
      this.removeClass(class2).addClass(class1);
    }
  };
```

```
  })(jQuery);

  $(document).ready(function() {
    $('table').click(function() {
      $('tr').swapClass('one', 'two');
    });
  });
```

Listing 8.8

In our plugin, we first test for the presence of `class1` on the matched element and substitute `class2` if it is found. Otherwise, we test for `class2` and switch in `class1` if necessary. If neither class is currently present, then we do nothing.

In the code that uses the plugin, we bind a `click` handler to the table, calling `.swapClass()` on every row when the table is clicked. We'd expect this to change the header row's `one` class to `two`, and to change the sum row's `two` class to `one`. However, this is not the effect:

Inventory

Product	Quantity	Price
Spam	4	2.50
Egg	12	4.32
Gourmet Spam	14	7.89
Total	**30**	
Average		*4.90*

Every row has received the `two` class. To fix this, we need to correctly handle jQuery objects with multiple selected elements.

Implicit iteration

We need to remember that a jQuery selector expression can always match zero, one, or multiple elements. We must allow for any of these scenarios when designing a plugin method. In this case, we are calling `.hasClass()`, which only examines the first matched element. Instead, we need to check each element independently and act on it.

The easiest way to guarantee proper behavior regardless of the number of matched elements is to always call `.each()` on the method context; this enforces **implicit iteration**, which is important for maintaining consistency between plugin and built-in methods.

Within the .each() call, this refers to each DOM element in turn, so we can adjust our code to separately test for and apply classes to each matched element, as shown in the following code snippet:

```
(function($) {
  $.fn.swapClass = function(class1, class2) {
    this.each(function() {
      var $element = $(this);
      if ($element.hasClass(class1)) {
        $element.removeClass(class1).addClass(class2);
      }
      else if ($element.hasClass(class2)) {
        $element.removeClass(class2).addClass(class1);
      }
    });
  };
})(jQuery);
```

Listing 8.9

The meaning of this

Caution! The keyword this refers to a jQuery object within the object method's body, but refers to a DOM element within the .each() invocation.

Now when we click on the table, the classes are switched without affecting the rows that have neither class applied:

Inventory

Product	Quantity	Price
Spam	4	2.50
Egg	12	4.32
Gourmet Spam	14	7.89
Total	30	
Average		4.90

Method chaining

In addition to implicit iteration, jQuery users should be able to rely on **chaining** behavior. This means that we need to return a jQuery object from all plugin methods, unless the method is clearly intended to retrieve a different piece of information. The returned jQuery object is usually just the one provided as this.

If we use `.each()` to iterate over `this`, then we can just return its result, as shown in the following code snippet:

```
(function($) {
  $.fn.swapClass = function(class1, class2) {
    return this.each(function() {
      var $element = $(this);
      if ($element.hasClass(class1)) {
        $element.removeClass(class1).addClass(class2);
      }
      else if ($element.hasClass(class2)) {
        $element.removeClass(class2).addClass(class1);
      }
    });
  };
})(jQuery);
```

Listing 8.10

Previously, when we called `.swapClass()` we had to start a new statement to do anything else with the elements. With the `return` statement in place, though, we can freely chain our plugin method with built-in methods.

Method parameters

In *Chapter 7, Using Plugins*, we saw some plugins that can be fine-tuned to do exactly what we want through the use of parameters. We saw that a cleverly-constructed plugin helps us by providing sensible defaults that can be independently overridden. When we make our own plugins, we should keep the user in mind the same way.

As our example, we'll start with a plugin method that provides a shadow on an element. This can be done with various advanced CSS techniques, but here we'll use a more brute force approach: we will create a number of elements that are partially transparent, overlaid in different positions on the page, as follows:

```
(function($) {
  $.fn.shadow = function() {
    return this.each(function() {
      var $originalElement = $(this);
      for (var i = 0; i < 5; i++) {
        $originalElement
          .clone()
```

```
        .css({
          position: 'absolute',
          left: $originalElement.offset().left + i,
          top: $originalElement.offset().top + i,
          margin: 0,
          zIndex: -1,
          opacity: 0.1
        })
        .appendTo('body');
    }
  });
  };
}) (jQuery);
```

Listing 8.11

For each element this method is called on, we make a number of clones of the element, adjusting their opacity. These clones are positioned absolutely, at varying offsets from the original element. For the moment, our plugin takes no parameters, so calling the method is simple, as follows:

```
$(document).ready(function() {
  $('h1').shadow();
});
```

Next we can introduce some flexibility to the plugin method. The operation of the method relies on several numeric values that the user might want to modify. We can make these into **parameters** so they can be changed on demand.

Parameter maps

We have seen many examples in the jQuery API of maps being provided as method parameters. This can be a much friendlier way to expose options to a plugin user than a simple parameter list we just used. A **map** provides a visual label for each parameter, and also makes the order of the parameters irrelevant. In addition, any time we can mimic the jQuery API in our plugins, we should do so to increase consistency and, therefore, ease-of-use:

```
(function($) {
  $.fn.shadow = function(options) {
    return this.each(function() {
      var $originalElement = $(this);
      for (var i = 0; i < options.copies; i++) {
        $originalElement
          .clone()
          .css({
            position: 'absolute',
            left: $originalElement.offset().left + i,
            top: $originalElement.offset().top + i,
            margin: 0,
            zIndex: -1,
            opacity: options.opacity
          })
          .appendTo('body');
      }
    });
  };
})(jQuery);
```

Listing 8.12

The number of copies made and their opacity are now customizable. Within our plugin, each value is accessed as a property of the `options` argument to the function.

Calling this method now requires us to provide a map of values:

```
$(document).ready(function() {
  $('h1').shadow({
    copies: 3,
    opacity: 0.25
  });
});
```

The configurability is an improvement, but we now have to provide both options every time. We'll address this issue in the following section.

Default parameter values

As the number of parameters for a method grows, it becomes less likely that we will always want to specify each one. A sensible set of default values can make a plugin interface much more usable. Fortunately, using a map for our parameters helps with this task as well; it is simple to omit any item from the map and replace it with a default.

```
(function($) {
  $.fn.shadow = function(opts) {
    var defaults = {
      copies: 5,
      opacity: 0.1
    };
    var options = $.extend(defaults, opts);

    // ...
  };
})(jQuery);
```

Listing 8.13

Here, we have defined a new map, called `defaults`, within our method definition. The utility function `$.extend()` lets us take the `opts` map provided as an argument and use it to override the items in `defaults`, leaving omitted items alone.

We still call our method using a map, but now we can specify only the parameters that we want to differ from their defaults, as follows:

```
$(document).ready(function() {
  $('h1').shadow({
    copies: 3
  });
});
```

Unspecified parameters use their default values. The `$.extend()` method even accepts null values, so if the default parameters are all acceptable, our method can be called very simply without errors.

```
$(document).ready(function() {
  $('h1').shadow();
});
```

Callback functions

Of course, some method parameters can be quite a bit more complicated than a simple numeric value. One common parameter type we have seen frequently throughout the jQuery API is the **callback function**. Callback functions can lend a large amount of flexibility to a plugin without requiring a great deal of preparation when creating the plugin.

To employ a callback function in our method, we need to simply accept the function object as a parameter and call that function, where appropriate, in our method implementation. As an example, we can extend our text shadow method to allow the user to customize the position of the shadow relative to the text:

```
(function($) {
  $.fn.shadow = function(opts) {
    var defaults = {
      copies: 5,
      opacity: 0.1,
      copyOffset: function(index) {
        return {x: index, y: index};
      }
    };
    var options = $.extend(defaults, opts);

    return this.each(function() {
      var $originalElement = $(this);
      for (var i = 0; i < options.copies; i++) {
        var offset = options.copyOffset(i);
        $originalElement
          .clone()
          .css({
            position: 'absolute',
            left: $originalElement.offset().left + offset.x,
            top: $originalElement.offset().top + offset.y,
            margin: 0,
            zIndex: -1,
            opacity: options.opacity
          })
          .appendTo('body');
      }
    });
  };
})(jQuery);
```

Listing 8.14

Each slice of the shadow has a different offset from the original text. Before, this offset has simply been equal to the index of the copy. Now, though, we're calculating the offset using the `copyOffset()` function, which is an option that the user can override. So, for example, we could provide negative values for the offset in both dimensions:

```
$(document).ready(function() {
  $('h1').shadow({
    copyOffset: function(index) {
      return {x: -index, y: -2 * index};
    }
  });
});
```

This will cause the shadow to be cast up and to the left rather than down and to the right:

The callback allows simple modifications to the shadow's direction, or much more sophisticated positioning if the plugin user supplies the appropriate callback. If the callback is not specified, then the default behavior is once again used.

Customizable defaults

We can improve the experience of using our plugins by providing reasonable default values for our method parameters, as we have seen. However, sometimes it can be difficult to predict what a reasonable default value will be. If a script will be calling our plugin multiple times with a different set of parameters than we set as the defaults, then the ability to customize these defaults could significantly reduce the amount of code that needs to be written.

To make the defaults customizable, we need to move them out of our method definition and into a location that is accessible by outside code, as follows:

```
(function($) {
  $.fn.shadow = function(opts) {
    var options = $.extend({}, $.fn.shadow.defaults, opts);
    // ...
  };

  $.fn.shadow.defaults = {
    copies: 5,
    opacity: 0.1,
    copyOffset: function(index) {
      return {x: index, y: index};
    }
  };
})(jQuery);
```

Listing 8.15

The defaults are now in the namespace of the shadow plugin, and can be directly referred to with `$.fn.shadow.defaults`. Our call to `$.extend()` had to change to accommodate this as well. As we are now reusing the same defaults map for every call to `.shadow()`, we can't allow `$.extend()` to modify it. Instead, we provide an empty map `{}` as the first argument to `$.extend()`, and it is this new object that gets modified.

Now code that uses our plugin can change the defaults that all subsequent calls to `.shadow()` will use. Options can also still be supplied at the time the method is invoked:

```
$(document).ready(function() {
  $.fn.shadow.defaults.copies = 10;
  $('h1').shadow({
    copyOffset: function(index) {
      return {x: -index, y: index};
    }
  });
});
```

This script will create a shadow using 10 copies of the element, because that is the new default value, but will also cast the shadow left and down, due to the `copyOffset` callback that is provided along with the method call:

The jQuery UI widget factory

As we saw in *Chapter 7*, jQuery UI houses an assortment of **widgets** — plugins that present a particular kind of UI element, such as a button or slider. These widgets present a very consistent API to a JavaScript programmer, which makes the job of learning to use one a snap. When a plugin we're writing will create a new user interface element, extending the jQuery UI library with a widget plugin is often the right choice.

A widget is an intricate piece of functionality, but fortunately we are not left completely to our own devices in creating one. The jQuery UI core contains a factory method called `$.widget()` which does a great deal of the work for us. Using this factory will help ensure that our code meets the API standards enjoyed by all jQuery UI widgets.

Plugins we create using the widget factory have many nice features. We get all of these perks (and more!) with very little effort on our part:

1. The plugin becomes "stateful," meaning that we can examine, alter, or even completely reverse the effects of the plugin after it has been applied.

2. User-supplied options are merged with customizable default options automatically.

3. Multiple plugin methods are seamlessly combined into a single jQuery method, accepting a string to identify which sub-method is being called.

4. Custom event handlers triggered by the plugin get access to the widget instance's data.

In fact, these advantages are so nice that we may wish to use the widget factory to construct any suitably complex plugin, UI-related or otherwise.

Creating a widget

For our example, we'll craft a plugin that adds custom tooltips to elements. A simple tooltip implementation creates a `<div>` container for each element on the page that gets a tooltip, and positions that container next to the element when the mouse cursor hovers over the target. We'll look at the following functioning plugin code, and then step through it piece by piece:

```
(function($) {
  $.widget('ljq.tooltip', {
    _create: function() {
      this._tooltipDiv = $('<div></div>')
        .addClass('ljq-tooltip-text ' +
          'ui-widget ui-state-highlight ui-corner-all')
        .hide().appendTo('body');
      this.element
        .addClass('ljq-tooltip-trigger')
        .bind('mouseenter.ljq-tooltip',
          $.proxy(this._open, this))
        .bind('mouseleave.ljq-tooltip',
          $.proxy(this._close, this));
    },

    _open: function() {
      var elementOffset = this.element.offset();
      this._tooltipDiv.css({
        left: elementOffset.left,
        top: elementOffset.top + this.element.height()
      }).text(this.element.data('tooltip-text'));
      this._tooltipDiv.show();
    },

    _close: function() {
      this._tooltipDiv.hide();
    }
  });
}) (jQuery);
```

Listing 8.16

A plugin is created by the widget factory each time $.widget() is called. This function accepts the name of the widget and a map of widget properties. The name of the widget must be namespaced; here, we've chosen a namespace of ljq and the plugin name tooltip. As a result, our plugin will be invoked by calling .tooltip() on a jQuery object.

In our example thus far, the widget properties are all functions. These function names all begin with underscores because they are **private**—we will discuss public functions later. The first function, _create, is special, and will be invoked by the widget factory whenever .tooltip() is called, once per matched element in the jQuery object.

Inside this creation function, we need to set up our tooltip for future displaying. To do this, we make the new <div> element and add it to the document. We're storing the created element in this._tooltipDiv for later use.

In the context of our function, this refers to the current widget instance, and we can add whatever properties we want to this object. The object has some built-in properties that can be handy for us as well; in particular, this.element gives us a jQuery object pointing to the element that was originally selected.

We use this.element to bind mouseenter and mouseleave handlers to the tooltip trigger element. We need these handlers to open the tooltip when the mouse begins hovering over the trigger, and to close it when the mouse leaves. Note that the events are namespaced with the name of our plugin. As we discussed in *Chapter 3, Handling Events*, namespacing makes it easier for us to add and remove event handlers without stepping on the toes of other code that also wants to bind handlers to the elements.

These .bind() calls contain another feature that is new to us: the event handlers are passed through the $.proxy() function. This function changes what this refers to in a method, so that in this case we can easily refer to the widget instance within the _open function.

The _open and _close functions themselves are fairly self-explanatory. These are not special names, but rather illustrate that we can create whatever private functions we need within our widget, so long as their names begin with underscores. When the tooltip is opened, we position it with CSS and show it; when it is closed, we simply hide it.

During the opening process, we need to populate the tooltip with information. We're using the .data() method for this, which can get and set arbitrary data associated with any element but here is returning the value of the data-tooltip-text attribute of each element.

With our plugin in place, the code $('a').tooltip() will cause a tooltip to be displayed when the mouse is over any anchor, as shown in the following screenshot:

The plugin is not very long, but densely packed with sophisticated concepts. To make this sophistication pay off, the first thing we can do is to make our widget stateful.

Destroying widgets

We've seen that the widget factory creates a new jQuery method, in our case called .tooltip(), that can be called with no arguments to apply the widget to a set of elements. There's much more that this method can do, though. When we give this method a string argument, it calls the **sub-method** with the appropriate name.

One of the built-in sub-methods is called destroy. Calling .tooltip('destroy') will remove the tooltip widget from the page. The widget factory does most of the work, but if we have modified parts of the document inside _create (as we have here by creating the tooltip text <div>); we need to clean up after ourselves.

```
destroy: function() {
  this._tooltipDiv.remove();
  this.element
    .removeClass('ljq-tooltip-trigger')
    .unbind('.ljq-tooltip');
  $.Widget.prototype.destroy.apply(this, arguments);
},
```

Listing 8.17

This new code is added as a new property of the widget. Note that destroy is not preceded with an underscore; this is a public sub-method that we can call with .tooltip('destroy'). The function then undoes the modifications we performed, then calls the prototype's version of destroy so that the automatic cleanup occurs.

Enabling and disabling widgets

In addition to being destroyed completely, any widget can be temporarily disabled and later re-enabled. The built-in sub-methods `enable` and `disable` assist us by setting the value of `this.options.disabled` to `true` or `false` as appropriate. All we have to do to support these sub-methods is to check this value before our widget takes any action:

```
_open: function() {
  if (!this.options.disabled) {
    var elementOffset = this.element.offset();
    this._tooltipDiv.css({
      left: elementOffset.left,
      top: elementOffset.top + this.element.height()
    }).text(this.element.data('tooltip-text'));
    this._tooltipDiv.show();
  }
},
```

Listing 8.18

With this extra check in place, the tooltips stop displaying once `.tooltip('disable')` is called, and display once again after `.tooltip('enable')` is invoked.

Accepting widget options

Now it's time to make our widget customizable. As we saw when constructing the `.shadow()` plugin, it's friendly to provide a customizable set of defaults for a widget, and then to override those defaults with options the user specifies. Nearly all of the work in this process is performed by the widget factory. All we need to do is to provide an `options` property, as follows:

```
options: {
  offsetX: 10,
  offsetY: 10,
  content: function() {
    return $(this).data('tooltip-text');
  }
},

_open: function() {
  if (!this.options.disabled) {
    var elementOffset = this.element.offset();
    this._tooltipDiv.css({
      left: elementOffset.left + this.options.offsetX,
```

```
        top: elementOffset.top + this.element.height()
          + this.options.offsetY
      }).text(this.options.content.call(this.element[0]));
      this._tooltipDiv.show();
    }
  },
```

Listing 8.19

The `options` property is a simple map. All of the valid options for our widget should be represented, so that none of them are mandatory for the user to provide. Here we're supplying x and y coordinates for the tooltip relative to its trigger element, as well as a function that generates the tooltip text for each element.

The only piece of our code that needs to examine these options is `_open`, so the other functions are unchanged. Inside a sub-method such as `_open`, we can access these properties using `this.options`. We will always get the correct value for the option this way: the default value or the overridden value if the user has provided one.

We can still add our widget without arguments, like `.tooltip()`, and get the default behavior. Now, though, we can supply options that override the default behavior: `.tooltip({offsetX: -10, offsetX: 25})`. The widget factory even lets us change these options after the widget is instantiated: `.tooltip('option', 'offsetX', 20)`. The next time the option is accessed, we will see the new value.

Reacting to option changes

If we need to immediately react to an option change, we can add a `_setOption` function to our widget that handles the change and then calls the default implementation of `_setOption`.

Adding sub-methods

The built-in sub-methods are convenient, but often we will want to expose more "hooks" to the users of our plugin. We've already seen how to create new private functions inside our widget. Creating public functions (sub-methods) is just the same, except that the widget property names do not begin with an underscore. We can use this to create sub-methods that manually open and close the tooltip quite simply:

```
open: function() {
  this._open();
},
```

```
close: function() {
  this._close();
},
```

Listing 8.20

That's it! By adding public sub-methods that call the private functions, we can now open a tooltip with `.tooltip('open')` and close it with `.tooltip('close')`. The widget factory even takes care of details for us like ensuring that chaining continues to work even if we don't return anything from our sub-method.

Triggering widget events

A great plugin not only extends jQuery, but also offers plenty of opportunities for other code to extend the plugin itself. One simple way to offer this extensibility is to support a set of custom events related to the plugin. The widget factory makes this a simple process, as follows:

```
_open: function() {
  if (!this.options.disabled) {
    var elementOffset = this.element.offset();
    this._tooltipDiv.css({
      left: elementOffset.left + this.options.offsetX,
      top: elementOffset.top + this.element.height()
        + this.options.offsetY
    }).text(this.options.content.call(this.element[0]));
    this._tooltipDiv.show();
    this._trigger('open');
  }
},
_close: function() {
  this._tooltipDiv.hide();
  this._trigger('close');
}
```

Listing 8.21

Calling `this._trigger()` in one of our functions allows code to listen for the new custom event. The event's name will be prefixed with our widget name, so we don't have to worry much about conflicts with other events. As we call `this._trigger('open')` in our tooltip's opening function, for example, the event called `tooltipopen` will be issued each time the tooltip opens. We can listen for this event by calling `.bind('tooltipopen')` on the element.

Chapter 8

This only scratches the surface of what's possible with a full-fledged widget plugin, but gives us the tools we need to build a widget that has the features and conforms to the standards that jQuery UI users have come to expect.

Plugin design recommendations

Now that we have examined common ways to extend jQuery and jQuery UI by creating plugins, we can review and supplement what we've learned with a list of recommendations.

- Protect the `$` alias from potential interference from other libraries by using `jQuery` instead or passing `$` into an **immediately invoked function expression** (**IIFE**) so that it can be used as a local variable.

- Whether extending the jQuery object with `$.myPlugin` or the jQuery prototype with `$.fn.myPlugin`, add no more than one property to the `$` namespace. Additional public methods and properties should be added to the plugin's namespace (for example, `$.myPlugin.publicMethod` or `$.fn.myPlugin.pluginProperty`).

- Provide a map of default options for the plugin: `$.fn.myPlugin.defaults = {size: 'large'}`.

- Allow the plugin user to optionally override any of the default settings for all subsequent calls to the method (`$.fn.myPlugin.defaults.size = 'medium';`) or for a single call (`$('div').myPlugin({size: 'small'});`).

- In most cases when extending the jQuery prototype (`$.fn.myPlugin`), return `this` to allow the plugin user to **chain** additional jQuery methods to it (for example, `$('div').myPlugin().find('p').addClass('foo')`).

- When extending the jQuery prototype (`$.fn.myPlugin`), enforce **implicit iteration** by calling `this.each()`.

- Employ callback functions when appropriate to allow for flexible modification of the plugin's behavior without having to change the plugin's code.

- If the plugin calls for user interface elements or needs to track elements' state, create it with the jQuery UI widget factory.

- Maintain a set of automated **unit tests** for the plugin with a testing framework such as **QUnit** to ensure that it works as expected. See *Appendix B* for more information about QUnit.

[223]

- Use a version control system such as Git to track revisions to the code. Consider hosting the plugin publicly on Github (`http://github.com/`) and allowing others to contribute.

- When making the plugin available for others to use, make the licensing terms clear. Consider using the MIT license, which jQuery also uses.

Plugin distribution

By following the preceding recommendations, we should arrive at a plugin we can be proud of. If it performs a useful, reusable task, then we may want to share it with the jQuery community.

In addition to properly preparing the plugin code as defined above, we should be sure to adequately **document** the operation of the plugin prior to distribution. We can choose a documentation format that suits our style, but may want to consider a standard such as **ScriptDoc** (described at `http://www.scriptdoc.org/`). Regardless of format, we must ensure that our documentation covers every parameter and option available for use with our plugin's methods.

Plugin code and documentation can be hosted anywhere; Github (`http://github.com/`) is a popular and free option. To publicize our work, we can submit information about it to the official **jQuery Plugin Repository** at `http://plugins.jquery.com/`. Here we can log in, or register if we need to, and follow the instructions to describe the plugin and specify where its code and documentation reside.

Summary

In this chapter, we have seen how the functionality that is provided by the jQuery core need not limit the library's capabilities. In addition to the readily available plugins we explored in *Chapter 7*, we now know how to extend the menu of features ourselves.

The plugins we've created contain various features, including global functions that use the jQuery library, new methods of the jQuery object for acting on DOM elements, and sophisticated jQuery UI widgets. With these tools at our disposal, we can shape jQuery—and our own JavaScript code—into whatever form we desire.

Exercises

To complete these exercises, you will need the `index.html` file for this chapter, as well as the finished JavaScript code as found in `complete.js`. These files can be downloaded from the Packt Publishing website at `http://www.packtpub.com/support`.

The challenge exercises may require use of the official jQuery documentation at `http://api.jquery.com/`.

1. Create new plugin methods called `.slideFadeIn()` and `.slideFadeOut()`, combining the opacity animations of `.fadeIn()` and `.fadeOut()` with the height animations of `.slideDown()` and `.slideUp()`.

2. Extend the customizability of the `.shadow()` method so that the z-index of the cloned copies can be specified by the plugin user. Add a new sub-method called `isOpen` to the tooltip widget. This sub-method should return `true` if the tooltip is currently displayed and `false` otherwise.

3. Add code that listens for the `tooltipopen` event that our widget fires, and logs a message to the console.

4. **Challenge**: Provide an alternative `content` option for the tooltip widget that fetches the content of the page and anchor's `href` points to via Ajax, and displays that content as the tooltip text.

5. **Challenge**: Provide a new `effect` option for the tooltip widget that, if specified, applies the named jQuery UI effect (such as `explode`) to the showing and hiding of the tooltip.

9
Advanced Selectors and Traversing

In January 2009, jQuery's creator John Resig introduced a new open source JavaScript project called **Sizzle**. A standalone **CSS selector engine**, Sizzle was written to allow any JavaScript library to use it with little or no modification to its codebase. In fact, jQuery has adopted Sizzle as its own selector engine ever since version 1.3.

Sizzle is the component within jQuery that is responsible for parsing the CSS selector expressions we put into the `$()` function. It determines which native DOM methods to use as it builds a collection of elements that we can then act on with other jQuery methods. The combination of Sizzle and jQuery's set of traversal methods makes jQuery an extremely powerful tool for finding elements on the page. It boasts a large set of features, an extensible architecture, and a finely-tuned set of internal functions for outstanding power, flexibility, and speed.

Selecting and traversing revisited

There are so many options provided by jQuery for locating elements on the page, we can't hope to discuss them all in detail in this volume. Instead, throughout *Chapter 2, Selecting Elements*, we looked at each of the basic types of selectors and traversal methods, so that we have a roadmap for what's available when we need to learn more. In order to kick off this more advanced look into selectors and traversing, we'll build a script that will provide yet more selecting and traversing examples to inspect.

For our sample, we'll build an HTML document containing a list of news items. We'll place those items in a table, so that we can experiment with selecting rows and columns in several ways, as follows:

```
<div id="topics">
  Topics:
  <a href="topics/all.html" class="selected">All</a>
```

```
      <a href="topics/community.html">Community</a>
      <a href="topics/conferences.html">Conferences</a>
      <!-- continues... -->
  </div>
  <table id="news">
    <thead>
      <tr>
        <th>Date</th> <th>Headline</th>
        <th>Author</th> <th>Topic</th>
      </tr>
    </thead>
    <tbody>
      <tr>
        <th colspan="4">2011</th>
      </tr>
      <tr>
        <td>Feb 24</td> <td>jQuery Conference 2011</td>
        <td>Ralph Whitbeck</td> <td>Conferences</td>
      </tr>
      <tr>
        <td>Jan 31</td> <td>jQuery 1.5 Released</td>
        <td>John Resig</td> <td>Releases</td>
      </tr>
      <!-- continues... -->
    </tbody>
  </table>
```

From this code fragment, we can see the structure of the document. The table has four columns, representing date, headline, author, and topic, but some table rows contain a "subheading" of a calendar year instead of those four items. We'll need to be mindful of this structure as we craft our JavaScript enhancements to the table:

Before the table, there is a set of links representing each of the news topics in the table. For our first task, we'll change the behavior of these links to perform filtering of the table in place rather than requiring navigation to different pages.

Dynamic table filtering

In order to use the topic links to filter the table, we need to defeat their default linking behavior. We should also give the user some feedback about the currently selected topic, as follows:

```
$(document).ready(function() {
  $('#topics a').click(function() {
    $('#topics a').removeClass('selected');
    $(this).addClass('selected');

    return false;
  });
});
```

Listing 9.1

We remove the `selected` class from all the topic links when one is clicked, and then add the `selected` class to the new topic. The `return false` statement prevents the link from being followed.

Next we need to actually perform the filtering operation. As a first pass at this problem, we can hide every row of the table that doesn't contain the text of the topic, as shown in the following code snippet:

```
// Unfinished code
$(document).ready(function() {
  $('#topics a').click(function() {
    var topic = $(this).text();

    $('#topics a.selected').removeClass('selected');
    $(this).addClass('selected');

    $('#news tr').show();
    if (topic != 'All') {
      $('#news tr:has(td):not(:contains("' + topic + '"))')
        .hide();
    }
    return false;
  });
});
```

Listing 9.2

We're now storing the text of the link in the variable `topic`, so that we can compare it against the text in the table itself. First we show all the table rows, and then if the topic is not `All` we hide the irrelevant ones. The selector we're using for this process is a little complex, though, and bears some discussion.

The selector starts straightforwardly, with `#news tr` locating all of the rows in the table. We then filter this element set, using the `:has()` custom selector. This selector winnows the currently selected elements down to those that contain the specified descendant. In this case, we're eliminating the header rows (such as the calendar years) from consideration, as they do not contain `<td>` cells.

Once we have found the rows of the table where the actual content lies, we need to find out which ones relate to the selected topic. The `:contains()` custom selector matches just the elements that have the given text string somewhere inside them; wrapping this in a `:not()` then gives us all the rows that don't have the topic string, so we can hide them.

This code works well enough, unless the topic happens to appear as part of a news headline, for instance. We also need to take care of the eventuality that one topic is a substring of another. In order to handle these cases, we will need to execute a little code for each of the rows, as follows:

```
if (topic != 'All') {
  $('#news').find('tr:has(td)').not(function() {
    return $(this).children(':nth-child(4)').text() == topic;
  }).hide();
}
```

Listing 9.3

This new code, which replaces the corresponding portion of Listing 9.2, eliminates some of the complex selector expression text with DOM traversal methods. The `.find()` method acts just like the space previously separating `#news` and `tr`, but the `.not()` method is doing something that `:not()` can't accomplish. Just as we saw with the `.filter()` method back in *Chapter 2*, `.not()` can accept a callback function, invoked once per element to be tested. If that function returns `true`, then the element is excluded from the result set.

Selectors vs. traversal methods

The choice of using a selector or its equivalent traversal method has performance ramifications, as well. We'll explore this further later in this chapter.

Inside the `.not()` method's filtering function, we examine the child elements of the row to find the fourth one (which is the cell in the `Topic` column). A simple check of the text of this cell tells us whether the row should be hidden, as follows:

Topics: All Community **Conferences** Documentation Plugins Releases Miscellaneous			
Date	**Headline**	**Author**	**Topic**
2011			
Feb 24	jQuery Conference 2011: San Francisco Bay Area	Ralph Whitbeck	Conferences
2010			
Aug 24	jQuery Conference 2010: Boston	Ralph Whitbeck	Conferences
Jun 14	Seattle jQuery Open Space and Hack Attack with John Resig	Rey Bango	Conferences
Mar 15	jQuery Conference 2010: San Francisco Bay Area	Mike Hostetler	Conferences
2009			
Oct 22	jQuery Summit	John Resig	Conferences

Table row striping

In *Chapter 2*, one of our selector investigations delved into ways we can apply colors to alternating row in a table. We saw that the `:even` and `:odd` custom selectors can make short work of this task, and that the CSS-native `:nth-child()` pseudo-class can accomplish it as well, as follows:

```
$(document).ready(function() {
  $('#news').find('tr:nth-child(even)').addClass('alt');
});
```

Listing 9.4

This straightforward selector finds every other table row, and since each year's news articles reside in their own `<tbody>` element, the alternation starts over again with each section, as shown in the following screenshot:

Date	**Headline**	**Author**	**Topic**
2011			
Apr 15	jQuery 1.6 Beta 1 Released	John Resig	Releases
Feb 24	jQuery Conference 2011: San Francisco Bay Area	Ralph Whitbeck	Conferences
Feb 7	New Releases, Videos & a Sneak Peek at the jQuery UI Grid	Addy Osmani	Plugins
Jan 31	jQuery 1.5 Released	John Resig	Releases
Jan 30	API Documentation Changes	Karl Swedberg	Documentation
2010			
Nov 23	Team Spotlight: The jQuery Bug Triage Team	Paul Irish	Community
Oct 4	New Official jQuery Plugins Provide Templating, Data Linking and Globalization	John Resig	Plugins

For a more complicated row-striping challenge, we can attempt to give the `alt` class to sets of two rows at a time. The first two rows will receive the class, and then the next two will not, and so on. To achieve this, we will need to revisit filtering functions:

```
$(document).ready(function() {
  $('#news tr').filter(function(index) {
    return (index % 4) < 2;
  }).addClass('alt');
});
```

Listing 9.5

In our `.filter()` examples in *Chapter 2* as well as the `.not()` example in Listing 9.3, our filtering functions examined each element (held in the keyword `this`) to determine whether to include it in the result set. Here, we don't need information about the element to determine if it should be included. Instead, we need to know its position within the original set of elements. This information is passed as an argument to the function, and we're calling it `index`.

The `index` parameter now holds the zero-based position of the element. With this, we can use the modulo operator (`%`) to determine whether we are in a pair of elements that should receive the `alt` class or not. Now we have stripes of two rows throughout the table.

There are a couple of loose ends to clean up, however. As we're no longer using `:nth-child()`, the alternation does not begin again within each `<tbody>`. Also, we should be skipping table header rows for a consistent appearance. These goals can be achieved by making a couple of small modifications, as follows:

```
$(document).ready(function() {
  $('#news tbody').each(function() {
    $(this).children().has('td').filter(function(index) {
      return (index % 4) < 2;
    }).addClass('alt');
  });
});
```

Listing 9.6

To treat each group of rows independently, we can loop over the `<tbody>` elements with an `.each()` call. Within the loop, we then exclude subheading rows just as we did in Listing 9.3, using `.has()`, as follows:

Date	Headline	Author	Topic
2011			
Apr 15	jQuery 1.6 Beta 1 Released	John Resig	Releases
Feb 24	jQuery Conference 2011: San Francisco Bay Area	Ralph Whitbeck	Conferences
Feb 7	New Releases, Videos & a Sneak Peek at the jQuery UI Grid	Addy Osmani	Plugins
Jan 31	jQuery 1.5 Released	John Resig	Releases
Jan 30	API Documentation Changes	Karl Swedberg	Documentation
2010			
Nov 23	Team Spotlight: The jQuery Bug Triage Team	Paul Irish	Community

Combining filtering and striping

Our advanced table striping now works nicely, but behaves strangely when the topic filter is used. For the two functions to play together well, we need to re-stripe the table each time a filter is used. We will also need to consider whether rows are currently hidden when calculating where to apply the `alt` class, as shown in the following code snippet:

```
$(document).ready(function() {
  function stripe() {
    $('#news').find('tr.alt').removeClass('alt');
    $('#news tbody').each(function() {
      $(this).children(':visible').has('td')
        .filter(function(index) {
          return (index % 4) < 2;
        }).addClass('alt');
    });
  }
  stripe();

  $('#topics a').click(function() {
    var topic = $(this).text();

    $('#topics a.selected').removeClass('selected');
    $(this).addClass('selected');

    $('#news').find('tr').show();
    if (topic != 'All') {
      $('#news').find('tr:has(td)').not(function() {
        return $(this).children(':nth-child(4)')
          .text() == topic;
      }).hide();
    }
```

```
        stripe();
        return false;
    });
});
```

Listing 9.7

Combining the filtering code from earlier with our row striping example, this script now defines a function called `stripe()` that is called once when the document is loaded, and again each time a topic link is clicked. Within the function, we take care of removing the `alt` class from rows that no longer need it, as well as limiting the selected rows to those that are currently shown. This `:visible` pseudo-class (and its counterpart, `:hidden`) are extremely useful, and respect whether elements are hidden for a variety of reasons, including having a `display` value of `none` or a `width` and `height` of `0`:

Date	Headline	Author	Topic
2011			
Feb 24	jQuery Conference 2011: San Francisco Bay Area	Ralph Whitbeck	Conferences
2010			
Aug 24	jQuery Conference 2010: Boston	Ralph Whitbeck	Conferences
Jun 14	Seattle jQuery Open Space and Hack Attack with John Resig	Rey Bango	Conferences
Mar 15	jQuery Conference 2010: San Francisco Bay Area	Mike Hostetler	Conferences
2009			

Topics: All   Community   Conferences   Documentation   Plugins   Releases   Miscellaneous

More selectors and traversal methods

Even after all the examples we've seen, we have not come close to exploring every way to find elements on a page using jQuery. There are dozens of selectors and DOM traversal methods available to us, and each has a particular utility we may need to call upon.

To find the appropriate selector or method for our needs, many resources are available to us. The quick reference at the end of this book lists each selector and method, with a very brief description of each. For lengthier descriptions and usage examples, though, we will need a more thorough guide, such as *jQuery Reference Guide* either in its printed form or online. This guide lists all selectors at `http://api.jquery.com/category/selectors/` and the traversal methods at `http://api.jquery.com/category/traversing/`.

Customizing and optimizing selectors

The many techniques we've seen give us a tool chest that can be used to find any page element we want to work with. The story doesn't end here, though; there is much to learn about performing our element-finding tasks efficiently. This efficiency can take the form of both code that is easier to write and read, and code that executes more quickly inside the web browser.

Writing a custom selector plugin

One way to improve legibility is to encapsulate code snippets in reusable components. We do this all the time by creating functions. In *Chapter 8*, we expanded on this idea by crafting jQuery plugins that added methods to jQuery objects. This isn't the only way plugins can help us reuse code, though. Plugins can also provide additional selector expressions, such as the :paused selector that Cycle gave us in *Chapter 7*.

The easiest type of selector expression to add is a pseudo-class; these are the expressions that start with a colon, such as :checked or :nth-child(). To illustrate the process of creating a selector expression, we'll build a pseudo-class called :group(). This new selector will encapsulate the code we used to find table rows to stripe back in Listing 9.6.

When using a selector expression to find elements, jQuery looks for instructions in an internal map called expr. The values in this map behave much like the filtering functions we pass to .filter() or .not(), containing JavaScript code that causes each element to be contained in the result set if, and only if, the function returns true. We can add new expressions to this map using the $.extend() function:

```
(function($) {
  $.extend($.expr[':'], {
    group: function(element, index, matches, set) {
      var num = parseInt(matches[3], 10);
      if (isNaN(num)) {
        return false;
      }
      return index % (num * 2) < num;
    }
  });
})(jQuery);
```

Listing 9.8

This code instructs jQuery that `group` is a valid string that can follow a colon in a selector expression, and that when it is encountered, the given function should be called to determine whether the element should be included in the result set.

The function that is evaluated here is passed four parameters:

1. `element`: The DOM element under consideration. This is needed for most selectors, but not ours.

2. `index`: The index of the DOM element within the result set.

3. `matches`: An array containing the result of the regular expression that was used to parse this selector. Typically, `matches[3]` is the only relevant item in the array; in a selector of the form `:a(b)`, the `matches[3]` item contains b, the text within the parentheses.

4. `set`: The entire set of DOM elements matched up to this point. This parameter is rarely needed.

Pseudo-class selectors need to use the information contained in these four arguments to determine whether or not the element belongs in the result set. In this case, `index` and `matches` are all that we require.

With the new `:group` selector, we now have a flexible way to select alternating groups of elements. For example, we could combine the selector expression and `.filter()` function from Listing 9.5 into a single selector expression: `$('#news tr:group(2)')`. Alternately, we could preserve the per-section behavior from Listing 9.7, and use `:group()` as an expression within a `.filter()` call. We can even change the number of rows to group by simply changing the number within parentheses, as follows:

```
$(document).ready(function() {
  function stripe() {
    $('#news').find('tr.alt').removeClass('alt');
    $('#news tbody').each(function() {
      $(this).children(':visible').has('td')
        .filter(':group(3)').addClass('alt');
    });
  }
  stripe();
});
```

Listing 9.9

Now we can see that the row striping alternates by groups of three:

Date	Headline	Author	Topic
2011			
Apr 15	jQuery 1.6 Beta 1 Released	John Resig	Releases
Feb 24	jQuery Conference 2011: San Francisco Bay Area	Ralph Whitbeck	Conferences
Feb 7	New Releases, Videos & a Sneak Peek at the jQuery UI Grid	Addy Osmani	Plugins
Jan 31	jQuery 1.5 Released	John Resig	Releases
Jan 30	API Documentation Changes	Karl Swedberg	Documentation
2010			
Nov 23	Team Spotlight: The jQuery Bug Triage Team	Paul Irish	Community

Selector performance

Whenever we develop websites, we need to keep in mind the time it takes to create the site, the ease and speed with which we can maintain our code and the performance of the site as users interact with it. In general, the first two of these concerns are more important than the third. Especially with client-side scripting, developers can easily fall into the traps of **premature optimization** and **micro-optimization**, spending countless hours tweaking their code to shave milliseconds off of their JavaScript execution times when there was no noticeable performance lag in the first place and the performance boost is barely perceptible to the human eye. Therefore, a good rule of thumb is to consider developers' time more valuable than the computer's time, unless we notice slowness in our application.

Even when performance is an issue, pinpointing the bottlenecks in our jQuery code can be difficult. As we hinted at earlier in this chapter, some selectors are generally faster than others, and moving part of a selector to a traversal method can help speed up the time it takes to find elements on the page. Selector and traversal performance is, therefore, often a good place to start examining our code to reduce the amount of delay that users may experience when interacting with the page. However, any decrees made about the relative speed of selectors and traversal methods are likely to become outdated with the release of newer, faster browsers and clever speed tweaks introduced in newer jQuery versions. With this in mind, we'll examine a couple of simple guidelines, understanding that everything is subject to change and even the most basic assumptions require evidence that is applied to the specific web browsers and versions, jQuery versions, and web pages being targeted.

Sizzle selector implementation

As noted in the beginning of this chapter, when we pass a selector expression into the $() function, jQuery's **Sizzle** implementation parses the expression and determines how to gather the elements represented by it. In its basic form, Sizzle applies the most efficient native **DOM method** that the browser supports to obtain a **nodeList**, a native array-like object of DOM elements that jQuery ultimately converts to a true array and adds to the jQuery object. The following is a list of DOM methods that jQuery uses internally, along with the recent browser versions that support them:

- `.getElementById()` selects the unique element with an ID that matches the given string. It is supported by IE 6+, Firefox 3+, Safari 3+, Chrome 4+, and Opera 10+.

- `.getElementsByTagName()` selects all elements with a tag name that matches the given string. It is supported by IE 6+, Firefox 3+, Safari 3+, Chrome 4+, and Opera 10+.

- `.getElementsByClassName()` selects all elements that have one of its class names matching the given string. It is supported by IE 9+, Firefox 3+, Safari 4+, Chrome 4+, and Opera 10+.

- `.querySelectorAll()` selects all elements that match the given selector expression. It is supported by IE 8+, Firefox 3.5+, Safari 3+, Chrome 4+, and Opera 10+.

If a part of the selector expression cannot be handled by one of these methods, then Sizzle falls back to looping through each element that has already been collected and testing each one against the expression part. If no part of the selector expression can be handled by a DOM method, then Sizzle starts with a collection of all elements in the document, represented by `document.getElementsByTagName('*')` and looping through each one in turn.

This looping and testing of each element is much more costly in terms of performance than any of the native DOM methods. Fortunately, the most recent versions of all modern desktop browsers include the native `.querySelectorAll()` method, and Sizzle uses it when it can't use the other, even speedier, native methods—with one exception. When the selector expression contains a custom jQuery selector, such as `:eq()` or `:odd` or `:even`, that has no CSS counterpart, Sizzle has no choice but to loop and test.

Testing selector speed

To get an idea of the performance difference between `.querySelectorAll()` and the **loop and test** procedure, consider a document in which we wish to select all `<input type="text">` elements. We could write the selector expression one of two ways: `$('input[type="text"]')`, which uses the CSS attribute selector, and `$('input:text')`, which uses the custom jQuery selector. When these two expressions are run through the JavaScript benchmarking site `http://jsperf.com/` the results are dramatic, as shown in the following diagram:

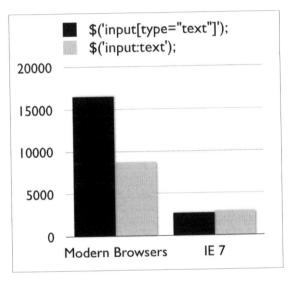

Figure 9.1

In `jsperf.com` tests, each test case is cycled to see how many times it can be completed in a certain amount of time, so the higher the number, the better. When tested in modern browsers that support `.querySelectorAll()` (Chrome 12, Firefox 4, and Safari 5) the selector that can take advantage of it is, on average, roughly twice as fast as the custom jQuery selector. Note, however, that the two selectors performed almost identically in Internet Explorer 7, because they both force jQuery to loop through and test each `<input>` element individually.

The performance difference is even greater between `$('input:eq(1)')` and `$('input').eq(1)`:

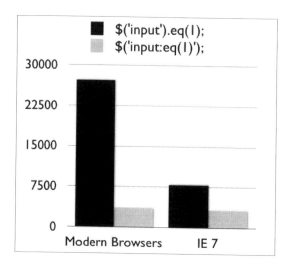

Figure 9.2

Even in Internet Explorer 7, moving the custom `:eq()` selector out into the `.eq()` method increases the speed by more than 100%. The reason? Whenever jQuery sees a single ID, tag name, or class name, the selector is fast tracked to the DOM method (as long as the browser supports it). In this case, using the simple `input` tag name as the argument for the `$()` function allows for a very speedy lookup. The `.eq()` method then simply calls an array function to retrieve the second element in the jQuery collection.

As a general rule of thumb, we should prefer selectors that are part of the CSS specification over jQuery's custom selectors whenever possible. Still, before changing our selectors, it makes sense to first confirm that there is a need to increase performance and then test just how much the change would boost performance with a benchmarking tool such as `http://jsperf.com`.

DOM traversal under the hood

In *Chapter 2*, and again at the beginning of this chapter, we looked at ways of traveling from one set of DOM elements to another by calling DOM traversal methods. Our (far from exhaustive) survey of such methods included simple ways to reach neighboring cells, such as `.next()` and `.parent()`, and more complex avenues of combining selector expressions, like `.find()` and `.filter()`. By now we should have a fairly strong grasp of these ways of getting from one DOM element to another step-by-step.

Each time we take one of these steps, though, jQuery takes note of our travels, laying down a trail of breadcrumbs we can follow back home if needed. A couple of the methods we briefly touched on in that chapter, `.end()` and `.andSelf()`, take advantage of this record-keeping. To be able to get the most out of these methods, and in general to write efficient jQuery code, we need to understand a bit more about how the DOM traversal methods do their jobs.

jQuery object properties

As we know, we typically construct a jQuery object instance by passing a selector expression to the `$()` function. Within the resulting object there lays an array structure containing references to each DOM element that matched that selector. What we haven't seen, though, is the other properties hidden in the object. Such properties include `.context`, a reference to the DOM node from which the search began (usually `document`), and `.selector`, a record of the selector expression that created the object. These two properties come into play when calling event delegation methods like `.live()`, which we'll investigate further in *Chapter 10*. When a DOM traversal method is called, though, a third property comes into play: `.prevObject` holds a reference to the jQuery object the traversal method was called upon.

To see this in action, we can highlight an arbitrary cell of our table and examine those properties:

```
$(document).ready(function() {
  var $cell = $('#release');

  $cell.addClass('highlight');
  console.log($cell.context);
  console.log($cell.selector);
  console.log($cell.prevObject);
});
```

Listing 9.10

The preceding snippet will highlight the single selected cell, as shown in the following screenshot:

Date	Headline	Author	Topic
2011			
Apr 15	jQuery 1.6 Beta 1 Released	John Resig	Releases
Feb 24	jQuery Conference 2011: San Francisco Bay Area	Ralph Whitbeck	Conferences
Feb 7	New Releases, Videos & a Sneak Peek at the jQuery UI Grid	Addy Osmani	Plugins
Jan 31	*jQuery 1.5 Released*	John Resig	Releases
Jan 30	API Documentation Changes	Karl Swedberg	Documentation

Three messages are also logged to the console, as follows:

Expression	Logged value
`$cell.context`	Document
`$cell.selector`	#release
`$cell.prevObject`	undefined

We can see that `.context` is the document object, `.selector` is exactly the string that we passed to the object, and `.prevObject` is undefined as this is a newly-created object. If we add a traversal method to the mix, though, then things get more interesting:

```
$(document).ready(function() {
    var $cell = $('#release').nextAll();

    $cell.addClass('highlight');
    console.log($cell.context);
    console.log($cell.selector);
    console.log($cell.prevObject);
});
```

Listing 9.11

This change alters which cells are highlighted, as shown in the following screenshot:

Date	Headline	Author	Topic
2011			
Apr 15	jQuery 1.6 Beta 1 Released	John Resig	Releases
Feb 24	jQuery Conference 2011: San Francisco Bay Area	Ralph Whitbeck	Conferences
Feb 7	New Releases, Videos & a Sneak Peek at the jQuery UI Grid	Addy Osmani	Plugins
Jan 31	jQuery 1.5 Released	John Resig	Releases
Jan 30	API Documentation Changes	Karl Swedberg	Documentation

The log messages also change as a result of the `.nextAll()` call, as follows:

Expression	Logged value
`$cell.context`	Document
`$cell.selector`	#release.nextAll()
`$cell.prevObject`	[td]

Now the two cells following the one we initially selected are highlighted. Within the jQuery object, `.context` still points to the document object, but `.selector` has been modified to reflect our call to `.nextAll()`, and `.prevObject` refers to the original jQuery object instance before the call to `.nextAll()`.

The DOM element stack

As each jQuery object instance has a `.prevObject` property pointing to the previous one, we have a linked list structure that implements a **stack**. Each traversal method call finds a new set of elements, and pushes this set onto the stack. This is only useful if we can do something with this stack, which is where the `.end()` and `.andSelf()` methods come into play.

The `.end()` method simply pops one element off the end of the stack, which is the same as fetching the value of the `.prevObject` property. We saw an example of this in *Chapter 2*, and we will see more later in this chapter. For a more interesting example, though, we'll investigate how `.andSelf()` manipulates the stack:

```
$(document).ready(function() {
  $('#release').nextAll().andSelf().addClass('highlight');
});
```

Listing 9.12

Once again, the highlighted cells have changed, as shown in the following screenshot:

Date	Headline	Author	Topic
2011			
Apr 15	jQuery 1.6 Beta 1 Released	John Resig	Releases
Feb 24	jQuery Conference 2011: San Francisco Bay Area	Ralph Whitbeck	Conferences
Feb 7	New Releases, Videos & a Sneak Peek at the jQuery UI Grid	Addy Osmani	Plugins
Jan 31	*jQuery 1.5 Released*	*John Resig*	*Releases*
Jan 30	API Documentation Changes	Karl Swedberg	Documentation

When `.andSelf()` is called, jQuery looks back one step on the stack, and combines the two element sets. In our example, this means that the highlighted cells include both the two cells found by the `.nextAll()` call and the original cell located using the selector. This new, merged element set is then pushed onto the stack.

This kind of stack manipulation can definitely come in handy. To make sure these techniques work when they are needed, each traversal method implementation must properly update the stack; this means that we need to understand some of the system's inner workings if we want to provide traversal methods of our own.

Writing a DOM traversal method plugin

Like any other jQuery object method, traversal methods can be added to jQuery by adding properties to $.fn. We saw in *Chapter 8* that new jQuery methods we define should operate on the matched set of elements, and then return the jQuery object so that users can chain on additional methods. When we create DOM traversal methods, the process is similar, but the jQuery object we return needs to point to a new set of matched elements.

As an example, we'll build a plugin that finds all of the table cells in the same column as a given cell. First we'll look at the plugin code in its entirety, as follows, and then examine it piece-by-piece to understand how it works:

```
(function($) {
  $.fn.column = function() {
    var $cells = $();
    this.each(function() {
      var $td = $(this).closest('td, th');
      if ($td.length) {
        var colNum = $td[0].cellIndex + 1;
        var $columnCells = $td
          .closest('table')
          .find('td, th')
          .filter(':nth-child(' + colNum + ')');
        $cells = $cells.add($columnCells);
      }
    });
    return this.pushStack($cells);
  };
})(jQuery);
```

Listing 9.13

Our .column() method could be called on a jQuery object pointing to zero, one, or more DOM elements. To account for all of these possibilities, we use the .each() method to loop over the elements, adding the columns of cells one by one into the variable $cells. This $cells variable starts out as an empty jQuery object, but then is expanded with the .add() method to point to more and more DOM elements as needed.

This explains the outer loop of the function; inside the loop, we need to understand how $columnCells gets populated with the DOM elements in the table column. First, we get a reference to the table cell being examined. We want to allow the .column() method to be called on table cells or on elements inside table cells. The .closest() method takes care of this for us; it travels up the DOM tree until it finds an element matching the selector we provide. This method will prove very useful to us in event delegation, which we'll revisit in *Chapter 10*.

With our table cell in hand, we find its column number using the DOM `.cellIndex` property. This gives us a zero-based index of the cell's column; we add 1 to this number as we'll be using it in a one-based context later. Then, from the cell, we travel up to the nearest `<table>` element, back down to the `<td>` and `<th>` elements, and filter these cells down to the appropriate column with an `:nth-child()` selector expression.

> **Handling nested tables**
>
> The plugin we're writing is limited to simple, non-nested tables, due to the `.find('td, th')` call. To support nested tables, we would need to determine whether `<tbody>` tags are present and move up and down the DOM tree by the appropriate amount, which would add more complexity than is appropriate for this example.

Once we've found all the cells in the column or columns, we need to return the new jQuery object. We could just return `$cells` from our method, but this wouldn't properly respect the DOM element stack. Instead, we pass `$cells` to the `.pushStack()` method and return the result. This method accepts an array of DOM elements and adds them to the stack, so that later calls to methods like `.andSelf()` and `.end()` behave correctly.

To see our plugin in action, we can react to clicks on cells and highlight the corresponding column, as follows:

```
$(document).ready(function() {
  $('#news td').click(function() {
    $('#news td.active').removeClass('active');
    $(this).column().addClass('active');
  });
});
```

Listing 9.14

The `active` class is added to the selected column, resulting in different shading when, for instance, one of the author names is clicked, as shown in the following screenshot:

Date	Headline	Author	Topic
2011			
Apr 15	jQuery 1.6 Beta 1 Released	John Resig	Releases
Feb 24	jQuery Conference 2011: San Francisco Bay Area	Ralph Whitbeck	Conferences
Feb 7	New Releases, Videos & a Sneak Peek at the jQuery UI Grid	Addy Osmani	Plugins
Jan 31	*jQuery 1.5 Released*	*John Resig*	*Releases*
Jan 30	API Documentation Changes	Karl Swedberg	Documentation

DOM traversal performance

The points raised in the preceding section about selector performance apply equally to DOM traversal performance. We should prioritize ease of code writing and code maintenance when possible, only sacrificing legibility for optimization when performance is a measurable problem. Again, sites such as http://jsperf.com/ are helpful in determining the best approach given several options.

In addition to this general advice, one tip that we can keep in mind is to minimize repetition of selectors and traversal methods. As these can be potentially expensive tasks, the fewer times we do them the better. Two strategies for avoiding this repetition are **chaining** and **object caching**.

Improving performance using chaining

We have spoken about chaining many times now, typically discussing the brevity it gives our code. There can be a performance benefit to chaining as well, however, if it allows us to reduce repetition.

Our `stripe()` function from Listing 9.9 located the element with ID `news` twice: once to remove the `alt` class from rows that no longer needed it, and once to apply that class to the new set of rows. Using chaining, we can combine these two thoughts into one and prevent this repetition:

```
$(document).ready(function() {
  function stripe() {
    $('#news')
      .find('tr.alt').removeClass('alt').end()
      .find('tbody').each(function() {
        $(this).children(':visible').has('td')
          .filter(':group(3)').addClass('alt');
    });
  }
  stripe();
});
```

Listing 9.15

In order to merge the two uses of `$('#news')`, we once again exploit the DOM element stack within the jQuery object. The first call to `.find()` pushes the table rows onto the stack, but then `.end()` pops this off the stack so that the next `.find()` call is operating on the `news` table once again. This kind of clever manipulation of the stack is a handy way of avoiding selector duplication.

Improving performance using caching

Caching is simply storing the result of an operation so that it can be used multiple times without running the operation again. In the context of selector and traversal performance, we can use caching by storing a jQuery object in a variable for later use rather than creating a new one.

Returning to our example, we can rewrite the `stripe()` function to avoid selector duplication with caching rather than chaining, as follows:

```
$(document).ready(function() {
  var $news = $('#news');
  function stripe() {
    $news.find('tr.alt').removeClass('alt');
    $news.find('tbody').each(function() {
      $(this).children(':visible').has('td')
        .filter(':group(3)').addClass('alt');
    });
  }
  stripe();
});
```

Listing 9.16

The two operations are separate JavaScript statements once again, rather than being chained together. We're still executing the `$('#news')` selector only once, though, by storing the result in `$news`.

This caching approach is a little more verbose than chaining, as we need to separately create the variable storing the jQuery object. On the other hand, it has the advantage of allowing the two uses of the selected elements to be far apart in the code, if we need them to be. Also, as we can cache the selected elements outside the `stripe()` function, the selector doesn't need to be re-run each time the function is called.

As selecting elements on the page by ID is extremely fast, neither of these examples will have a big performance impact, and in practice we'd choose the approach that seemed the most legible and maintainable. These techniques are useful tools, though, when performance is found to be a concern.

Summary

In this chapter, we've delved deeper into jQuery's extensive capabilities for finding elements in a document. We've looked at some of the details of how the Sizzle selector engine works, and the implications this has on designing effective and efficient code. In addition, we have explored the ways in which we can extend and enhance jQuery's selectors and DOM traversal methods.

Further reading

A complete list of available selectors and traversal methods is available in *Appendix C* of this book, in *jQuery Reference Guide*, or in the official jQuery documentation at `http://api.jquery.com/`.

Exercises

To complete these exercises, you will need the `index.html` file for this chapter, as well as the finished JavaScript code as found in `complete.js`. These files can be downloaded from the Packt Publishing website at `http://www.packtpub.com/support`.

The challenge exercise may require use of the official jQuery documentation at `http://api.jquery.com/`.

1. Modify the table row striping routine so that it gives no class to the first row, a class of `alt` to the second row, and a class of `alt-2` to the third row. Repeat this pattern for every set of three rows in a section.

2. Create a new selector plugin called `:containsExactly()` that selects elements with text content that exactly matches what is put inside the parentheses.

3. Use this new `:containsExactly()` selector to rewrite the filtering code from Listing 9.3.

4. Create a new DOM traversal plugin method called `.grandparent()` that moves from an element or elements to their grandparent elements in the DOM.

5. **Challenge**: Using `http://jsperf.com/`, paste in the content of `index.html` and compare the performance of finding the closest ancestor table element of `<td id="release">` using the following:

    ◦ The `.closest()` method

    ◦ The `.parents()` method, limiting the result to the first table found

6. **Challenge**: Using `http://jsperf.com/`, paste in the content of `index.html` and compare the performance of finding the final `<td>` element in each row using the following:

    ◦ The `:last-child` pseudo-class

    ◦ The `:nth-child()` pseudo-class

    ◦ The `.last()` method within each row (using `.each()` to loop over the rows)

    ◦ The `:last` pseudo-class within each row (using `.each()` to loop over the rows)

10
Advanced Events

Our applications are only interactive when we can observe the user's activities and respond to them. In *Chapter 3, Handling Events*, we touched on a number of the features jQuery provides for handling events. In the subsequent chapters, we have used the event system many times. Many details remain to be discovered, though.

In this chapter, we will take a closer look at event delegation and some of the challenges it presents. We will investigate the performance hazards of certain events, and explore a technique for keeping the browser responsive during these operations. We will also revisit custom events and even take advantage of the special event system that jQuery uses internally.

Events revisited

For our sample document, we will create a simple photo gallery. The gallery will display a set of photos, with an option to display additional photos upon the click of a link. We will also use jQuery's event system to display textual information about each photo when the user's mouse cursor is over it:

```
<div id="container">
  <h1>Photo Gallery</h1>

  <div id="gallery">
    <div class="photo">
      <img src="photos/skyemonroe.jpg">
      <div class="details">
        <div class="description">The Cuillin Mountains,
          Isle of Skye, Scotland.</div>
        <div class="date">12/24/2000</div>
        <div class="photographer">Alasdair Dougall</div>
      </div>
```

```
      </div>
      <div class="photo">
        <img src="photos/dscn1328.jpg">
        <div class="details">
          <div class="description">Mt. Ruapehu in summer</div>
          <div class="date">01/13/2005</div>
          <div class="photographer">Andrew McMillan</div>
        </div>
      </div>
      <div class="photo">
        <img src="photos/024.JPG">
        <div class="details">
          <div class="description">midday sun</div>
          <div class="date">04/26/2011</div>
          <div class="photographer">Jaycee Barratt</div>
        </div>
      </div>
      <!-- Code continues -->
    </div>
    <a id="more-photos" href="pages/1.html">More Photos</a>
</div>
```

Downloadable code examples

As with many of the HTML, CSS, and JavaScript examples in this book, the preceding markup is merely a fragment of the complete document. In order to experiment with the examples, we can download them from the Packt Publishing website at http://www.packtpub.com/support. In addition, the examples can be viewed in an interactive browser at http://book.learningjquery.com/.

When we apply styles to the photos, arranging them into rows of three, the gallery looks similar to one shown in the following screenshot:

More Photos

Loading additional pages of data

By now, we are experts at the common task of reacting to a click on a page element. When the **More Photos** link is clicked, we need to perform an Ajax request for the next set of photos and append them to `<div id="gallery">`. We also need to update the destination of the **More Photos** link to point to the next page of photos as follows:

```
$(document).ready(function() {
  var pageNum = 1;
  $('#more-photos').click(function() {
    var $link = $(this);
    var url = $link.attr('href');
    if (url) {
      $.get(url, function(data) {
        $('#gallery').append(data);
      });
    }
    pageNum++;
    if (pageNum < 20) {
```

```
        $link.attr('href', 'pages/' + pageNum + '.html');
      }
      else {
        $link.remove();
      }
    }
    return false;
  });
});
```

Listing 10.1

Our .click() handler uses the pageNum variable to track the next page of photos to request and uses this to build the new href value for the link. As pageNum is defined outside the function, its value persists between clicks of the link. We remove the link once we have reached the last page of photos.

Progressive enhancement

Our example is constructed to work offline, without a web server. In a practical implementation, the data would likely be delivered from a database. With server-side code, we would deliver an entire HTML page when a set of photos is requested normally by the browser and only the HTML fragment with the photo markup when an Ajax request is made. This way, we would have an interface that is friendly to clients with and without JavaScript available.

Displaying data on hover

Next, we need to display the details relating to each photo when the user's mouse is in that area of the page. For our first pass at displaying this information, we can use the .hover() method as follows:

```
$(document).ready(function() {
  $('div.photo').hover(function() {
    $(this).find('.details').fadeTo('fast', 0.7);
  }, function() {
    $(this).find('.details').fadeOut('fast');
  });
});
```

Listing 10.2

When the user's mouse enters a photo, the information fades in to 70% opacity, and when it leaves, the information fades back out:

There are, of course, multiple ways to perform this task. As a portion of each handler is the same, it is possible to combine the two handlers to reduce code duplication. We can bind a handler to both `mouseenter` and `mouseleave` at the same time by separating the event names with a space as follows:

```
$(document).ready(function() {
  $('div.photo')
    .bind('mouseenter mouseleave', function(event) {
      var $details = $(this).find('.details');
      if (event.type == 'mouseenter') {
        $details.fadeTo('fast', 0.7);
      } else {
        $details.fadeOut('fast');
      }
    });
});
```

Listing 10.3

With the same handler bound to both events, we check for the event's type to determine whether to fade the details in or out. The code locating the `<div>`, however, is the same for both events, so we can write it just once.

This example is admittedly a little contrived, as the shared code in this instance is so brief. In other cases, though, this technique can significantly reduce the code complexity. If we had chosen to add a class on `mouseenter` and remove it on `mouseleave`, for example, rather than animate opacity, then we could have taken care of it with a single statement inside the handler as follows:

```
$(this).find('.details')
       .toggleClass('entered', event.type == 'mouseenter');
```

In any case, our script is now working as intended, except that we have not accounted for the additional photos that we load when the user clicks on the **More Photos** link. As we noted in Chapter 3, event handlers are only attached to the elements that are there when we make the `.bind()` call. Elements added later, such as from an Ajax call, won't have the behavior. We saw that two approaches to addressing this issue are to "rebind" event handlers after the new content is introduced, or to initially bind the handlers to a containing element instead and rely on **event bubbling**. The second approach, **event delegation**, is the one we will pursue here.

Event delegation

Recall that in order to implement event delegation, we check the `target` property of the `event` object to see if it matches the element that we want to trigger the behavior. The event target represents the innermost, or most deeply nested, element that is receiving the event. With our sample HTML this time, however, we are presented with a new challenge. The `<div class="photo">` elements are unlikely to be the event target as they contain other elements, such as the image itself and the image details. In order to find this `<div>` from an element it contains, we can use the `.closest()` method, which works its way up the DOM from parent to parent until it finds an element that matches a given selector expression. If no elements are found, then it acts like any other DOM traversal method, returning a new "empty" jQuery object, as follows:

```
// Unfinished code
$(document).ready(function() {
  $('#gallery').bind('mouseover mouseout', function(event) {
    var $target = $(event.target).closest('div.photo');
    var $details = $target.find('.details');
    var $related = $(event.relatedTarget)
                     .closest('div.photo');

    if ( event.type == 'mouseover' && $target.length ) {
      $details.fadeTo('fast', 0.7);
    } else if (event.type == 'mouseout' && !$related.length) {
      $details.fadeOut('fast');
    }
  });
});
```

Listing 10.4

Note that we also needed to change the event types from `mouseenter` and `mouseleave` to `mouseover` and `mouseout`, because the former types are only triggered when the mouse first enters the gallery `<div>` and finally leaves it, and we need the handlers to be fired whenever the mouse enters any of the photos *within* that wrapping `<div>`. However, the latter types introduce yet another problem in that the detail `<div>` will fade in and out repeatedly unless we include an additional check for the `event` object's `relatedTarget` property. Even with the additional code, repeated quick mouse movements over and out of photos are handled unsatisfactorily, leaving an occasional detail `<div>` visible when it should have faded out.

Using jQuery's delegation methods

Event delegation can be frustratingly difficult to manage when the tasks become more complex. Fortunately, jQuery's **delegation methods** smooth over the rough spots for us. Using these methods, our code can return to the simplicity it had in Listing 10.3:

```
$(document).ready(function() {
  $('#gallery').delegate('div.photo', 'mouseenter mouseleave',
  function(event) {
    var $details = $(this).find('.details');
    if (event.type == 'mouseenter') {
      $details.fadeTo('fast', 0.7);
    } else {
      $details.fadeOut('fast');
    }
  });
});
```

Listing 10.5

The selector, `'#gallery'`, remains the same as in Listing 10.4, but the event types return to the `mouseenter` and `mouseleave` of Listing 10.3. When we pass in `'div.photo'` to the first argument, the `.delegate()` method maps the `this` keyword to the element(s) matched by that selector within `'#gallery'`.

Choosing a delegation method

When jQuery introduced the `.live()` method in Version 1.3, it was generally intended as a drop-in replacement for `.bind()`. Any developers who needed their event handlers to work with elements inserted into the DOM at a later time, or those who wanted to avoid the performance penalty of binding event handlers to a large number of elements, could simply replace their `.bind()` methods with `.live()` methods, and they would just work.

For example, other than the substitution of `.live()` for `.bind()`, the following code in Listing 10.6 is identical to the code in Listing 10.3:

```
$(document).ready(function() {
  $('div.photo')
    .live('mouseenter mouseleave', function(event) {
      var $details = $(this).find('.details');
      if (event.type == 'mouseenter') {
        $details.fadeTo('fast', 0.7);
      } else {
        $details.fadeOut('fast');
      }
    });
});
```

Listing 10.6

For all of its convenience, however, `.live()` is not a perfect mirror of `.bind()` with a little delegation magic thrown in. Unlike `.bind()`, for example, `.live()` cannot be called reliably after most DOM traversal methods. So, while `$('div').filter('.photo').bind('click', fn)` would work as expected, `$('div').filter('.photo').live('click', fn)` would not.

Additionally, the `.live()` method under certain circumstances can suffer some of the same performance issues as its `.bind()` counterpart. Even though it avoids binding handlers to many elements, `.live()` does initially select all of those elements. In our photo gallery example, this is not much of a concern. However, if we were binding handlers to specific elements within a table of many columns and hundreds of rows, for example, just the expense of the initial selection of elements might cause the script to become unresponsive. Oddly enough, `.live()` does not even use the set of matched elements collected by the `$()` function. Instead, it uses the selector expression, the actual string value, to match against the `event.target` or its ancestors.

Another potential performance drain of `.live()` is that it binds events to `document`. In a DOM of deeply nested elements, relying on events to bubble all the way up a multitude of ancestor elements could be costly. With `.delegate()`, events are bound to whichever elements are matched in the `$()` function's selector expression, so the part of the page that registers the event can be more precise and the event bubbling can be reduced.

Especially because of these performance concerns — initial element selection and excessive event bubbling — some developers have sworn off `.live()` in favor of `.delegate()` when it became available as of jQuery 1.4.2. Yet, we don't have to do away with `.live()` entirely. If we use it judiciously, either by calling it early or by supplying a **context** for it, we can enjoy the convenience of `.live()` while avoiding some of its drawbacks.

Delegating early

One way to avoid a performance hit caused by the `$()` function's selection of elements is to place our `.live()` handler outside of `$(document).ready()`. If the script is referenced in the `<head>` of the document, as it is in our example, the selector has very little work to do, as at that moment, nearly the entire DOM has yet to be registered. Of course, document, which `.live()` uses, is always available.

```
(function($) {
  $('div.photo').live('mouseenter mouseleave',
  function(event) {
    var $details = $(this).find('.details');
    if (event.type == 'mouseenter') {
      $details.fadeTo('fast', 0.7);
    } else {
      $details.fadeOut('fast');
    }
  });
})(jQuery);
```

Figure 10.7

As we are not waiting for the entire DOM to be ready, we can be assured that the mouseenter and mouseleave behaviors will apply to all `<div class="photo">` elements immediately, as soon as they are rendered on the page. In order to see the benefit of this technique, consider a click handler that, among other things, prevents the default action on a link. If we were to wait until the document was ready, we would run the risk of the user clicking on that link before the handler was registered and thereby leaving the current page, rather than get the enhanced treatment provided by the script. In any case, we now have the benefit of binding the event early without the cost of having to scan through a complex DOM structure.

> **Immediately invoked function expression**
>
> In place of $(document).ready(), we are using an **immediately invoked function expression** (IIFE) to act as a closure, as discussed in *Chapter 8*. This allows us to avoid potential naming conflicts with other scripts when we define variables and functions inside of it (as variables are "scoped" within functions).

Using a context argument

Another technique we can employ with .live() is to provide a **context** argument to the $() function. By doing so, we can limit event bubbling in the same way that .delegate() does. For example, rather than $('div.photo').live..., we could write $('div.photo', $('#gallery')[0]).live.... The context argument used with .live() must be a single DOM element. We can achieve this by using the array index operator, as in $('#gallery')[0], or by using the underlying DOM method itself, such as document.getElementById('gallery').

If we decide that this kind of precision is necessary, however, we must place the script back inside a $(document).ready() call as long as the script is being referenced in the <head>, in which case we lose the benefit of delegating early. For this reason, our example script will stick with the system represented in Listing 10.7.

Custom events

The events that are triggered naturally by the DOM implementations of browsers are crucial to any interactive web application. However, we are not limited to this set of events in our jQuery code. We can freely add our own **custom events** to the repertoire. We saw this briefly in *Chapter 8, Developing Plugins* when we saw how jQuery UI widgets trigger events, but we will investigate here how we can create and use custom events even outside plugins.

Custom events must be triggered manually by our code. In a sense, they are like regular functions that we define, in that we can cause a block of code to be executed when we invoke it from another place in the script. The .bind() call corresponds to a function definition and the .trigger() call to a function invocation.

However, event handlers are **decoupled** from the code that triggers them. This means that we can trigger events at any time, without knowing in advance what will happen when we do. We might cause a single bound event handler to execute, as with a regular function. We also might cause multiple handlers to run or even none at all.

In order to illustrate this, we can revise our Ajax loading feature to use a custom event. We will trigger a `nextPage` event whenever the user requests more photos and bind handlers that watch for this event and perform the work previously done by the `.click()` handler as follows:

```
$(document).ready(function() {
  $('#more-photos').click(function() {
    $(this).trigger('nextPage');
    return false;
  });
});
```

Listing 10.8

The `.click()` handler now does very little work itself. After triggering the custom event, it prevents the default behavior by returning `false`. The heavy lifting is transferred to the new event handlers for the `nextPage` event as follows:

```
(function($) {
  $(document).bind('nextPage', function() {
    var url = $('#more-photos').attr('href');
    if (url) {
      $.get(url, function(data) {
        $('#gallery').append(data);
      });
    }
  });

  var pageNum = 1;
  $(document).bind('nextPage', function() {
    pageNum++;
    if (pageNum < 20) {
      $('#more-photos')
        .attr('href', 'pages/' + pageNum + '.html');
    }
    else {
      $('#more-photos').remove();
    }
  });
})(jQuery);
```

Listing 10.9

Most of this code is the same as in Listing 10.1. The largest difference is that we have split what was once a single function into two. This is simply to illustrate that a single event trigger can cause multiple bound handlers to fire.

The other point to note is that we are illustrating another application of event bubbling here. Our `nextPage` handlers could be bound to the link that triggers the event, but we would need to wait to do this until the DOM was ready. Instead, we are binding the handlers to the document itself, which is available immediately, so we can do the binding outside of `$(document).ready()`. This is, in fact, the same principle we took advantage of in Listing 10.6 when we moved the `.live()` method outside of `$(document).ready()`. The event bubbles up and, so long as another handler does not stop the event propagation, our handlers will be fired.

Infinite scrolling

Just as multiple event handlers can react to the same triggered event, the same event can be triggered in multiple ways. We can demonstrate this by adding an **infinite scrolling** feature to our page. This popular technique lets the user's scroll bar manage the loading of content, fetching additional content whenever the user reaches the end of what has been loaded thus far.

We will begin with a simple implementation, and then improve it in successive examples. The basic idea is to observe the `scroll` event, measure the current scroll bar position when scrolling occurs, and load the new content if needed, as follows:

```
(function($) {
  var $window = $(window);
  function checkScrollPosition() {
    var distance = $window.scrollTop() + $window.height();
    if ($('#container').height() <= distance) {
      $(document).trigger('nextPage');
    }
  }

  $(document).ready(function() {
    $window.scroll(checkScrollPosition).scroll();
  });
})(jQuery);
```

Listing 10.10

The new `checkScrollPosition()` function is set as a handler for the window's `scroll` event. This function computes the distance from the top of the document to the bottom of the window, and then compares this distance to the total height of the main container in the document. As soon as these reach equality, we need to fill the page with additional photos, so we trigger the `nextPage` event.

As soon as we bind the `scroll` handler, we immediately trigger it with a call to `.scroll()`. This kick-starts the process, so that if the page is not initially filled with photos, an Ajax request is made right away.

Custom event parameters

When we define functions, we can set up any number of parameters to be filled with argument values when we actually call the function. Similarly, when triggering a custom event, we may want to pass along additional information to any registered event handlers. We can accomplish this by using **custom event parameters**.

The first parameter defined for any event handler, as we have seen, is the DOM event object as enhanced and extended by jQuery. Any additional parameters we define are available for our discretionary use.

To see this action, we will add a new option to the `nextPage` event allowing us to scroll the page down to display the newly added content as follows:

```
(function($) {
  $(document).bind('nextPage',
    function(event, scrollToVisible) {
      var url = $('#more-photos').attr('href');
      if (url) {
        $.get(url, function(data) {
          var $data = $(data).appendTo('#gallery');
          if (scrollToVisible) {
            var newTop = $data.offset().top;
            $(window).scrollTop(newTop);
          }
          checkScrollPosition();
        });
      }
    }
  );
});
```

Listing 10.11

We have now added a `scrollToVisible` parameter to the event callback. The value of this parameter determines whether we perform the new functionality, which entails measuring the position of the new content and scrolling to it. Measurement is easy using the `.offset()` method, which returns the top and left coordinates of the new content. In order to move down the page, we call the `.scrollTop()` method.

Now we need to pass an argument into the new parameter. All that is required is providing an extra value when invoking the event using `.trigger()`. When `newPage` is triggered through scrolling, we don't want the new behavior to occur, as the user is already manipulating the scroll position directly. When the **More Photos** link is clicked, on the other hand, we want the newly added photos to be displayed on the screen, so we will pass a value of `true` to the handler as follows:

```
$(document).ready(function() {
  $('#more-photos').click(function() {
    $(this).trigger('nextPage', [true]);
    return false;
  });


  $window.scroll(checkScrollPosition).scroll();
});
```

Listing 10.12

In the call to `.trigger()`, we are now providing an array of values to pass to event handlers. In this case, the value of `true` will be given to the `scrollToVisible` parameter of the event handler in Listing 10.11.

Note that custom event parameters are optional on both sides of the transaction. We have two calls to `.trigger()` in our code, only one of which provides argument values; when the other is called, this does not result in an error, but rather the value of `null` is passed to each parameter. Similarly, the lack of a `scrollToVisible` parameter in one of our `.bind('nextPage')` calls is not an error; if a parameter does not exist when an argument is passed, that argument is simply ignored.

Throttling events

A major issue with the infinite scrolling feature as we have implemented it in Listing 10.10 is its performance impact. While our code is brief, the `checkScrollPosition()` function does need to do some work to measure the dimensions of the page and window. This effort can accumulate rapidly, because in some browsers the `scroll` event is triggered repeatedly during the scrolling of the window. The result of this combination could be choppy or sluggish performance.

Several native events have the potential for frequent triggering. Common culprits include `scroll`, `resize`, and `mousemove`. To account for this, we need to limit our expensive calculations, so that they only occur after some of the event instances, rather than each one. This technique is known as **event throttling**.

```
$(document).ready(function() {
  var timer = 0;
  $window.scroll(function() {
    if (!timer) {
      timer = setTimeout(function() {
        checkScrollPosition();
        timer = 0;
      }, 250);
    }
  }).scroll();
});
```

Listing 10.13

Rather than setting `checkScrollPosition()` directly as the `scroll` event handler, we are using the JavaScript `setTimeout` function to defer the call by 250 milliseconds. More importantly, we are checking for a currently running timer first before performing any work. As checking the value of a simple variable is extremely fast, most of the calls to our event handler will return almost immediately. The `checkScrollPosition()` call will only happen when a timer completes, which will at most be every 250 milliseconds.

We can easily adjust the `setTimeout()` value to a comfortable number that strikes a reasonable compromise between instant feedback and low performance impact. Our script is now a good web citizen.

Other ways to perform throttling

The throttling technique we have implemented is efficient and simple, but it is not the only solution. Depending on the performance characteristics of the action being throttled and typical interaction with the page, we may for instance want to institute a single timer for the page rather than create one when an event begins:

```
$(document).ready(function() {
  var scrolled = false;
  $window.scroll(function() {
    scrolled = true;
  });
  setInterval(function() {
```

```
    if (scrolled) {
      checkScrollPosition();
      scrolled = false;
    }
  }, 250);
  checkScrollPosition();
});
```

Listing 10.14

Unlike our previous throttling code, this polling solution uses a single `setInterval()` call to begin checking the state of the `scrolled` variable every 250 milliseconds. Any time a scroll event occurs, `scrolled` is set to true, ensuring that the next time the interval passes, `checkScrollPosition()` will be called. The result is similar to that of Listing 10.13.

A third solution for limiting the amount of processing performed during frequently repeated events is **debouncing**. This technique, named after the post-processing required handling repeated signals sent by electrical switches, ensures that only a single, final event is acted upon even when many have occurred. We will see an example of this technique in *Chapter 13, Advanced Ajax*.

Special events

Some events, such as `mouseenter` and `ready`, are designated as **special events** by the jQuery internals. Such events get the opportunity to take action at various times in the life cycle of an event handler. They may react to handlers being bound or unbound, and they can even have preventable default behaviors like those that clicked links or submitted forms do. The special event API lets us create sophisticated new events that act much like native DOM events.

The throttling behavior we implemented for scrolling in Listing 10.13 is useful and could be generalized for use elsewhere. One way to accomplish this is to create a new event that encapsulates the throttling technique within the special event hooks.

In order to implement a special behavior for an event, we add a property to the `$.event.special` object. This property, whose key is our event name, has a value which is itself an object. This special event object has five special properties we may define if we wish, each of which holds a callback function:

1. `add` is called every time a handler for this event is bound.
2. `remove` is called every time a handler for the event is unbound.

3. `setup` is called when a handler is bound for the event, but only if no other handlers for that event are bound to the element.

4. `teardown` is the converse of `setup`, called when the last handler for the event is unbound from an element.

5. `_default` becomes the default behavior of the event, called unless the default action is prevented by an event handler.

These callbacks can be used in some very creative ways. A fairly common scenario, which we will explore in our example code, is to automatically trigger the event in response to some browser condition. It would be wasteful to monitor the state and trigger events if no handlers are listening for the event, so we can use the `setup` callback to initiate this work only when needed as follows:

```
(function($) {
  $.event.special.throttledScroll = {
    setup: function(data) {
      var timer = 0;
      $(this).bind('scroll.throttledScroll', function(event) {
        if (!timer) {
          timer = setTimeout(function() {
            $(this).triggerHandler('throttledScroll');
            timer = 0;
          }, 250);
        }
      });
    },
    teardown: function() {
      $(this).unbind('scroll.throttledScroll');
    }
  };
})(jQuery);
```

Listing 10.15

For our scroll-throttling event, we need to bind a regular `scroll` handler that uses the `setTimeout` technique we developed in Listing 10.13. Whenever a timer completes, the custom event will be triggered. As we only need one timer per element, the `setup` callback will serve our needs. By namespacing the `scroll` handler, we can easily remove the handler when `teardown` is called.

In order to use this new behavior, all we have to do is bind handlers to the `throttledScroll` event as follows:

```
$(document).ready(function() {
  $window
    .bind('throttledScroll', checkScrollPosition)
    .trigger('throttledScroll');
});
```

Listing 10.16

This greatly simplifies the event binding code and gives us a nice reusable throttling mechanism.

More about special events

While this chapter covers advanced techniques for dealing with events, special event creation is a tool that is very advanced indeed, and a detailed investigation is beyond the scope of this book. The preceding `throttledScroll` example covers the simplest and most common usage of the facility. Other possible applications include the following:

- Modifying the event object, so that event handlers have different information available to them

- Causing events that occur in one place in the DOM to trigger behaviors associated with different elements

- Reacting to new and browser-specific events that are not standard DOM events, and allowing jQuery code to react to them as if they are

- Changing the way event bubbling and delegation are handled

Many of these tasks can be quite complicated. For an in-depth take on the possibilities offered by special events, read Ben Alman's article "jQuery Special Events" at the following URL:

```
http://benalman.com/news/2010/03/jquery-special-events/
```

Summary

The jQuery event system can be very powerful if we choose to leverage it fully. In this chapter, we have seen several aspects of the system, including event delegation methods, custom events, and the special event framework. We have also found ways of sidestepping pitfalls associated with delegation and with events that are triggered frequently.

Further reading

A complete list of available event methods is available in *Appendix C* of this book, in *jQuery Reference Guide*, or in the official jQuery documentation at the following URL:

```
http://api.jquery.com/
```

Exercises

In order to complete these exercises, you will need the `index.html` file for this chapter, as well as the finished JavaScript code as found in `complete.js`. These files can be downloaded from the Packt Publishing website at `http://www.packtpub.com/support`.

The challenge exercise may require use of the official jQuery documentation at `http://api.jquery.com/`.

1. When the user clicks on a photo, add or remove the `selected` class on the photo `<div>`. Make sure this behavior works even for photos added later using the **Next Page** link.

2. Add a new custom event named `pageLoaded` that fires when a new set of images has been added to the page.

3. Using `nextPage` and `pageLoaded` handlers, show a **Loading** message at the bottom of the page only while a new page is being loaded.

4. Bind a `mousemove` handler to photos that logs the current mouse position (using `console.log()`).

5. Revise this handler to perform the logging no more than five times a second.

6. **Challenge**: Create a new special event named `tripleclick` that fires when the mouse button is clicked three times within 500 milliseconds. In order to test the event, bind a `tripleclick` handler to the `<h1>` element which hides and reveals the contents of `<div id="gallery">`.

11
Advanced Effects

Since learning about jQuery's animation capabilities in *Chapter 4, Styling and Animating* we have found many uses for them. We can hide and reveal objects on the page with ease, we can gracefully resize elements, and we can smoothly reposition items. As this effects library is so versatile, it contains even more techniques and specialized abilities than we have seen so far.

In this chapter, we will investigate a few of these advanced features. We will learn how to better keep an eye on animations as they run, both by reacting to the progress and conclusion of animations and by querying the current animation state. We will see how to interrupt animations in progress and how to globally alter all effects on the page. We will also dive further into the topic of easing, allowing us to fine-tune the progress of any effect.

Animation revisited

In order to refresh our memories about jQuery's effect methods and set up a baseline from which to build in this chapter, we will start with a simple hover animation. By using a document with a number of photo thumbnails on it, we will make each photo "grow" slightly when the user's mouse is over it and shrink back to its original size when the mouse leaves. The HTML, which follows, also contains some textual information that is hidden for now, which we will use later in the chapter:

```
<div class="team">
  <div class="member">
    <img class="avatar" src="photos/rey.jpg" alt="" />
    <div class="name">Rey Bango</div>
    <div class="location">Florida</div>
    <p class="bio">Rey Bango is a consultant living in South
      Florida, specializing in web application development...</p>
  </div>
```

```
<div class="member">
  <img class="avatar" src="photos/scott.jpg" alt="" />
  <div class="name">Scott González</div>
  <div class="location">North Carolina</div>
  <div class="position">jQuery UI Development Lead</div>
  <p class="bio">Scott is a web developer living in
    Raleigh, NC...</p>
</div>
<!-- Code continues ... -->
</div>
```

The HTML and CSS for this example produce a vertically arranged list of images, as shown in the following screenshot. The text associated with each image is initially hidden by the CSS:

Executive Board

The Executive Board is responsible for the day-to-day operations of the jQuery project, and has powers delegated to it by our governance plan or a regular vote of the voting membership. The Executive Board is made up of seven members of the voting membership, elected twice annually by the voting membership, in October and April.

In order to alter the size of the image, we will increase its height and width from 75 pixels to 85 pixels. At the same time, to keep the image centered, we will decrease its padding from 5 pixels to 0 pixels as follows:

```
$(document).ready(function() {
  $('div.member')
  .bind('mouseenter mouseleave', function(event) {
    var size = event.type == 'mouseenter' ? 85 : 75;
```

```
    var padding = event.type == 'mouseenter' ? 0 : 5;
    $(this).find('img').animate({
      width: size,
      height: size,
      paddingTop: padding,
      paddingLeft: padding
    });
  })
});
```

Listing 11.1

Here we repeat a pattern we saw in *Chapter 10*. Because much of the work we are performing when the mouse enters the region is the same as when it leaves, we are combining the handlers for `mouseenter` and `mouseleave` into one function rather than calling `.hover()` with two separate callbacks. Inside this joint handler, we determine the values of `size` and `padding` based on which of the two events is being triggered, and pass these property values on to the `.animate()` method.

Now, when the mouse cursor is over an image, it is slightly larger than the rest, as shown in the following screenshot:

Observing and interrupting animations

Our basic animation already reveals a problem. As long as the user is careful about drawing the mouse over and out of the images slowly and avoiding triggering repeated `mouseenter` and `mouseleave` events too quickly, the animations proceed as intended. When the events are triggered quickly and repeatedly, however, we see that the images also grow and shrink repeatedly, well after the last event is triggered. This occurs because, as discussed in *Chapter 4*, animations on a given element are added to a **queue** and called in order. The first animation is called immediately, completes in the allotted time, and then is shifted off the queue. At this point, the next animation becomes first in line, is called, completes, is shifted, and so on until the queue is empty.

There are many cases in which this animation queue, known within jQuery as `fx`, is desirable. In the case of hover actions such as ours, though, it needs to be circumvented.

Determining the animation state

One way to avoid the undesirable queuing of animations is to employ jQuery's custom `:animated` selector. Inside the `mouseenter`/`mouseleave` event handler, we can use the selector to check the image and see if it is currently being animated. When the user's mouse enters the member `<div>`, the image will only animate if it is not already being animated. When the mouse leaves, the animation will occur regardless of its state because we always want it to ultimately restore to the original dimensions and padding, as follows:

```
$(document).ready(function() {
  $('div.member')
  .bind('mouseenter mouseleave', function(event) {
    var $image = $(this).find('img');
    if (!$image.is(':animated')
        || event.type == 'mouseleave') {
      var size = event.type == 'mouseenter' ? 85 : 75;
      var padding = event.type == 'mouseenter' ? 0 : 5;
      $image.animate({
        width: size,
        height: size,
        paddingTop: padding,
        paddingLeft: padding
      });
    }
  });
});
```

Listing 11.2

We have successfully avoided the runaway animations that occur in Listing 11.1, but the animations still need improvement. When the mouse quickly enters and leaves the <div>, the image still has to complete the entire mouseenter animation (growing) before it starts the mouseleave animation (shrinking). This is not ideal, to be sure, but the :animated check has introduced an even greater problem: If the mouse enters the <div> while the image is *shrinking*, the image will fail to grow again. Only a subsequent mouseleave and mouseenter, after the animation has stopped, will execute another animation. While checking the animated state of an element with the :animated selector can be useful in some situations, here it does not help enough.

Halting a running animation

Fortunately, jQuery has a method to help us with both of the problems evident in Listing 11.2. The .stop() method can halt an animation in its tracks. In order to employ it, we can return the code to the way it was in Listing 11.1 and simply insert .stop() between .find() and .animate() as follows:

```
$(document).ready(function() {
  $('div.member').bind('mouseenter mouseleave', function(event) {
    var size = event.type == 'mouseenter' ? 85 : 75;
    var padding = event.type == 'mouseenter' ? 0 : 5;
    $(this).find('img').stop().animate({
      width: size,
      height: size,
      paddingTop: padding,
      paddingLeft: padding
    });
  });
});
```

Listing 11.3

It is worth noting that we stop the current animation *before* proceeding with the new one. Now when the mouse enters and leaves repeatedly, the undesirable effect of our previous attempts is gone. The current animation always completes immediately, so there is never more than one in the fx queue. When the mouse finally rests, the final animation completes, so the image is either fully-grown (mouseenter) or restored to its original dimensions (mouseleave) depending on the last triggered event.

Caution when halting animations

As the `.stop()` method, by default, halts animations at their current position, it can lead to surprising results when used with shorthand animation methods. Before animating, these shorthand methods determine the final value and then animate to that value. For example, if `.slideDown()` is halted with `.stop()` midway through its animation and then `.slideUp()` is called, the next time `.slideDown()` is called on the element, it will only slide down to the height at which it stopped the previous time. In order to mitigate this type of problem, the `.stop()` method can accept two Boolean (`true`/`false`) arguments, the second of which is known as `goToEnd`. If we set this argument to `true`, then the current animation not only stops, but also jumps immediately to the final value. Still, this can look "jerky," so a better solution would be to store the final value in a variable and animate to it explicitly using `.animate()` rather than relying on jQuery to determine that value.

Global effect properties

The effects module in jQuery includes a handy `$.fx` object that we can access when we want to change characteristics of our animations across the board. Although some of this object's properties are undocumented and intended for use solely within the library itself, others are provided as tools for globally altering the way our animations run.

Globally disabling all effects

We already discussed a way to halt animations that are currently running, but what if we need to disable all animations entirely? We may, for example, wish to provide animations by default, but disable those animations for low-resource devices, such as feature phones, in which animations could look choppy or for users who find animations distracting. In order to do so, we can simply set the `$.fx.off` property to `true`. For our demonstration, we will display a previously hidden button to allow the user to toggle animations on and off as follows:

```
$('#fx-toggle').show().bind('click', function() {
  $.fx.off = !$.fx.off;
});
```

Listing 11.4

The hidden button is displayed between the introductory paragraph and the subsequent images, as follows:

Executive Board

The Executive Board is responsible for the day-to-day operations of the jQuery project, and has powers delegated to it by our governance plan or a regular vote of the voting membership. The Executive Board is made up of seven members of the voting membership, elected twice annually by the voting membership, in October and April.

Toggle Animations

When the user clicks on the button to toggle animations off, subsequent animations, such as our growing and shrinking images, will occur with duration of 0 and any callback functions will be called virtually instantly.

Fine-tuning animation smoothness

The `$.fx` object also exposes an `interval` property which determines the number of milliseconds between each step of an animation. The default value for `$.fx.interval` is `13`, which translates to an attempted frame rate of roughly 77 frames per second. As not all JavaScript timers are that precise and are subject to momentary interruption, the actual frame rate can vary. Some developers have reported that increasing the interval (or, decreasing the frame rate) can make animations appear smoother, especially on low-resource devices, as it reduces the number of times functions are executed during the lifespan of the animation. Demonstrable differences, however, are hard to confirm, so changing the interval may not be worth doing. In addition, some versions of jQuery use the "timer-less" DOM method named `requestAnimationFrame()` in browsers that support it instead of `setInterval()`, so changing `$.fx.interval` would have no effect in those cases.

Defining effect durations

Another property of the `$.fx` object is `speeds`. This property is an object itself, consisting of three properties, as evidenced by this part of the jQuery core file:

```
speeds: {
  slow: 600,
  fast: 200,
  // Default speed
  _default: 400
}
```

We have already learned that all of jQuery's animation methods provide an optional speed, or duration, argument. Looking at the $.fx.speeds object, we see that the strings 'slow' and 'fast' map to 600 milliseconds and 200 milliseconds, respectively. Each time an animation method is called, jQuery goes through the following steps to determine the duration of the effect, in this order:

1. Checks if $.fx.off is true. If so, sets duration to 0.

2. Checks if the duration passed is a number; if so, sets duration to that number of milliseconds.

3. Checks if the duration pass matches one of the property keys of the $.fx.speeds object. If so, sets duration to the value of the property.

4. If the duration is not set by any of the above checks, then sets duration to the value of $.fx.speeds._default.

Given this information, we now know that passing any string duration other than 'slow' or 'fast' will result in a duration of 400 milliseconds. We can also see that adding our own custom speed is as easy as adding another property to $.fx.speeds. If we write $.fx.speeds.crawl = 1200, for example, we can use 'crawl' for any animation method's speed argument to run the animation for 1200 milliseconds, like so:

```
$(someElement).animate({width: '300px'}, 'crawl');
```

Although typing 'crawl' is no easier than typing 1200, custom speeds can come in handy in larger projects when a number of animations that share a certain speed need to change. In such cases, we could just change the value of $.fx.speeds.crawl rather than search throughout the project for 1200 and replace each one only if it represents an animation speed.

While custom speeds can be useful, perhaps even more useful is the ability to change the default speed. We can do this by setting the _default property as follows:

```
$.fx.speeds._default = 250;
```

Listing 11.5

Now that we have defined a new faster default speed, any new animations we add will use it unless we override their durations. In order to see this at work, we will introduce another interactive element to the page. When the user clicks on one of the portraits, we want to display the details associated with that person. We will create the illusion of the details "unfolding" from the portrait by moving them out from under the portrait into their final positions as follows:

```
$(document).ready(function() {
  function showDetails() {
```

```
    $(this).find('div').css({
      display: 'block',
      left: '-300px',
      top: 0
    }).each(function(index) {
      $(this).animate({
        left: 0,
        top: 25 * index
      });
    });
  }

  $('div.member').click(showDetails);
});
```

Listing 11.6

When a member is clicked, we use the `showDetails()` function as a handler. This function first sets the detail `<div>` elements in their starting positions, underneath the member's portrait. Then, it animates each of the elements into its final position. By calling `.each()`, we can calculate a separate final `top` position for each element:

As the `.animate()` calls are made on different elements, they happen simultaneously rather than being queued. Moreover, as the calls do not specify duration, they all use the new default duration of 250 milliseconds.

When another member is clicked, we want to hide the previously displayed one. We can easily track which details are currently on the screen with the use of a class as follows:

```
var $member = $(this);
if ($member.hasClass('active')) {
```

```
      return;
   }

   $('div.member.active')
      .removeClass('active')
      .children('div').fadeOut();
   $member.addClass('active');
```

Listing 11.7

This new code, placed at the beginning of `showDetails()`, adds an `active` class to members that are clicked. By finding this class, we can easily locate the elements that are visible and fade them away. We can also use the class to return without taking action if the clicked member is already active.

Note that our `.fadeOut()` call also uses the faster 250 second duration we have defined. The defaults apply to jQuery's pre-packaged effects just as they do to custom `.animate()` calls.

Multi-property easing

The `showDetails()` function almost accomplishes the "unfolding" effect we set out to achieve, but because the `top` and `left` properties are animating at the same rate, it looks more like a "sliding in" effect. We can subtly alter the effect by changing the easing equation to `easeInQuart` for the `top` property only, causing the element to follow a curved path rather than a straight one. Remember, however, that using any easing other than `swing` or `linear` requires a plugin, such as the effects core of jQuery UI (`http://jqueryui.com/`) or the standalone jQuery Easing plugin (`http://gsgd.co.uk/sandbox/jquery/easing/`), as follows:

```
$member.find('div').css({
   display: 'block',
   left: '-300px',
   top: 0
}).each(function(index) {
   $(this).animate({
      left: 0,
      top: 25 * index
   }, {
      duration: 'slow',
      specialEasing: {
```

```
        top: 'easeInQuart'
      }
    });
  });
```

Listing 11.8

The `specialEasing` option allows us to set a different acceleration curve for each property that is being animated. Any properties that are not included in the option will use the `easing` option's equation if it is provided or the default `swing` equation if not.

We now have an attractive animation presenting most of the details associated with a team member. We are not yet displaying a member's biography, however. Before we do this, we need to take a small digression to talk about jQuery's deferred object mechanism.

Deferred objects

In jQuery 1.5, a concept known as a **deferred object** was introduced to the library. A deferred object encapsulates an operation that takes some time to complete. These objects allow us to easily handle situations in which we want to act when a process completes, but we don't necessarily know how long the process will take or even if it will be successful.

A new deferred object can be created at any time by calling the `$.Deferred()` constructor. Once we have such an object, we can perform long-lasting operations and then call the `.resolve()` or `.reject()` methods on the object to indicate the operation was successful or unsuccessful. It is somewhat unusual to do this manually, however. Typically, rather than creating our own deferred objects by hand, jQuery or its plugins will create the object and take care of resolving or rejecting it. We just need to learn how to use the object that is created.

Creating deferred objects is a very advanced topic—more advanced than is appropriate for the scope of this book. Rather than detailing how the `$.Deferred()` constructor operates, we will focus here on how jQuery effects take advantage of deferred objects. In *Chapter 13*, we will further explore deferred objects in the context of Ajax requests.

Every deferred object makes a **promise** to provide data to other code. This promise is represented as another object, with its own set of methods. From any deferred object, we can obtain its promise object by calling its `.promise()` method. Then, we can call methods of the promise to attach handlers that are executed when the promise is fulfilled:

- The `.done()` method attaches a handler that is called when the deferred object is resolved successfully.
- The `.fail()` method attaches a handler that is called when the deferred object is rejected.
- The `.always()` method attaches a handler that is called when the deferred object completes its task, either by being resolved or by being rejected.

These handlers are much like the callbacks we provide to `.bind()`, in that they are functions called when some event happens. We can also attach multiple handlers to the same promise, and all will be called at the appropriate time. There are a few important differences, however. Promise handlers will only ever be called once; the deferred object cannot resolve a second time. A promise handler will also be called immediately if the deferred object is already resolved at the time we attach the handler.

Now we can put this powerful tool to use by investigating one of the deferred objects created by jQuery for us.

Animation promises

Every jQuery collection has a set of deferred objects associated with it, tracking the status of queued operations on the elements in the collection. By calling the `.promise()` method on the jQuery object, we get a promise object that is resolved when a queue completes. In particular, we can use this promise to take an action upon the completion of all of the animations running on any of the matched elements.

Just as we have a `showDetails()` function to display a member name and location information, we can write a `showBio()` function for bringing the biographical information into view. First, we will append a new `<div>` to the `<body>` and set up a couple of map options as follows:

```
var $movable = $('<div id="movable"></div>')
  .appendTo('body');

var bioBaseStyles = {
    display: 'none',
    height: '5px',
    width: '25px'
  },
```

```
bioEffects = {
  duration: 800,
  easing: 'easeOutQuart',
  specialEasing: {
    opacity: 'linear'
  }
};
```

Listing 11.9

This new "movable" <div> is the one that we will actually animate after injecting it with a copy of a biography. Having a wrapper element such as this is particularly useful when animating an element's width and height. We can set its overflow property to hidden and set an explicit width and height for the biographies within it to avoid a continual reflowing of text that would have occurred if we had instead animated the biography <div>s themselves.

We will use the showBio() function to determine what the movable <div>'s starting and ending styles should be based on the member that is clicked. Note that we are using the $.extend() method to merge the set of base styles that remain constant with the top and left properties that vary depending on the member's position. Then, it is just a matter of using .css() to set the starting styles and .animate() for the ending styles as follows:

```
function showBio() {
  var $member = $(this).parent(),
      $bio = $member.find('p.bio'),
      startStyles = $.extend(bioBaseStyles, $member.offset()),
      endStyles = {
        width: $bio.width(),
        top: $member.offset().top + 5,
        left: $member.width() + $member.offset().left - 5,
        opacity: 'show'
      };

  $movable
    .html($bio.clone())
    .css(startStyles)
    .animate(endStyles, bioEffects)
    .animate({height: $bio.height()}, {
      easing: 'easeOutQuart'
    });
}
```

Listing 11.10

We are queuing two `.animate()` methods, so that the biography first flies from the left as it grows wider and fully opaque and then slides down to its full height once it is in position.

Recall from *Chapter 4* that callback functions in jQuery's animation methods are called when the animation completes *for each element in the collection*. We want to show the member's biography after the other `<div>` elements appear. Before jQuery introduced the `.promise()` method, this would have been an onerous task, requiring us to count down from the total number of elements for each time the callback was executed until the last time, at which point we could execute the code to animate the biography. Now we can simply chain the `.promise()` and `.done()` methods to the `.each()` method inside our `showDetails()` function as follows:

```
function showDetails() {
  var $member = $(this).parent();
  if ($member.hasClass('active')) {
    return;
  }
  $movable.fadeOut();

  $('div.member.active')
    .removeClass('active')
      .children('div').fadeOut();

  $member.addClass('active');
  $member.find('div').css({
    display: 'block',
    left: '-300px',
    top: 0
  }).each(function(index) {
    $(this).animate({
      left: 0,
      top: 25 * index
    }, {
      duration: 'slow',
      specialEasing: {
        top: 'easeInQuart'
      }
    });
  }).promise().done(showBio);
}
```

Listing 11.11

The .done() method takes a reference to our showBio() function as its argument. Now clicking on an image brings all of that member's information into view with an attractive animation sequence as shown in the following screenshots:

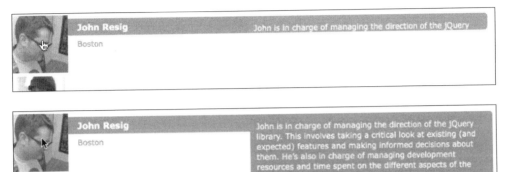

Notice that we also slipped in $movable.fadeOut() near the top of the function. This has no visible effect the first time showDetails() is called, but in subsequent calls, it nicely fades the currently visible biography away along with the other information before the new information is animated into view.

Summary

In this chapter, we have further investigated several techniques that can assist us in designing beautiful animations that are helpful to our users. We can now individually control the acceleration and deceleration of each property we are animating, and halt these animations individually or globally if needed. We learned about the properties jQuery's effects library defines internally and the way to change some of them to suit our needs. We also made our first foray into the jQuery deferred object system, which we will explore further in *Chapter 13*.

Further reading

A complete list of available effect and animation methods is available in *Appendix C* of this book, in *jQuery Reference Guide*, or in the official jQuery documentation at the following URL:

```
http://api.jquery.com/
```

Exercises

In order to complete these exercises, you will need the `index.html` file for this chapter, as well as the finished JavaScript code as found in `complete.js`. These files can be downloaded from the Packt Publishing website at `http://www.packtpub.com/support`.

The challenge exercises may require use of the official jQuery documentation at `http://api.jquery.com/`.

1. Define a new animation speed constant named `zippy` and apply this to the biography display effect.

2. Change the easing of the horizontal movement of member details, so that they "bounce" into place.

3. Add a second deferred callback function to the promise that adds a `highlight` class to the current member's location `<div>`.

4. **Challenge**: Add a delay of two seconds before animating the biography. Use the jQuery `.delay()` method.

5. **Challenge**: When the active photo is clicked, collapse the bio details. Stop any running animation before doing so.

Advanced DOM Manipulation

12

In *Chapter 5*, we were introduced to jQuery's powerful mechanisms for altering the content of the DOM. We now have seen several ways in which we can insert new content, move existing content around, or remove content from the document. We also know how to alter the attributes and properties of elements to suit our needs.

In this chapter, we will continue our examination of jQuery's DOM manipulation features and delve into some more advanced techniques. We'll look at ways to store and retrieve data related to DOM elements, and use this data to restructure page content on demand. By building our understanding of the inner workings of the jQuery's DOM manipulation faculties, we will also learn how to optimize the performance of our code and to alter the library to enable advanced CSS features.

Sorting table rows

The majority of the topics we're investigating in this chapter can be demonstrated through sorting the rows of a table. This common task is a very useful way to assist users in quickly finding the information they need. There are, naturally, a number of ways in which the task can be accomplished.

Server-side sorting

A common solution for data sorting is to perform it on the server. Data in tables often comes from a **database**, which means that the code that pulls it out of the database can request it in a given sort order (using, for example, the **SQL** language's ORDER BY clause). If we have server-side code at our disposal, then it is straightforward to begin with a reasonable default sort order.

Sorting is most useful, though, when the user can determine the sort order. A common user interface for this is to make the table headers (`<th>`) of sortable columns into links. These links can go to the current page, but with a query string appended indicating the column to sort by, as follows:

```
<table id="my-data">
  <thead>
    <tr>
      <th class="name">
        <a href="index.php?sort=name">Name</a>
      </th>
      <th class="date">
        <a href="index.php?sort=date">Date</a>
      </th>
    </tr>
  </thead>
  <tbody>
    ...
  </tbody>
</table>
```

The server can react to the query string parameter by returning the database contents in a different order.

Ajax sorting

This setup is simple, but requires a page refresh for each sort operation. As we have seen, jQuery allows us to eliminate such page refreshes by using Ajax methods. If we have the column headers set up as links as before, then we can add jQuery code to change those links into Ajax requests:

```
$(document).ready(function() {
  $('#my-data th a').click(function() {
    $('#my-data tbody').load($(this).attr('href'));
    return false;
  });
});
```

Now when the anchors are clicked, jQuery sends an Ajax request to the server for the same page. When jQuery is used to make a page request using Ajax, it sets the X-Requested-With HTTP header to XMLHttpRequest so that the server can determine that an Ajax request is being made. The server code can be written to send back only the content of the `<tbody>` element itself, and not the surrounding page, when this parameter is present. This way we can use the response to replace the content of the existing `<tbody>` element.

This is an example of **progressive enhancement**. The page works perfectly well without any JavaScript at all, as the links for server-side sorting are still present. When JavaScript is available, however, the Ajax hijacks the page request and allows the sort to occur without a full page load.

JavaScript sorting

There are times, though, when we either don't want to wait for server responses when sorting or don't have a server-side scripting language available to us. A viable alternative, in this case, is to perform the sorting entirely on the browser using JavaScript client-side scripting.

In order to demonstrate the various techniques in this chapter, we will set up three separate JavaScript sorting mechanisms. Each will accomplish the same goal, but in a unique way. The tables we'll be sorting will have different HTML structures to accommodate the varying JavaScript techniques, but each contains columns listing books, their author names, release dates, and prices. The first table has this simple structure:

```html
<table id="t-1" class="sortable">
  <thead>
    <tr>
      <th></th>
        <th class="sort-alpha">Title</th>
        <th class="sort-alpha">Author(s)</th>
        <th class="sort-date">Publish Date</th>
        <th class="sort-numeric">Price</th>
    </tr>
  </thead>
  <tbody>
    <tr>
      <td><img src="images/2862_OS.jpg" alt="Drupal 7"></td>
      <td>Drupal 7</td>
      <td>David <span class="sort-key">Mercer</span></td>
      <td>September 2010</td>
      <td>$44.99</td>
    </tr>
    <!-- code continues -->
  </tbody>
</table>
```

Before we enhance the table with JavaScript, the first few rows look like the following screenshot:

Title	Author(s)	Publish Date	Price
Drupal 7	David Mercer	September 2010	$44.99
Amazon SimpleDB: LITE	Prabhakar Chaganti, Rich Helms	May 2011	$9.99
Object-Oriented JavaScript	Stoyan Stefanov	July 2008	$39.99

Moving and inserting elements, revisited

Over the course of the coming examples, we will build a flexible sorting mechanism that works on each of the columns. In order to do this, we will use the jQuery DOM manipulation methods to insert some new elements and move other existing elements to new homes. We will start with the most straightforward piece of the puzzle: linking the table headers.

Adding links around existing text

We'd like to turn the table headers into links that sort the data by their respective columns. We can use jQuery's `.wrapInner()` method to add them; we recall from *Chapter 5* that `.wrapInner()` places a new element (in this case an `<a>` element) inside the matched element, but around child elements:

```
$(document).ready(function() {
  var $table1 = $('#t-1');
  var $headers = $table1.find('thead th').slice(1);
  $headers
    .wrapInner('<a href="#"></a>')
    .addClass('sort');
  });
});
```

Listing 12.1

We skipped the first `<th>` of each table (using `.slice()`) because it contains no text other than white space, as there is no need to either label, or sort, the cover photos. We've added a class of `sort` to the remaining `<th>` elements as well, so we can distinguish them in our CSS from their non-sortable counterparts. Now the header rows look like the following screenshot:

This is an example of progressive enhancement's counterpart, **graceful degradation**. Unlike the Ajax solution discussed earlier, this technique cannot function without JavaScript; we are assuming the server has no scripting language available to it for the purposes of this example. As JavaScript is required for the sort to work, we are adding the `sort` class and the anchors through code only, thereby making sure that the interface indicates that sorting is possible only if the script can run. And as we're actually creating links, rather than simply adding visual styles to indicate that the headers can be clicked, we provide the added benefit of accessibility for users who need to navigate to the headers with the keyboard (by pressing the *Tab* key). The page **degrades** into one that is still functional, albeit without sorting available.

Sorting simple JavaScript arrays

To perform the sort, we will be taking advantage of JavaScript's built in `.sort()` method. It does an in-place sort on an array, and can take a **comparator function** as an argument. This function compares two items in the array and should return a positive or negative number depending on which item should come first in the sorted array.

For example, take a simple array of numbers, as follows:

```
var arr = [52, 97, 3, 62, 10, 63, 64, 1, 9, 3, 4];
```

We can sort this array by calling `arr.sort()`. After this, the items are in the order:

```
[1, 10, 3, 3, 4, 52, 62, 63, 64, 9, 97]
```

By default, as we see here, the items are sorted **lexicographically** (in alphabetical order). In this case it might make more sense to sort the items **numerically**. To do this, we can supply a comparator function to the `.sort()` method:

```
arr.sort(function(a,b) {
  if (a < b) {
    return -1;
  }
  if (a > b) {
    return 1;
  }
  return 0;
});
```

This function returns a negative number if a should come first in the sorted array, a positive number if b should come first, and zero if the order of the items does not matter. With this information in hand, the `.sort()` method can sequence the items appropriately:

```
[1, 3, 3, 4, 9, 10, 52, 62, 63, 64, 97]
```

We will next apply this `.sort()` method to our table rows.

Sorting DOM elements

Let's perform a sort on the **Title** column of the table. Note that while we added the `sort` class to it and the others, this column's header cell already has a `sort-alpha` class that was output in the HTML. The other header cells received similar treatment, depending on the type of sorting for each, but for now we'll focus on the **Title** header, which requires a straightforward alphabetic sort.

```
$headers.bind('click', function(event) {
  event.preventDefault();
  var column = $(this).index();
  var rows = $table1.find('tbody > tr').get();
  rows.sort(function(a, b) {
    var keyA = $(a).children('td').eq(column).text();
    keyA = $.trim(keyA).toUpperCase();
    var keyB = $(b).children('td').eq(column).text();
```

```
    keyB = $.trim(keyB).toUpperCase();
    if (keyA < keyB) return -1;
    if (keyA > keyB) return 1;
    return 0;
  });

  $.each(rows, function(index, row) {
    $table1.children('tbody').append(row);
  });
});
```

Listing 12.2

Once we have found the index of the clicked header cell, we retrieve an array of all of the data rows. This is a great example of how `.get()` is useful in transforming a jQuery object into an array of DOM nodes; even though jQuery objects act like arrays in many respects, they don't have all of the native array methods available, such as `.pop()` or `.shift()`.

> Internally, jQuery actually does define a few methods that act like native array methods. In version 1.6, for example, `.sort()`, `.push()`, and `.splice()` are methods of jQuery objects. However, as these methods are for internal use and not publicly documented, we cannot rely on them behaving in expected ways in our own code and should, thus, avoid calling them on jQuery objects.

Now that we have an array of DOM nodes, we can sort them, but to do this we need to write an appropriate **comparator function**. We want to sort the rows according to the textual contents of the relevant table cells, so this will be the information the comparator function will examine. We know which cell to look at because we captured the column index with the `.index()` call. We use jQuery's `$.trim()` function to strip out leading and trailing white space, and then we convert the text to uppercase because string comparisons in JavaScript are **case-sensitive** while our sort should be **case-insensitive**. We store the key values in variables to avoid redundant calculations, compare them, and return a positive or negative number as discussed earlier.

Our array is now sorted, but note that this has not changed the DOM itself. To do this, we need to call DOM manipulation methods to move the rows around. We do this one row at a time, reinserting each into the table as we loop through them. As `.append()` does not clone nodes, this moves them rather than copying them. Our table is now sorted, as follows:

	⬍ Title	⬍ Author(s)	⬍ Publish Date	⬍ Price
	Amazon SimpleDB: LITE	Prabhakar Chaganti, Rich Helms	May 2011	$9.99
	CakePHP 1.3 Application Development Cookbook	Mariano Iglesias	March 2011	$39.99
	Cocoa and Objective-C Cookbook	Jeff Hawkins	May 2011	$39.99

Storing data alongside DOM elements

Our code works, but it is quite slow. The culprit is the comparator function, which is performing a fair amount of work. This comparator will be called many times during the course of a sort, which means that every extra moment it spends on processing will be magnified.

Array sorting performance

The actual **sort algorithm** used by JavaScript is not defined by the standard. It may be a simple sort like a **bubble sort** (worst case of $\Theta(n^2)$ in computational complexity terms) or a more sophisticated approach like **quick sort** (which is $\Theta(n \log n)$ on average). It is safe to say, though, that doubling the number of items in an array will more than double the number of times the comparator function is called.

The remedy for our slow comparator is to **pre-compute** the keys for the comparison. We can do most of the expensive work in an initial loop and store the result with jQuery's `.data()` method, which sets or retrieves arbitrary information associated with page elements. Then we can simply examine the keys within the comparator function, and our sort is markedly faster, as follows:

```
var rows = $table1.find('tbody > tr').each(function() {
    var key = $(this).children('td').eq(column).text();
```

```
    $(this).data('sortKey', $.trim(key).toUpperCase());
}).get();

rows.sort(function(a, b) {
  var keyA = $(a).data('sortKey');
  var keyB = $(b).data('sortKey');
  if (keyA < keyB) return -1;
  if (keyA > keyB) return 1;
  return 0;
});
```

Listing 12.3

The `.data()` method, paired with its complement `.removeData()`, provides a data storage mechanism that is a convenient alternative to **expando properties**, or non-standard properties added directly to DOM elements. Using `.data()` instead of expando properties avoids potential problems with Internet Explorer memory leaks.

Performing additional precomputation

Now, we want to apply the same kind of sorting behavior to the **Author(s)** column of our table. As its table header cell has the `sort-alpha` class, the **Author(s)** column can be sorted with our existing code. Ideally, though, authors should be sorted by last name, not first. As some books have multiple authors, and some authors have middle names or initials listed, we need outside guidance to determine what part of the text to use as our sort key. We can supply this guidance by wrapping the relevant part of the cell in a tag, as follows:

```
<td>David <span class="sort-key">Mercer</span></td>
```

Now, we have to modify our sorting code to take this tag into account without disturbing the existing behavior for the **Title** column, which is already working well. By prepending the marked sort key to the key we have previously calculated, we can sort first on the last name if it is called out, but on the whole string as a fallback:

```
var rows = $table1.find('tbody > tr').each(function() {
  var $cell = $(this).children('td').eq(column);
  var key = $cell.find('span.sort-key').text() + ' ';
  key += $.trim($cell.text()).toUpperCase();
  $(this).data('sortKey', key);
}).get();
```

Listing 12.4

Sorting by the **Author(s)** column now uses the provided key, thereby sorting by last name:

⇕ Title	⇕ Author(s)	⇕ Publish Date	⇕ Price
WordPress 3 Plugin Development Essentials	Brian Bondari, Everett Griffiths	March 2011	$39.99
Magento 1.4 Themes Design	Richard Carter	January 2011	$39.99
Amazon SimpleDB: LITE	Prabhakar Chaganti, Rich Helms	May 2011	$9.99

If two last names are identical, then the sort uses the entire string as a tiebreaker for positioning.

Storing non-string data

Our user should be able to sort not just by the **Title** and **Author(s)** columns, but the **Publish Date** and **Price** columns as well. Since we streamlined our comparator function, it can handle all kinds of data, but first the computed keys will need to be adjusted for other data types. For example, in the case of prices we need to strip off the leading $ character and parse the rest so that we can compare them numerically, as follows:

```
var key = parseFloat($cell.text().replace(/^[^\d.]*/, ''));
if (isNaN(key)) {
  key = 0;
}
```

The regular expression used here removes any leading characters other than numbers and decimal points, passing the result on to `parseFloat()`. The result of `parseFloat()` then needs to be checked, because if no number can be extracted from the text, NaN (**not a number**) is returned. This can wreak havoc on `.sort()`, so we set any non-number to 0.

For the date cells, we can use the JavaScript `Date` object, as follows:

```
var key = Date.parse('1 ' + $cell.text());
```

The dates in this table contain a month and year only; `Date.parse()` requires a fully-specified date, so we prepend the string with 1. This provides a day to accompany the month and year, and the combination is then converted into a **timestamp**, which can be sorted using our normal comparator.

We can apportion these expressions across separate functions, so that later we can call the appropriate one based on the class applied to the table header:

```
$headers
  .each(function() {
    var keyType = this.className.replace(/^sort-/,'');
    $(this).data('keyType', keyType);
  })
  .wrapInner('<a href="#"></a>')
  .addClass('sort');

var sortKeys = {
  alpha: function($cell) {
    var key = $cell.find('span.sort-key').text() + ' ';
    key += $.trim($cell.text()).toUpperCase();
    return key;
  },
  numeric: function($cell) {
    var num = $cell.text().replace(/^[^\d.]*/, '');
    var key = parseFloat(num);
    if (isNaN(key)) {
      key = 0;
    }
    return key;
  },
  date: function($cell) {
    var key = Date.parse('1 ' + $cell.text());
    return key;
  }
};
```

Listing 12.5

We've modified the script a bit to store `keyType` data for each column header cell based on its class name before we add the `sort` class. We strip off the `sort-` portion of the class so that we're left with `alpha`, `numeric`, or `date`. By making each sort function a method of the `sortKeys` map, we can use **array notation** and pass in the value of the header cell's `keyType` data to call the appropriate function.

Typically when we call methods, we use **dot notation**. This is, in fact, the way we call methods of the jQuery object throughout this book. For example, to add a class of `bar` to `<div class="foo">` we write `$('div.foo').addClass('bar')`. As JavaScript allows properties and methods to be represented in either dot or array notation, we could also write it as `$('div.foo')['addClass']('bar')`. It doesn't make much sense to do this most of the time, but it can be a great way to conditionally call methods without using a bunch of `if` statements. For our `sortKeys` map, we could call the `alpha` method like `sortKeys.alpha($cell)` or `sortKeys['alpha']($cell)` or, if the method name is stored in a `keyType` variable, `sortKeys[keyType]($cell)`. We'll use the third variation inside the `click` handler, as follows:

```
var $header = $(this),
    column = $header.index(),
    keyType = $header.data('keyType');

if ( !$.isFunction(sortKeys[keyType]) ) {
  return;
}

var rows = $table1.find('tbody > tr').each(function() {
  var $cell = $(this).children('td').eq(column);
  $(this).data('sortKey', sortKeys[keyType]($cell));
}).get();
```

Listing 12.6

To be safe and avoid JavaScript errors, we also made sure that the `sortKeys[keyType]` method exists before continuing on. We can now sort on date or price, as well:

	⬍ Title	⬍ Author(s)	⬍ Publish Date	⬍ Price
	Object-Oriented JavaScript	Stoyan Stefanov	July 2008	$39.99
	jQuery 1.4 Reference Guide	Karl Swedberg, Jonathan Chaffer	January 2010	$39.99
	Drupal 7	David Mercer	September 2010	$44.99

Alternating sort directions

Our final sorting enhancement is to allow for both **ascending** and **descending** sort orders. When the user clicks on a column that is already sorted, we want to reverse the current sort order.

To reverse a sort, all we have to do is to invert the values returned by our comparator. We can do this with a simple variable, as follows:

```
if (keyA < keyB) return -sortDirection;
if (keyA > keyB) return sortDirection;
return 0;
```

If `sortDirection` equals 1, then the sort will be the same as before. If it equals -1, then the sort will be reversed. Combining this concept with some classes to keep track of the current sort order of a column, achieving alternating sort directions is simple.

```
$headers.bind('click', function(event) {
  event.preventDefault();
  var $header = $(this),
    column = $header.index(),
    keyType = $header.data('keyType'),
    sortDirection = 1;

  if ( !$.isFunction(sortKeys[keyType]) ) {
    return;
  }

  if ($header.hasClass('sorted-asc')) {
    sortDirection = -1;
  }

  var rows = $table1.find('tbody > tr').each(function() {
    var $cell = $(this).children('td').eq(column);
    $(this).data('sortKey', sortKeys[keyType]($cell));
  }).get();

  rows.sort(function(a, b) {
    var keyA = $(a).data('sortKey');
    var keyB = $(b).data('sortKey');
    if (keyA < keyB) return -sortDirection;
    if (keyA > keyB) return sortDirection;
    return 0;
  });
```

```
$headers.removeClass('sorted-asc sorted-desc');
$header.addClass(sortDirection == 1 ? 'sorted-asc' : 'sorted-
  desc');


$.each(rows, function(index, row) {
  $table1.children('tbody').append(row);
});
});
```

Listing 12.7

As a side benefit, because we use classes to store the sort direction, we can style the column headers to indicate the current order, as well:

	⬍ Title	⬍ Author(s)	⬍ Publish Date	⬌ Price
	Amazon SimpleDB: LITE	Prabhakar Chaganti, Rich Helms	May 2011	$9.99
	Object-Oriented JavaScript	Stoyan Stefanov	July 2008	$39.99
	jQuery 1.4 Reference Guide	Karl Swedberg, Jonathan Chaffer	January 2010	$39.99

Using HTML5 custom data attributes

So far, we've been relying on the content within the table cells to determine the sort order. While we've managed to sort the rows correctly by manipulating that content, we can make our code more efficient by outputting more HTML from the server in the form of **HTML5 data-* attributes**. The second table in our example page includes the following attributes:

```
<h3>Table 2</h3>
<table id="t-2" class="sortable">
  <thead>
    <tr>
      <th></th>
      <th data-sort='{"key":"title"}'>Title</th>
      <th data-sort='{"key":"authors"}'>Author(s)</th>
```

```
    <th data-sort='{"key":"publishedYM"}'>Publish Date</th>
    <th data-sort='{"key":"price"}'>Price</th>
  </tr>
</thead>

<tbody>
  <tr data-book='{"img":"2862_OS.jpg","title":"DRUPAL
    7","authors":"MERCER DAVID","published":"September
    2010","price":44.99,"publishedYM":"2010-09"}'>
    <td><img src="images/2862_OS.jpg" alt="Drupal 7">
    </td>
    <td>Drupal 7</td>
    <td>David Mercer</td>
    <td>September 2010</td>
    <td>$44.99</td>
  </tr>
  <!-- code continues -->
</tbody>
</table>
```

Notice that each `<th>` element (except the first) has a `data-sort` attribute and each `<tr>` element has a `data-book` attribute. When we use the `.data()` method to get the value of a data attribute, jQuery converts the value to a number, array, object, Boolean, or null if it determines that it is one of those types. For both the `<th>` and the `<tr>` elements, jQuery will interpret the values as objects.

In order for jQuery to convert a data attribute's value to an object, the string must use valid JSON format. This is why we surround the value in single quotes and put each key and string value in double quotes (actually, the server-side code has encoded an associative array to JSON format). To retrieve the value, we pass the part of the attribute's name after `data-` to the `.data()` method. For example, we write `$('th').first().data('sort')` to get the value of the first `<th>` element's `data-sort` attribute. To get the value of the `key` property specifically (`"title"`), we write `$('th').first().data('sort').key`. Once a custom data attribute is retrieved in this way, the data is stored internally by jQuery and the HTML `data-*` attribute itself is no longer accessed or modified.

One great benefit of using data attributes here is that the values can be output differently from the table cell content. In other words, all of the work that we had to do in the first table to finesse the sorting—converting strings to uppercase, changing the date format, converting the price to a number—is already taken care of. This allows us to write much simpler and more efficient sorting code:

```
$(document).ready(function() {
  var $table2 = $('#t-2');
```

```
    var $headers = $table2.find('thead th').slice(1);
    $headers
        .wrapInner('<a href="#"></a>')
        .addClass('sort');

    var rows = $table2.find('tbody > tr').get();

    $headers.bind('click', function(event) {
        event.preventDefault();
        var $header = $(this),
            sortKey = $header.data('sort').key,
            sortDirection = 1;

        if ($header.hasClass('sorted-asc')) {
            sortDirection = -1;
        }

        rows.sort(function(a, b) {
            var keyA = $(a).data('book')[sortKey];
            var keyB = $(b).data('book')[sortKey];

            if (keyA < keyB) return -sortDirection;
            if (keyA > keyB) return sortDirection;
            return 0;
        });

        $headers.removeClass('sorted-asc sorted-desc');
        $header.addClass(sortDirection == 1 ? 'sorted-asc' : 'sorted-
            desc');

        $.each(rows, function(index, row) {
            $table2.children('tbody').append(row);
        });
    });
});
```

Listing 12.8

The simplicity of this approach is clear: the `sortKey` variable is set with `$header.data('sort').key` and is then used to compare the rows' sort values with `$(a).data('book')[sortKey]` and `$(a).data('book')[sortKey]`. The efficiency is evident in that there is no need to loop through the rows first and call one of the `sortKeys` functions each time before calling the `sort` function. With this combination of simplicity and efficiency, we've also improved the code's performance and made it easier to maintain.

Sorting and building rows with JSON

So far in this chapter we have been moving in the direction of outputting more and more information from the server into the HTML so that our client-side scripts can remain as lean and efficient as possible. Now let's consider a different scenario, one in which a whole new set of information is displayed when JavaScript is available. Increasingly, full-fledged web applications are relying on JavaScript to deliver content as well as manipulate it once it arrives. In our third table sorting example, we'll do the same.

> **Graceful degradation note**
>
> To clarify this example, our HTML document contains no body content for this table. In a real-world situation, we'd prepopulate the table with content so that users without JavaScript could see the (unsortable) table data.

We'll start by writing two functions: `buildRow()`, which builds the HTML for a single table row, and `buildRows()`, which uses `$.map()` to loop through all of the rows in the dataset, calling `buildRow()` for each one. Although for our purposes we could get by with a single function to handle both tasks, by using two separate functions we leave open the possibility of building and inserting a single row at some other point. These functions will get their data from the response to an Ajax request, as follows:

```
(function($) {
  function buildRow(row) {
    var authors = [];
    $.each(row.authors, function(index, auth) {
      authors[index] = auth.first_name + ' ' + auth.last_name;
    });

    var html = '<tr>';
      html += '<td><img src="images/' + row.img + '"></td>';
      html += '<td>' + row.title + '</td>';
      html += '<td>' + authors.join(', ') + '</td>';
      html += '<td>' + row.published + '</td>';
      html += '<td>$' + row.price + '</td>';
    html += '</tr>';

    return html;
  }

  function buildRows(rows) {
```

```
            var allRows = $.map(rows, buildRow);
            return allRows.join('');
        }


        $.getJSON('books.json', function(json) {
            $(document).ready(function() {
                var $table3 = $('#t-3');
                $table3.find('tbody').html(buildRows(json));
            });
        });
    })(jQuery);
```

Listing 12.9

A few things are worth pointing out in this code. First, notice that the functions are defined outside of `$(document).ready()`. By waiting until the callback function of `$.getJSON()` to call `$(document).ready()`, we give the part of our code that doesn't rely on the DOM a head start.

Also worth noting is that we need to treat the `authors` data differently because it comes from the server as an array of objects with `first_name` and `last_name` properties, while everything else arrives as a string or a number. We loop through the array of authors—even though for most rows the array consists of only one—and concatenate the first name and the last. After the `$.each()` loop, we join the array values with a comma and a space to end up with a nicely formatted list of names.

The `buildRow()` function assumes that the text we're getting from the JSON file is safe for consumption. As we're concatenating `<img>`, `<td>`, and `<tr>` tags along with the text content into a single text string, we need to be sure that the text content has no `<`, `>`, or `&` characters. One way to ensure HTML-safe strings is to process them on the server, converting all instances of `<` to `&lt;` and so on.

Finally, although we are lovingly crafting our table rows by hand with these two functions, JavaScript template systems such as Mustache (`https://github.com/janl/mustache.js`) and Handlebars (`http://handlebars.strobeapp.com/`) could do a lot of the string processing and concatenation for us. Using templates can be especially beneficial as the size and complexity of a project grows.

Modifying the JSON object

The work we're doing with the `authors` array is fine if we only plan to call the `buildRows()` function once. However, as we intend to call it each time the rows are sorted, it's a good idea to have the author information formatted ahead of time. While we're at it, we can format the title and the author information for sorting as well. Unlike the second table, in which each row had sortable data in the `data-book` attribute and display data in the table cells, the JSON data we're retrieving for the third table comes in only one flavor. Still, by writing one more function, we can include modified values for sorting and displaying before we ever get to the table building functions:

```
function prepRows(rows) {
  $.each(rows, function(i, row) {
    var authors = [],
      authorsFormatted = [];

    rows[i].titleFormatted = row.title;
    rows[i].title = row.title.toUpperCase();

    $.each(row.authors, function(j, auth) {
      authors[j] = auth.last_name + ' ' + auth.first_name;
      authorsFormatted[j] = auth.first_name +
        ' ' + auth.last_name;
    });
    rows[i].authorsFormatted = authorsFormatted.join(', ');
    rows[i].authors = authors.join(' ').toUpperCase();
  });

  return rows;
}
```

Listing 12.10

By passing our JSON data through this function, we add two properties to each row's object: `authorsFormatted` and `titleFormatted`. These properties will be used for the displayed table contents, preserving the original `authors` and `title` properties for sorting. The properties used for sorting are also converted to uppercase to make the sort operation case insensitive.

When we call this `prepRows()` function immediately inside the `$.getJSON()` callback function, we store the returned value of the modified JSON object in the `rows` variable and use that one for sorting and building. This means that we also need to change the `buildRow()` function to take advantage of the simplicity that our advance preparation has afforded it:

```
function buildRow(row) {
  var html = '<tr>';
    html += '<td><img src="images/' + row.img + '"></td>';
    html += '<td>' + row.titleFormatted + '</td>';
    html += '<td>' + row.authorsFormatted + '</td>';
    html += '<td>' + row.published + '</td>';
    html += '<td>$' + row.price + '</td>';
    html += '</tr>';

  return html;
}

$.getJSON('books.json', function(json) {
  $(document).ready(function() {
    var $table3 = $('#t-3');
    var rows = prepRows(json);
    $table3.find('tbody').html(buildRows(rows));
  });
});
```

Listing 12.11

Rebuilding content on demand

Now that we've prepared the content for both sorting and displaying, we're ready again to implement the column heading modification and the sorting routine:

```
$.getJSON('books.json', function(json) {
  $(document).ready(function() {
    var $table3 = $('#t-3');
    var rows = prepRows(json);
    $table3.find('tbody').html(buildRows(rows));

    var $headers = $table3.find('thead th').slice(1);
    $headers
      .wrapInner('<a href="#"></a>')
```

```
        .addClass('sort');

    $headers.bind('click', function(event) {
      event.preventDefault();
      var $header = $(this),
        sortKey = $header.data('sort').key,
        sortDirection = 1;

      if ($header.hasClass('sorted-asc')) {
        sortDirection = -1;
      }

      rows.sort(function(a, b) {
        var keyA = a[sortKey];
        var keyB = b[sortKey];

        if (keyA < keyB) return -sortDirection;
        if (keyA > keyB) return sortDirection;
        return 0;
      });

      $headers.removeClass('sorted-asc sorted-desc');
      $header.addClass(sortDirection == 1 ? 'sorted-asc' :
        'sorted-desc');

      $table3.children('tbody').html(buildRows(rows));
    });
  });
});
```

Listing 12.12

The code inside the `click` handler is nearly identical to the handler for the second table in Listing 12.8. The one notable difference is that here we insert elements into the DOM only once per sort. In tables one and two, even after our other optimizations, we sorted the actual DOM elements and then looped through them one by one, appending each one in turn to arrive at the new order. For example, in Listing 12.8, table rows are reinserted in a loop like the following:

```
$.each(rows, function(index, row) {
  $table2.children('tbody').append(row);
});
```

This type of repetitive DOM insertion can be quite costly from a performance perspective, especially with a large number of rows. Compare that with our latest approach in Listing 12.12, as follows:

```
$table3.children('tbody').html(buildRows(rows));
```

The `buildRows()` function returns a string of HTML representing the rows and inserts it in one fell swoop, replacing the rows instead of moving the existing ones around.

Measuring performance

To get a sense of the performance difference among the techniques we used for the three tables, we can look at the tests on `http://jsperf.com/sort-and-insert/2`. Don't be surprised, however, if the code there does not exactly match what we've done here. Testing code such as ours can be tricky, as it's doing a number of tasks. The most accurate tests attempt to reduce the code as much as possible so that each case is measuring the right thing.

Advanced attribute manipulation

By now we are very used to getting and setting values that are associated with DOM elements. We have done this with simple methods like `.attr()`, `.prop()`, and `.css()`, convenient shorthands such as `.addClass()`, `.css()`, and `.val()`, and complex bundles of behavior such as `.animate()`. Even the simple methods, though, do quite a bit of work for us behind the scenes. We can get yet more utility out of them if we better understand what they do.

Shorthand element creation

We often create new elements in our jQuery code by providing an HTML string to the `$()` function or to DOM insertion functions. For example, we create quite a large HTML fragment in Listing 12.9. This technique is fast and concise. There are circumstances when it is not ideal, however: we might, for instance, want to escape special characters from text before it is used, or apply style rules that are browser-dependent. In these cases, we could create the element and then chain on additional jQuery methods to alter it. The `$()` function itself provides an alternative syntax that might be more appealing, though.

Suppose we want to introduce headings prior to each of the tables in our document. We can use an `.each()` loop to iterate over the tables, and create an appropriately-named heading prior to each one:

```
$(document).ready(function() {
  $('table').each(function(index) {
```

```
        var $table = $(this);
        $('<h3></h3>', {
           id: 'table-title-' + index,
           'class': 'table-title',
           text: 'Table ' + (index + 1),
           data: {'index': index},
           click: function() {
             $table.fadeToggle();
             return false;
           },
           css: {glowColor: '#00ff00'}
        }).insertBefore($table);
      });
   });
```

Listing 12.13

Providing a map of options as the second argument to the $() function has the same effect as first creating the element, then passing that map to the .attr() method. As we know, this method lets us set DOM attributes, such as the id of the element.

The rest of the options in our example, however, might be a little confusing at first. We are specifying the text of the heading, additional data, and a click handler, for instance. These are not DOM attributes, yet they get set all the same. It turns out that this shorthand $() syntax, along with the .attr() function, can handle a large number of additional DOM features through the use of **hooks**.

DOM manipulation hooks

Many jQuery methods that get and set properties can be extended for special cases by defining the appropriate hooks. These hooks are arrays in the jQuery namespace, with names like $.cssHooks, $.attrHooks, and $.attrFn. In general, hooks are objects holding a get method that retrieves the requested value, and a set method that provides a new value.

The $.attrFn map is an exception; it powers the example we saw in Listing 12.13, and simply contains a list of .attr() keys that send their values to the corresponding jQuery methods. For example, as text is listed in $.attrFn, the string we give for the value of that key is passed on to the .text() method.

The other hook types are:

- `$.attrHooks`, which alters `.attr()`. For example, this prevents the `type` attribute of an element from being changed.

- `$.cssHooks`, which alters `.css()`. For example, this provides special handling for `opacity` in Internet Explorer.

- `$.propHooks`, which alters `.prop()`. For example, this corrects the behavior of the `selected` property in Safari.

- `$.valHooks`, which alters `.val()`. For example, this allows radio buttons and checkboxes to report a consistent value across browsers.

Usually the work performed by these hooks is completely hidden to us, and we can receive their benefits without thinking much about what is going on. Sometimes, though, we might want to extend the behavior of jQuery's methods by adding hooks of our own.

Writing a CSS hook

The code in Listing 12.13 injects a CSS property called `glowColor` onto the page. This has no effect on the page at the moment, as such a property does not exist. Instead, we are going to extend `$.cssHooks` to add support for this newly-invented property. We will add a soft glow around the text using the CSS3 `text-shadow` property when `glowColor` is set on an element. As `text-shadow` is not supported in Internet Explorer, we will implement the glow there using Microsoft's proprietary `filter` property:

```
(function($) {
  var div = document.createElement('div');
  $.support.textShadow = div.style.textShadow === '';
  $.support.filter = div.style.filter === '';
  div = null;

  if ($.support.textShadow) {
    $.cssHooks.glowColor = {
      set: function(elem, value) {
        if (value == 'none') {
          elem.style.textShadow = '';
        }
        else {
          elem.style.textShadow = '0 0 2px ' + value;
        }
      }
```

```
      };
    }
  else {      $.cssHooks.glowColor = {
      set: function(elem, value) {
        if (value == 'none') {
          elem.style.filter = '';
        }
        else {
          elem.style.zoom = 1;
          elem.style.filter =
            'progid:DXImageTransform.Microsoft' +
            '.Glow(Strength=2, Color=' + value + ');';
        }
      }
    };
  }
})(jQuery);
```

Listing 12.14

A hook consists of a `get` and a `set` method for an element. In order to keep our example as brief and simple as possible, we are only defining `set` at this time. We run some feature compatibility tests before defining any hooks. If `text-shadow` is supported by the browser, then we define a version of the hook that uses that property. If not, then we check for support for DirectX filters and use those if possible. If neither is available, then the hook is not defined at all, so `glowColor` will do nothing.

With this hook in place, we now have a two pixel soft green glow around the heading text:

Table 1

While the new hook works as advertised, it lacks many features that we might expect. Some of these shortcomings include the following:

- The size of the glow is not customizable
- The effect is mutually exclusive with other uses of `text-shadow` or `filter`
- The `get` callbacks are unimplemented, so we cannot test for the current value of the property
- The property cannot be animated

With enough work and additional code, we could surmount all of these obstacles. In practice, we do not often have to define our own hooks, however; skilled plugin developers have created hooks for a wide variety of needs, including most CSS3 properties.

Finding hooks

The plugin landscape changes rapidly, so new hooks will crop up all the time and we cannot hope to list them all here. For a sampling of what is possible, see Brandon Aaron's collection of CSS hooks: `https://github.com/brandonaaron/jquery-cssHooks`

Summary

In this chapter, we have solved a common problem — sorting a data table — in three different ways, comparing the benefits of each approach. In doing so, we practiced the DOM modification techniques we learned earlier, and explored the `.data()` method for getting and setting data associated with any DOM element or attached using HTML5 data attributes. We also pulled back the curtain on several DOM modification routines, learning how to extend them for our own purposes.

Further reading

A complete list of available DOM manipulation methods is available in *Appendix C* of this book, in *jQuery Reference Guide*, or in the official jQuery documentation at `http://api.jquery.com/`.

Exercises

To complete these exercises, you will need the `index.html` file for this chapter, as well as the finished JavaScript code as found in `complete.js`. These files can be downloaded from the Packt Publishing website at `http://www.packtpub.com/support`.

The challenge exercise may require use of the official jQuery documentation at `http://api.jquery.com/`.

1. Modify the key computation for the first table so that titles and authors are sorted by length, rather than alphabetically.

2. Use the HTML5 data in the second table to compute the sum of all of the book prices, and insert this sum into the heading for that column.

3. Change the comparator used for the third table so that titles containing the word `jQuery` come first when sorted by title.

4. **Challenge**: Implement `get` callbacks for the `glowColor` CSS hook.

13
Advanced Ajax

Many web applications require frequent network communication. In *Chapter 6*, we investigated ways for our web pages to exchange information with the server without requiring new pages to be loaded in the browser. These Ajax techniques are very useful, and include some of the most sophisticated things we can do with jQuery.

In this chapter, we will dive deeper into the capabilities of the jQuery Ajax framework. We'll consider proper error-handling techniques for dealing with network interruptions, explore the interactions between Ajax and the jQuery deferred object system, and develop ways to keep our network traffic to a minimum through caching and throttling. Finally, we'll look at some of the inner workings of the Ajax system so that we can extend its functionality when needed.

Progressive enhancement with Ajax

Many times now we have encountered the concept of **progressive enhancement**. To reiterate, this philosophy ensures a positive user experience for all users by mandating that a working product be put in place first, before additional embellishments are added for users with modern browsers.

Ajax-heavy applications run a particular risk of being unusable without JavaScript enabled. To combat this, we can initially construct a traditional client-server page architecture using forms, and then change these forms to be more efficient if JavaScript is there to help us.

As an example, we'll build a form that searches the jQuery API documentation. As a form already exists for this purpose on the jQuery site, we can piggy-back on that form for our own purposes:

```
<form id="ajax-form"
    action="http://api.jquery.com/" method="get">
  <fieldset>
```

```
      <div class="text">
        <label for="title">Search</label>
        <input type="text" id="title" name="s">
      </div>
      <div class="actions">
        <button type="submit">Request</button>
      </div>
    </fieldset>
</form>
```

The search form has some styling applied via our CSS file, but is otherwise a normal form element with a text input and submit button:

When the **Request** button of this form is clicked, the form submits as normal, the user's browser is directed to http://api.jquery.com/, and the results are displayed, as follows:

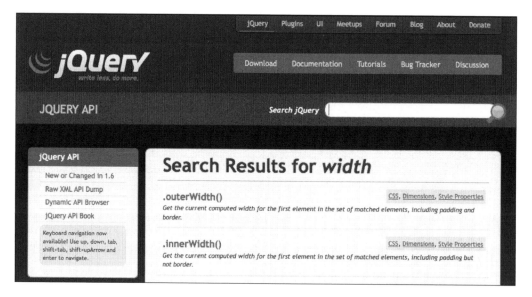

When JavaScript is available, we want to load this content into the `#response` container of our search page rather than leaving the page. Were the data on the same server as our search form, we could harvest the relevant portion of the page using the `.load()` method:

```
$(document).ready(function() {
  var $ajaxForm = $('#ajax-form'),
    $response = $('#response');

  $ajaxForm.bind('submit', function(event) {
    event.preventDefault();
    $response.load('http://api.jquery.com/ #content',
      $ajaxForm.serialize());
  });
});
```

Listing 13.1

However, as the API site is under a different hostname, the cross-domain policy of the browser will not allow this transaction to take place. Instead, we need to use a method that is cross-domain friendly. Fortunately, the API site exposes its data in JSONP format, which is perfect for our use.

Cross-domain requests with Yahoo! Query Language

Some third-party sites, of course, don't expose a JSONP search API. When we need to access data from such sites and setting up our own server-side proxy is not an option, Yahoo! Query Language (YQL) can bridge the gap. It effectively sets its own proxy, so we can send our request to the YQL service with the proper parameters and receive JSONP in response. More information on YQL is available at `http://developer.yahoo.com/yql/`, and a blog entry with instructions and examples for using YQL with jQuery can be found at `http://www.wait-till-i.com/2010/01/10/loading-external-content-with-ajax-using-jquery-and-yql/`

Harvesting JSONP data

In *Chapter 6*, we saw that JSONP is simply JSON with an added layer of server behavior allowing requests to be made from a different site. When a request is made for the JSONP data, a special query string parameter is provided that allows the requesting script to harvest the data. This parameter can be called anything the JSONP server wishes; in the case of the jQuery API site, the parameter is called **callback**, the default name.

Because the default callback name is used, the only setup required to make a JSONP request is to declare to jQuery that `jsonp` is the data type we are expecting:

```
$(document).ready(function() {
  var $ajaxForm = $('#ajax-form'),
    $response = $('#response');

  $ajaxForm.bind('submit', function(event) {
    event.preventDefault();

    $.ajax({
      url: 'http://api.jquery.com/jsonp/',
      dataType: 'jsonp',
      data: {
        title: $('#title').val()
      },
      success: function(data) {
        console.log(data);
      }
    });
  });
});
```

Listing 13.2

Now we can inspect the JSON data in the console. The data, in this case, is an array of objects, each describing a jQuery method, as follows:

```
{
  "url": "http://api.jquery.com/innerWidth/",
  "name": "innerWidth",
  "title": ".innerWidth()",
  "type": "method",
  "signatures": [
    {
      "added": "1.2.6"
    }
  ],
  "desc": "Get the current computed width for the first element in
    the set of matched elements, including padding but not
    border.",
  "longdesc": "<p>This method returns the width of the element,
    including left and right padding, in pixels.</p>\n<p>This
    method is not applicable to <code>window</code> and
```

```
      <code>document</code>     objects; for these, use <code><a
      href=\"/width\">.width()</a></code> instead.</p>\n<p
      class=\"image\"><img src=\"/images/0042_04_05.png\"/></p>",
    "categories": [
      "CSS",
      "Dimensions",
      "Manipulation > Style Properties",
      "Version > Version 1.2.6"
    ],
    "download": ""
  }
```

All of the data we need to display about a method is included in this object. We simply need to format it appropriately for display. Creating the HTML for an item is somewhat involved, so we'll break that step out into its own helper function, as follows:

```
var buildItem = function(item) {
  var title = item.name,
    args = [],
    output = '<li>';

  if (item.type == 'method' || !item.type) {
    if (item.signatures[0].params) {
      $.each(item.signatures[0].params, function(index, val) {
        args.push(val.name);
      });
    }
    title = (/^jQuery|deferred/).test(title)
      ? title : '.' + title;
    title += '(' + args.join(', ') + ')';
  } else if (item.type == 'selector') {
    title += ' selector';
  }
  output += '<h3><a href="' + item.url + '">' +
    title + '</a></h3>';
  output += '<div>' + item.desc + '</div>';
  output += '</li>';

  return output;
};
```

Listing 13.3

The `buildItem()` function converts the JSON object into an HTML list item. We have to handle the possibility of multiple method arguments and multiple function signatures, so we use loops and `.join()` calls to handle these situations. Once this is done, we create a link to the main documentation, and output the item description.

Now we have a function that creates the HTML for a single item. When our Ajax call completes, we'll need to call this function on every returned object, and display all of the results:

```
$(document).ready(function() {
  var $ajaxForm = $('#ajax-form'),
      $response = $('#response'),
      noresults = 'There were no search results.';

  var response = function(json) {
    var output = '';
    if (json && json.length) {
      output += '<ol>';
      $.each(json, function(index, val) {
        output += buildItem(val);
      });
      output += '</ol>';
    } else {
      output += noresults;
    }

    $response.html(output);
  };

  $ajaxForm.bind('submit', function(event) {
    event.preventDefault();

    $.ajax({
      url: 'http://api.jquery.com/jsonp/',
      dataType: 'jsonp',
      data: {
        title: $('#title').val()
      },
      success: response
    });
  });
});
```

Listing 13.4

We've pulled the success handler out of the $.ajax() options so that we can reference it by its variable name. Even though we often use inline anonymous functions in these situations for code brevity, there is nothing stopping us from separating and labeling functions to make our code clearer.

Now that we have a functional success handler, performing a search nicely presents the results in a column next to our form:

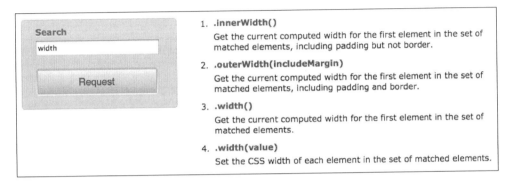

Ajax error handling

Introducing any kind of network interaction into an application brings along some degree of uncertainty. The user's connection could drop in the middle of an operation, or a temporary server issue could interrupt communications. Due to these reliability concerns, we should always plan for the worst case, and prepare for error scenarios.

The $.ajax() function can take a callback function named error to be called in these situations. In this callback, we should provide some kind of feedback to the user indicating that an error has occurred:

```
$(document).ready(function() {
  var $ajaxForm = $('#ajax-form'),
      $response = $('#response'),
      noresults = 'There were no search results.',
      failed = 'Sorry, but the request could not ' +
        'reach its destination. Try again later.';

  $ajaxForm.bind('submit', function(event) {
    event.preventDefault();

    $.ajax({
      url: 'http://api.jquery.com/jsonp/',
```

```
      dataType: 'jsonp',
      data: {
        title: $('#title').val()
      },
      success: response,
      error: function() {
        $response.html(failed);
      }
    });
  });
});
```

Listing 13.5

The error callback can be triggered for a number of reasons. Among these are the following:

- The server returned an error status code, such as **403 Forbidden**, **404 Not Found**, or **500 Internal Server Error**.

- The server returned a redirection status code, such as **301 Moved Permanently**. An exception is **304 Not Modified**, which does not trigger an error because the browser can handle this condition correctly.

- The data returned by the server could not be parsed as specified (for example, it is not valid JSON data when `dataType` is `json`).

- The `.abort()` method is called on the `XMLHttpRequest` object.

Detecting and responding to these conditions is important in providing the best possible user experience. We saw in *Chapter 6* that the error code, if any, is provided to us in the `.status` property of the `jqXHR` object that is passed to the error callback. We can use the value of `jqXHR.status` to react differently to different kinds of errors, if that is appropriate.

However, the server errors are only useful when they are actually observed. Some errors are immediately detected, but other conditions can cause a long delay between the request and eventual error response.

When a reliable server timeout mechanism is not available, we can enforce our own client-side request timeout. By providing a time in milliseconds to the timeout option, we tell `$.ajax()` to trigger `.abort()` on its own if that amount of time elapses before a response is received:

```
$.ajax({
  url: 'http://api.jquery.com/jsonp/',
  dataType: 'jsonp',
```

```
    data: {
      title: $('#title').val()
    },
    timeout: 15000,
    success: response,
    error: function() {
      $response.html(failed);
    }
  });
```

Listing 13.6

With the timeout in place, we can be assured that within 15 seconds either the data will be loaded, or the user will receive an error message.

The jqXHR object

When an Ajax request is made, jQuery determines the best mechanism available for retrieving the data. This **transport** could be the standard XMLHttpRequest object, the Microsoft ActiveX XMLHTTP object, or a `<script>` tag.

As the transport used can vary from request to request, we need a common interface in order to interact with the communication. The jqXHR object provides this interface for us: it is a wrapper for the XMLHttpRequest object when that transport is used, and in other cases it simulates XMLHttpRequest as best it can. Among the properties and methods it exposes are:

- `.responseText` or `.responseXML`, containing the returned data
- `.status` and `.statusText`, containing a status code and description
- `.setRequestHeader()`, to manipulate the HTTP headers sent with the request
- `.abort()`, to prematurely halt the transaction

This jqXHR object is returned from all of jQuery's Ajax methods, so we can store the result if we need access to any of these properties or methods.

Ajax promises

Perhaps a more important aspect of jqXHR than the XMLHttpRequest interface, however, is that it also acts as a **promise**. In *Chapter 11*, we learned about deferred objects, which allow us to set callbacks to be fired when certain operations complete. Ajax calls are just such an operation, and the jqXHR object provides the methods we expect from a deferred object's promise.

Using the promise's methods, we can rewrite our `$.ajax()` call to replace the `success` and `error` callbacks with an alternate syntax, as follows:

```
$.ajax({
  url: 'http://api.jquery.com/jsonp/',
  dataType: 'jsonp',
  data: {
    title: $('#title').val()
  },
  timeout: 15000
})
.done(response)
.fail(function() {
  $response.html(failed);
});
```

Listing 13.7

At first glance, calling `.done()` and `.fail()` doesn't seem any more useful than the callback syntax we used previously. However, the promise methods offer several advantages. First, the methods can be called multiple times to add more than one handler if desired. Second, if we store the result of the `$.ajax()` call in a variable, then we can attach the handlers later if that makes our code structure more readable. Third, the handlers will be invoked immediately if the Ajax operation is already complete when they are attached. Finally, we should not discount the readability advantage of using a syntax that is consistent with other parts of the jQuery library.

As another example of using the promise methods, we can add a loading indicator when a request is made. Since we want to hide the indicator when the request completes successfully or otherwise, the `.always()` method will come in handy:

```
$ajaxForm.bind('submit', function(event) {
  event.preventDefault();

  $response.addClass('loading').empty();

  $.ajax({
    url: 'http://api.jquery.com/jsonp/',
    dataType: 'jsonp',
    data: {
      title: $('#title').val()
    },
    timeout: 15000
  })
```

```
  .done(response)
  .fail(function() {
    $response.html(failed);
  })
  .always(function() {
    $response.removeClass('loading');
  });
});
```

Listing 13.8

Before we issue the $.ajax() call, we add the loading class to the response container. Once the load is complete, we remove it again. In this way, we have further enhanced the user experience.

To really get a grasp of how the promise behavior can help us, though, we need to look at what we can do if we store the result of our $.ajax() call in a variable for later use.

Caching responses

If we need to use the same piece of data repeatedly, then it is wasteful to make an Ajax request each time. To prevent this, we can **cache** the returned data in a variable. When we need to use some data, we can check to see if the data is already in the cache. If so, then we act on this data. If not, then we need to make an Ajax request, and in its .done() handler we store the data in the cache and act on the returned data.

This is a lot of steps. If we exploit the properties of promises, though, then it can be quite simple, as shown in the following code snippet:

```
var api = {};

$ajaxForm.bind('submit', function(event) {
  event.preventDefault();

  $response.empty();

  var search = $('#title').val();
  if (search == '') {
    return;
  }

  $response.addClass('loading');
```

```
     if (!api[search]) {
       api[search] = $.ajax({
         url: 'http://api.jquery.com/jsonp/',
         dataType: 'jsonp',
         data: {
           title: search
         },
         timeout: 15000
       });
     }
     api[search].done(response).fail(function() {
       $response.html(failed);
     }).always(function() {
       $response.removeClass('loading');
     });
   });
```

Listing 13.9

We've introduced a new variable named `api` to hold the `jqXHR` objects we create. This variable is an object, with keys corresponding to the searches being performed. When the form is submitted, we look to see if there is already a `jqXHR` object stored for that key. If not, then we do the query as before, storing the resulting object inside `api`.

The `.done()`, `.fail()`, and `.always()` handlers are then attached to the `jqXHR` object. Note that this happens regardless of whether an Ajax request was made. There are two possible situations to consider here.

First, the Ajax request might be sent, if it hasn't before. This is just like the previous behavior: the request is issued, and we use the promise methods to attach handlers to the `jqXHR` object. When a response comes back from the server, the appropriate callbacks are fired, and the result is printed to the screen.

On the other hand, if we have performed this search in the past, the `jqXHR` object is already stored in `api`. In this case no new search is performed, but we still call the promise methods on the stored object. This attaches new handlers to the object, but as the deferred object has already been resolved, the relevant handlers are fired immediately.

The jQuery deferred object system handles all of the hard work for us. With a couple of lines of code, we have eliminated duplicated network requests from the application.

Throttling Ajax requests

An increasingly common feature of searches is to display a dynamic list of results as the user is typing. We can emulate this live search feature for our jQuery API search by binding a handler to the `keyup` event, as follows:

```
$('#title').bind('keyup', function(event) {
  $ajaxForm.triggerHandler('submit');
});
```

Listing 13.10

Here we simply trigger the form's `submit` handler whenever the user types something in the **Search** field. This could have the effect of sending many requests across the network in rapid succession, depending on the speed at which the user types. This behavior could bog down JavaScript's performance, it could clog the network connection, and the server might not be able to handle that kind of demand. We're already limiting the number of requests with the request caching that we've just put in place. We can further ease the burden on the server, however, by **throttling** the requests. In *Chapter 10* we introduced the concept of throttling when we created a special `throttledScroll` event to reduce the number of times the native `scroll` event is fired. In this case, we want to make a similar reduction in activity, this time with the `keyup` event:

```
var searchTimeout,
  searchDelay = 300;

$('#title').bind('keyup', function(event) {
  clearTimeout(searchTimeout);
  searchTimeout = setTimeout(function() {
    $ajaxForm.triggerHandler('submit');
  }, searchDelay);
});
```

Listing 13.11

Our technique here is a bit different from the one we used in *Chapter 10*. Whereas in that example we needed our `scroll` handler to take effect multiple times as scrolling continued, here we only need the `keyup` behavior to happen one time, after typing has ceased. To do this, we keep track of a JavaScript timer that starts whenever the user presses a key. Each keystroke resets that timer, so only once the user stops typing for the designated amount of time (300 milliseconds) does the `submit` handler get triggered and the Ajax request performed.

Extending Ajax capabilities

The jQuery Ajax framework is powerful, as we've seen, but even so there are times when we might want to change the way it behaves. Unsurprisingly, it offers multiple hooks that can be used by plugins to give the framework brand new capabilities.

Data type converters

In *Chapter 6*, we saw that the `$.ajaxSetup()` function allows us to change the defaults used by `$.ajax()`, thus potentially affecting many Ajax operations with a single statement. This same function can also be used to add to the range of data types that `$.ajax()` can request and interpret.

As an example, we can add a converter that understands the **YAML** data format. YAML (`http://www.yaml.org/`) is a popular data representation with implementations in many programming languages. In case our script needs to interact with an alternative format such as this, jQuery allows us to build compatibility for them right into the native Ajax functions.

A simple YAML file containing jQuery method categories and subcategories looks like the following:

```
Ajax:
 - Global Ajax Event Handlers
 - Helper Functions
 - Low-Level Interface
 - Shorthand Methods
Effects:
 - Basics
 - Custom
 - Fading
 - Sliding
```

We can wrap jQuery around an existing YAML parser such as Diogo Costa's (`http://code.google.com/p/javascript-yaml-parser/`) to make `$.ajax()` speak this language as well.

Defining a new Ajax data type involves passing three properties to `$.ajaxSetup()`: `accepts`, `contents`, and `converters`. The `accepts` property adds headers to be sent to the server, declaring to the server that particular MIME types are understood by our script. The `contents` property handles the other side of the transaction, providing a regular expression that is matched against the response MIME type to attempt to auto-detect the data type from this metadata.

Finally, `converters` contains the actual functions that parse the returned data:

```
$.ajaxSetup({
  accepts: {
    yaml: 'application/x-yaml, text/yaml'
  },
  contents: {
    yaml: /yaml/
  },
  converters: {
    'text yaml': function(textValue) {
      console.log(textValue);
      return '';
    }
  }
});

$.ajax({
  url: 'categories.yml',
  dataType: 'yaml'
});
```

Listing 13.12

The partial implementation in Listing 13.12 uses `$.ajax()` to read in the YAML file, and declares its data type as `yaml`. As the incoming data is parsed as `text`, jQuery needs a way to convert one data type to the other. The `converters` key of `'text yaml'` tells jQuery that this conversion function will accept data that has been received as `text` and reinterpret it as `yaml`.

Inside the conversion function, we are simply logging out the contents of the text to ensure that the function is called correctly. To actually perform the conversion, we need to load the third-party YAML parsing library and call its methods, as follows:

```
$.ajaxSetup({
  accepts: {
    yaml: 'application/x-yaml, text/yaml'
  },
  contents: {
    yaml: /yaml/
  },
```

```
    converters: {
      'text yaml': function(textValue) {
        var result = YAML.eval(textValue);
        var errors = YAML.getErrors();
        if (errors.length) {
          throw errors;
        }
        return result;
      }
    }
  });

  $.getScript('yaml.js').done(function() {
    $.ajax({
      url: 'categories.yml',
      dataType: 'yaml'
    }).done(function (data) {
      var cats = '';
      $.each(data, function(category, subcategories) {
        cats += '<li><a href="#">' + category + '</a></li>';
      });

      $(document).ready(function() {
        var $cats = $('#categories').removeClass('hide');
        $('<ul></ul>', {
          html: cats
        }).appendTo($cats);
      });
    });
  });
```

Listing 13.14

The `yaml.js` file includes an object named YAML with `.eval()` and `.getErrors()` methods. We use these methods to parse the incoming text, and return the result which is a JavaScript object containing all of the `categories.yml` file's data in an easily-traversable structure.

Since the file we're loading contains categories of jQuery methods, we use the parsed structure to print out the top-level categories and later will allow the user to filter their search results by clicking on the categories:

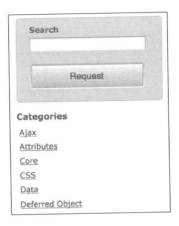

Note that when we insert the category names, we need to wrap that portion of the code in a `$(document).ready()` call. The Ajax operations may run immediately, without access to the DOM, but once we have a result from them, we need to wait until the DOM is available before proceeding. Structuring our code in this way allows the work to be performed as early as possible, likely improving the user's perception of the page's loading time.

Next, we need to handle clicks on the category links, as follows:

```
$('#categories a').live('click', function(event) {
  event.preventDefault();
  $(this).parent().toggleClass('active')
    .siblings('.active').removeClass('active');
  $('#ajax-form').triggerHandler('submit');
});
```

Listing 13.14

By using `.live()` to bind our `click` handler, we avoid some costly repetition, and we also can run the code right away, without concerning ourselves with waiting for the Ajax call to complete.

Inside the handler, we make sure the right category is highlighted, and then trigger the `submit` handler on the form. We haven't yet made the form understand our category list, but the highlighting works already:

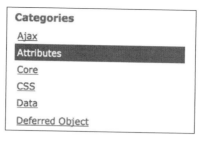

Finally, we need to update the form's `submit` handler to respect the active category, if there is one:

```
$ajaxForm.bind('submit', function(event) {
  event.preventDefault();

  $response.empty();

  var title = $('#title').val(),
    category = $('#categories').find('li.active').text(),
    search = category + '-' + title;
  if (search == '-') {
    return;
  }

  $response.addClass('loading');

  if (!api[search]) {
    api[search] = $.ajax({
      url: 'http://api.jquery.com/jsonp/',
      dataType: 'jsonp',
      data: {
        title: title,
        category: category
      },
      timeout: 15000
    });
  }
  api[search].done(response).fail(function() {
```

```
    $response.html(failed);
  }).always(function() {
    $response.removeClass('loading');
  });
});
```

Listing 13.15

Instead of simply fetching the value of the search field, now we retrieve the text of the active category as well, passing both pieces of information on through the Ajax call. We also change the `search` variable to contain both the category and the title. This way, our cache of search results correctly distinguishes searches on the same text in different categories.

We can now view all methods in a category by clicking on that category's name, or use the category list to filter the results we obtain by typing in the search field:

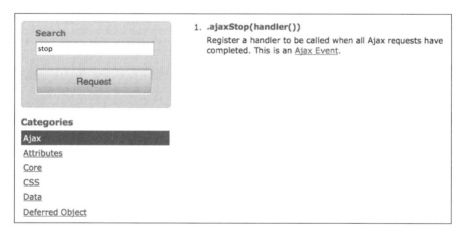

Additional data types can be defined in a similar fashion to our YAML example here. We can, thus, shape jQuery's Ajax library to our specific project's needs.

Ajax prefilters

The `$.ajaxPrefilter()` function can add **prefilters**, which are callback functions that allow us to manipulate requests before they are sent. Prefilters are invoked before `$.ajax()` changes or uses any of its options, so they are a good place to change the options or act on new, custom options.

Prefilters can also manipulate the data type of the request by simply returning the name of the new data type to use. In our YAML example, we specified `yaml` as the data type because we didn't want to rely on the server supplying the correct MIME type for the response. We could, though, provide a prefilter that ensures the data type is `yaml` if the corresponding file extension (`.yml`) is in the URL we request, as follows:

```
$.ajaxPrefilter(function(options) {
  if (/\.yml$/.test(options.url)) {
    return 'yaml';
  }
});
```

Listing 13.16

A short regular expression tests whether `.yml` is at the end of `options.url` and, if so, defines the data type as `yaml`. With this prefilter in place, our Ajax call to fetch the YAML document no longer needs to explicitly define its data type.

Alternate transports

We've seen that jQuery uses `XMLHttpRequest`, ActiveX or `<script>` tags as appropriate to handle Ajax transactions. If we wish, we can further extend this arsenal with new **transports**.

A transport is an object that handles the actual transmission of Ajax data. New transports are defined as factory functions that return an object with `.send()` and `.abort()` methods. The `.send()` method is responsible for issuing the request, handling the response, and sending the data back through a callback function. The `.abort()` method should stop the request immediately.

A custom transport can, for example, use `<img>` elements to fetch external data. This allows image loading to be handled in the same way as other Ajax requests, which can help make our code more internally consistent. The JavaScript required to create such a transport is a little involved, so we will look at the finished product, as follows, and then discuss its components:

```
$.ajaxTransport('img', function(settings) {
  var $img, img, prop;
  return {
    send: function(headers, complete) {
      function callback(success) {
        if (success) {
```

```
        complete(200, 'OK', {img: img});
      } else {
        $img.remove();
        complete(404, 'Not Found');
      }
    }

    $img = $('<img>', {
      src: settings.url
    });
    img = $img[0];
    prop = typeof img.naturalWidth === 'undefined' ?
      'width' : 'naturalWidth';
    if (img.complete) {
      callback( !!img[prop] );
    } else {
      $img.bind('load error', function(event) {
        callback(event.type == 'load');
      });
    }

  },
  abort: function() {
    if ($img) {
      $img.remove();
    }
  }
};
});
```

Listing 13.17

When defining a transport, we first pass a data type name into `$.ajaxTransport()`. This tells jQuery when to use our transport rather than the built-in mechanisms. Then we provide a function that returns the new transport object containing appropriate `.send()` and `.abort()` methods.

For our `img` transport, the `.send()` method needs to create a new `<img>` element, which we give a `src` attribute to. The value of this attribute comes from `settings.url`, which jQuery passes along from the `$.ajax()` call. The browser will react to the creation of this `<img>` element by loading the referenced image file, so we just need to detect when this load is complete and fire the completion callback.

Correctly detecting the completion of an image load is tricky, if we want to handle a wide variety of browsers and versions. In some browsers, we can simply attach `load` and `error` event handlers to the image element. In others, though, when the image is cached, `load` and `error` are not triggered as expected. Our code in Listing 13.17 handles these unusual browser behaviors by examining the values of the `.complete`, `.width`, and `.naturalWidth` properties as appropriate for each browser. Once we have detected that the image load has completed (successfully or in error), we call the `callback()` function which in turn calls the `complete()` function that was passed to `.send()`. This allows `$.ajax()` to react to the image load.

Handling aborted loads is much simpler. Our `.abort()` method simply needs to clean up after `.send()` by removing the `<img>` element if it has been created.

Next, we need to write the `$.ajax()` call that uses our new transport:

```
$(document).ready(function() {
  $.ajax({
    url: 'missing.jpg',
    dataType: 'img'
  }).done(function(img) {
    $('<div></div>', {
      id: 'picture',
      html: img
    }).appendTo('body');
  }).fail(function(xhr, textStatus, msg ) {
    $('<div></div>', {
      id: 'picture',
      html: textStatus + ': ' + msg
    }).appendTo('body');
  });
});
```

Listing 13.18

To use a particular transport, `$.ajax()` needs to be given a corresponding `dataType` value. Then the success and failure handlers need to take into account the kind of data that is passed to them. Our `img` transport returns an `<img>` DOM element when it is successful, so our `.done()` handler uses this element as the html contents of a newly-created `<div>` element that is inserted into the document.

However, in this case, the specified image file (`missing.jpg`) does not actually exist. We take into account such a possibility with an appropriate `.fail()` handler, which inserts an error message into the `<div>` where the image would otherwise go:

We can correct this error by referencing an image that does exist, as follows:

```
$(document).ready(function() {
  $.ajax({
    url: 'sunset.jpg',
    dataType: 'img'
  }).done(function(img) {
    $('<div></div>', {
      id: 'picture',
      html: img
    }).appendTo('body');
  }).fail(function(xhr, textStatus, msg ) {
    $('<div></div>', {
      id: 'picture',
      html: textStatus + ': ' + msg
    }).appendTo('body');
  });
});
```

Listing 13.19

Now our transport is able to successfully load the image, and we see this result on the page:

Creating a new transport is an unusual need, but even in this case jQuery's Ajax functions can be bent to our needs.

Summary

In this final chapter, we have taken an in-depth look at jQuery's Ajax framework. We can now craft a seamless user experience on a single page, fetching external resources when needed with proper attention to error handling, caching, and throttling. We learned details of the inner operations of the Ajax framework, including promises, transports, prefilters, and converters. We also learned how to extend these mechanisms to serve the needs of our scripts.

Further reading

A complete list of available Ajax methods is available in *Appendix C* of this book, in *jQuery Reference Guide*, or in the official jQuery documentation at `http://api.jquery.com/`.

Exercises

To complete these exercises, you will need the `index.html` file for this chapter, as well as the finished JavaScript code as found in `complete.js`. These files can be downloaded from the Packt Publishing website at `http://www.packtpub.com/support`.

The challenge exercises may require use of the official jQuery documentation at `http://api.jquery.com/`.

1. Alter the `buildItem()` function so that it includes the long description of each jQuery method it displays.

2. **Challenge**: Add a form to the page that points to a Flickr public photo search (`http://www.flickr.com/search/`) and make sure it has an `<input name="q">` and a submit button. Use progressive enhancement to retrieve the photos from Flickr's JSONP feed service at `http://api.flickr.com/services/feeds/photos_public.gne` instead and insert them into the content area of the page. When sending `data` to this service, use `tags` instead of q, and set `format` to `json`. Also note that rather than `callback`, the service expects the JSONP callback name to be `jsoncallback`.

3. **Challenge**: Add error handling for the Flickr request in case it results in a `parsererror`. Test it by setting the JSONP callback name back to `callback`.

A
JavaScript Closures

Throughout this book, we have seen many jQuery methods that take functions as parameters. Our examples have thus created, called, and passed around functions repeatedly. While usually we can do this with only a cursory understanding of the inner JavaScript mechanics at work, at times side effects of our actions can seem strange if we do not have knowledge of the language features. In this appendix, we will study one of the more esoteric (yet prevalent) function-based constructs named **closures**.

Our discussion will involve many small code examples, from each of which we will want to print out a set of messages. Rather than use a browser-specific logging mechanism (such as `console.log()`), or create a series of `alert()` dialogs, we will use a small plugin method as follows:

```
$.print = function(message) {
  $(document).ready(function() {
    $('<div class="result"><div>')
      .text(String(message))
      .appendTo('#results');
  });
};
```

With this method defined, we can call `$.print('hello')` to add the message `hello` within `<div id="results">`.

Inner functions

JavaScript is fortunate to number itself among the programming languages that support **inner function** declarations. Many traditional programming languages, such as C, collect all functions in a single top-level scope. Languages with inner functions, on the other hand, allow us to gather small utility functions where they are needed, avoiding **namespace pollution**.

An inner function is simply a function that is defined inside of another function. For example:

```
function outerFn() {
  function innerFn() {

  }
}
```

Here, `innerFn()` is an inner function, contained within the scope of `outerFn()`. This means that a call to `innerFn()` is valid within `outerFn()`, but not outside of it. The following code results in a JavaScript error:

```
function outerFn() {
  $.print('Outer function');
  function innerFn() {
    $.print('Inner Function');
  }
}
$.print('innerFn():');
innerFn();
```

We can successfully run the code, though, by calling `innerFn()` from within `outerFn()` as follows:

```
function outerFn() {
  $.print('Outer function');
  function innerFn() {
    $.print('Inner function');
  }
  innerFn();
}
$.print('outerFn():');
outerFn();
```

This results in the output:

```
outerFn():
Outer function
Inner function
```

This technique is especially handy for small, single-purpose functions. For example, algorithms that are **recursive**, but have a non-recursive API wrapper, are often best expressed with an inner function as a helper.

The great escape

The plot thickens when **function references** come into play. Some languages, such as Pascal, allow the use of inner functions for the purpose of **code hiding** only; those functions are forever entombed within their parent functions. JavaScript, on the other hand, allows us to pass functions around just as if they were any other kind of data. This means inner functions can escape their captors.

The escape route can wind in many different directions. For example, suppose the function is assigned to a **global variable** as follows:

```
var globalVar;

function outerFn() {
  $.print('Outer function');
  function innerFn() {
    $.print('Inner function');
  }
  globalVar = innerFn;
}
$.print('outerFn():');
outerFn();
$.print('globalVar():');
globalVar();
```

The call to outerFn() after the function definition modifies the global variable globalVar. It is now a reference to innerFn(). This means that the later call to globalVar() operates just as an inner call to innerFn() would, and the print statements are reached:

```
outerFn():
Outer function
globalVar():
Inner function
```

Note that a call to innerFn() from outside of outerFn() still results in an error! Though the function has escaped by way of the reference stored in the global variable, the function name is still trapped inside the scope of outerFn().

A function reference can also find its way out of a parent function through a **return value** as follows:

```
function outerFn() {
  $.print('Outer function');
  function innerFn() {
    $.print('Inner function');
```

```
    }
    return innerFn;
  }
  $.print('var fnRef = outerFn():');
  var fnRef = outerFn();
  $.print('fnRef():');
  fnRef();
```

Here, there is no global variable modified inside `outerFn()`. Instead, `outerFn()` returns a reference to `innerFn()`. The call to `outerFn()` results in this reference, which is stored and called itself in turn, triggering the message again:

```
var fnRef = outerFn():
Outer function
fnRef():
Inner function
```

The fact that inner functions can be invoked through a reference, even after the function has gone out of scope, means that JavaScript needs to keep referenced functions available as long as they could possibly be called. Each variable that refers to the function is tracked by the JavaScript **runtime** and once the last has gone away, the JavaScript **garbage collector** comes along and frees up that bit of memory.

Variable scoping

Inner functions can, of course, have their own variables, which are restricted in scope to the function itself:

```
function outerFn() {
  function innerFn() {
    var innerVar = 0;
    innerVar++;
    $.print('innerVar = ' + innerVar);
  }
  return innerFn;
}
var fnRef = outerFn();
fnRef();
fnRef();
var fnRef2 = outerFn();
fnRef2();
fnRef2();
```

Each time this inner function is called, through a reference or otherwise, a new variable `innerVar` is created, incremented, and displayed as follows:

```
innerVar = 1
innerVar = 1
innerVar = 1
innerVar = 1
```

Inner functions can reference global variables in the same way as any other function can:

```
var globalVar = 0;
function outerFn() {
   function innerFn() {
      globalVar++;
      $.print('globalVar = ' + globalVar);
   }
   return innerFn;
}
var fnRef = outerFn();
fnRef();
fnRef();
var fnRef2 = outerFn();
fnRef2();
fnRef2();
```

Now our function will consistently increment the variable with each call:

```
globalVar = 1
globalVar = 2
globalVar = 3
globalVar = 4
```

However, what if the variable is local to the parent function? As the inner function inherits its parent's scope, this variable can be referenced too:

```
function outerFn() {
   var outerVar = 0;
   function innerFn() {
      outerVar++;
      $.print('outerVar = ' + outerVar);
   }
   return innerFn;
}
var fnRef = outerFn();
fnRef();
```

```
   fnRef();
   var fnRef2 = outerFn();
   fnRef2();
   fnRef2();
```

Now our function calls have more interesting behavior:

```
   outerVar = 1
   outerVar = 2
   outerVar = 1
   outerVar = 2
```

This time we get a mix of the two earlier effects. The calls to `innerFn()` through each reference increment `outerVar` independently. Note that the second call to `outerFn()` is not resetting the value of `outerVar`, but rather creating a new **instance** of `outerVar`, bound to the scope of the second function call. The upshot of this is that after the above calls, another call to `fnRef()` will print the value 3, and a subsequent call to `fnRef2()` will also print 3. The two counters are completely separate.

When a reference to an inner function finds its way outside of the scope in which the function was defined, this creates a **closure** on that function. We call variables that are neither parameters nor local to the inner function **free variables**, and the environment of the outer function call **closes** them. Essentially, the fact that the function refers to a local variable in the outer function grants the variable a stay of execution. The memory is not released when the function completes, as it is still needed by the closure.

Interactions between closures

When more than one inner function exists, closures can have effects that are not as easy to anticipate. Suppose we pair our incrementing function with another function, this one incrementing by two:

```
function outerFn() {
  var outerVar = 0;
  function innerFn1() {
    outerVar++;
    $.print('(1) outerVar = ' + outerVar);
  }
  function innerFn2() {
    outerVar += 2;
    $.print('(2) outerVar = ' + outerVar);
  }
  return {'fn1': innerFn1, 'fn2': innerFn2};
}
```

```
var fnRef = outerFn();
fnRef.fn1();
fnRef.fn2();
fnRef.fn1();
var fnRef2 = outerFn();
fnRef2.fn1();
fnRef2.fn2();
fnRef2.fn1();
```

We return references to both functions using a **map** to do so (this illustrates another way in which reference to an inner function can escape its parent). Both functions are called through the references:

```
(1) outerVar = 1
(2) outerVar = 3
(1) outerVar = 4
(1) outerVar = 1
(2) outerVar = 3
(1) outerVar = 4
```

The two inner functions refer to the same local variable, so they share the same **closing environment**. When `innerFn1()` increments `outerVar` by 1, this sets the new starting value of `outerVar` when `innerFn2()` is called, and vice versa. Once again, though, we see that any subsequent call to `outerFn()` creates new instances of these closures with a new closing environment to match. Those familiar with **object-oriented programming** will note that we have in essence created a new **object**, with the free variables acting as **instance variables** and the closures acting as **instance methods**. The variables are also **private**, as they cannot be directly referenced outside of their enclosing scope, enabling true object-oriented data privacy.

Closures in jQuery

The methods we have seen throughout the jQuery library often take at least one function as a parameter. For convenience, we often use **anonymous functions**, so that we can define the function behavior right when it is needed. This means that functions are rarely in the top-level namespace; they are usually inner functions, which means they can quite easily create closures.

Arguments to $(document).ready()

Nearly all of the code we write using jQuery ends up getting placed inside a function passed as an argument to `$(document).ready()`. We do this to guarantee that the DOM has loaded before the code is run, which is usually a requirement for interesting jQuery code. When a function is created and passed to `.ready()`, a reference to the function is stored as part of the global `jQuery` object. This reference is then called at a later time, when the DOM is ready.

We usually place the `$(document).ready()` construct at the top level of the code structure, so this function is not really part of a closure. However, as our code is usually written inside this function, everything else is an inner function:

```
$(document).ready(function() {
  var readyVar = 0;
  function innerFn() {
    readyVar++;
    $.print('readyVar = ' + readyVar);
  }
  innerFn();
  innerFn();
});
```

This looks like many of our earlier examples, except that in this case, the outer function is the callback passed to `$(document).ready()`. As `innerFn()` is defined inside of it, and refers to `readyVar` which is in the scope of the callback function, `innerFn()` and its environment create a closure. We can see this by noting that the value of `readyVar` persists between calls to the function.

```
readyVar = 1
readyVar = 2
```

The fact that most jQuery code is inside a function body is useful, because this can protect against some **namespace collisions**. For example, it is this feature that allows us to use `jQuery.noConflict()` to free up the `$` shortcut for other libraries, while still being able to define the shortcut locally for use within `$(document).ready()`.

Event handlers

The `$(document).ready()` construct usually wraps the rest of our code, including the assignment of **event handlers**. As handlers are functions, they become inner functions. As those inner functions are stored and called later, they can create closures. A simple `click` handler can illustrate this:

```
$(document).ready(function() {
  var counter = 0;
  $('#button-1').click(function() {
    counter++;
    $.print('counter = ' + counter);
    return false;
  });
});
```

As the variable `counter` is declared inside of the `.ready()` handler, it is only available to the jQuery code inside this block and not to outside code. It can be referenced by the code in the `click` handler, however, which increments and display the variable's value. As a closure is created, the same instance of `counter` is referenced each time the link is clicked. This means that the messages displays a continuously incrementing set of values, not just 1 each time as follows:

```
counter = 1
counter = 2
counter = 3
```

Event handlers can share their closing environments, just like other functions:

```
$(document).ready(function() {
  var counter = 0;
  $('#button-1').click(function() {
    counter++;
    $.print('counter = ' + counter);
    return false;
  });
  $('#button-2').click(function() {
    counter--;
    $.print('counter = ' + counter);
    return false;
  });
});
```

As both of the functions reference the same counter variable, the incrementing and decrementing operations of the two links affect the same value rather than being independent:

```
counter = 1
counter = 2
counter = 1
counter = 0
```

Binding handlers in loops

Looping constructs can pose interesting challenges due to the way closures operate. Consider a scenario in which we create elements in a loop and bind behaviors to those elements based on the loop's index as follows:

```
$(document).ready(function() {
  for (var i = 0; i < 5; i++) {
    $('<div>Print ' + i + '</div>')
      .click(function() {
        $.print(i);
      }).insertBefore('#results');
  }
});
```

The variable i is set to the numbers 0 through 4 in turn, and a new `<div>` element is created each time. The elements each have a unique text label, as we would expect:

```
Print 0
Print 1
Print 2
Print 3
Print 4
```

However, clicking on any of these items will result in the number 5 being printed on the page and not the number matching the item label as we might expect. Each click handler's reference to i is the same; even though the value of i is different at the time the handler is bound, the variable is the same one and so the final value of i (5) is fetched when a click actually happens.

We can get around this problem in a number of ways. First, we could replace the for loop with the jQuery $.each() function as follows:

```
$(document).ready(function() {
  $.each([0, 1, 2, 3, 4], function(index, value) {
    $('<div>Print ' + value + '</div>')
      .click(function() {
        $.print(value);
      }).insertBefore('#results');
  });
});
```

Function parameters are like variables defined within functions: the variable `value` is actually a different variable each time through the loop. As a result of this, each `click` handler is pointing to a different `value` variable, and clicks on the elements print numbers corresponding to the element labels, as we planned.

We can also exploit the same properties of function parameters to solve this problem without calling `$.each()`. Inside the `for` loop, we can define and execute a new function that takes care of separating the values of `i` apart into distinct variables as follows:

```
$(document).ready(function() {
  for (var i = 0; i < 5; i++) {
    (function(value) {
      $('<div>Print ' + value + '</div>')
        .click(function() {
          $.print(value);
        }).insertBefore('#results');
    })(i);
  }
});
```

We have seen this construct, named **immediately invoked function expression (IIFE)**, before as a means of redefining the `$` alias for the `jQuery` object after `$.noConflict()` has been called. Here, we use it to pass in `i` as a parameter named `value` that is distinct for each `click` handler.

Finally, we can use a feature of the jQuery event system to solve the problem a different way. The `.bind()` method accepts an object parameter that is passed along to the event handler as `event.data`:

```
$(document).ready(function() {
  for (var i = 0; i < 5; i++) {
    $('<div>Print ' + i + '</div>')
      .bind('click', {value: i}, function(event) {
        $.print(event.data.value);
      }).insertBefore('#results');
  }
});
```

In this case, `i` is provided as data to the `.bind()` method, and can be retrieved inside the handler by inspecting `event.data.value`. Once again, as `event` is a function parameter, it is a unique entity each time a handler is invoked, rather than a single value being shared across them all.

Named and anonymous functions

These examples have used **anonymous functions**, as has been our custom in jQuery code. This makes no difference in the construction of closures; closures can come from named or anonymous functions. For example, we can write an anonymous function to report the index of an item within a jQuery object as follows:

```
$(document).ready(function() {
  $('input').each(function(index) {
    $(this).click(function() {
      $.print('index = ' + index);
      return false;
    });
  });
});
```

As the innermost function is defined within the .each() callback, this code actually creates as many functions as there are buttons. Each of these functions is attached as a click handler to one of the buttons. The functions have index in their closing environment, as it is a parameter to the .each() callback. This behaves the same way as if the click handler were written as a named function:

```
$(document).ready(function() {
  $('input').each(function(index) {
    function clickHandler() {
      $.print('index = ' + index);
      return false;
    }

    $(this).click(clickHandler);
  });
});
```

The version with the anonymous function is just a bit shorter. The position of this named function is still relevant, however:

```
$(document).ready(function() {
  function clickHandler() {
    $.print('index = ' + index);
    return false;
  }

  $('input').each(function(index) {
    $(this).click(clickHandler);
  });
});
```

This version will trigger a JavaScript error whenever a button is clicked, because `index` is not found in the closing environment of `clickHandler()`. It remains a free variable, and so is undefined in this context.

Memory leak hazards

JavaScript manages its memory using a technique known as **garbage collection**. This is in contrast to low-level languages such as C, which require programmers to explicitly **reserve** blocks of memory and free them when they are no longer being used. Other languages such as Objective-C assist the programmer by implementing a **reference counting** system, which allows the user to note how many pieces of the program are using a particular piece of memory so it can be cleaned up when no longer used. JavaScript is a high-level language, on the other hand, and generally takes care of this bookkeeping behind the scenes.

Whenever a new memory-resident item such as an object or function comes into being in JavaScript code, a chunk of memory is set aside for this item. As the object is passed around to functions and assigned to variables, more pieces of code begin to point to the object. JavaScript keeps track of these **pointers**, and when the last one is gone, the memory taken by the object is released. Consider a chain of pointers as shown in the following diagram:

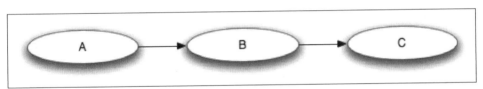

Here object *A* has a property that points to *B*, and *B* has a property that points to *C*. Even if object *A* here is the only one that is a variable in the current scope, all three objects must remain in memory because of the pointers to them. When *A* goes out of scope, however (such as at the end of the function it was declared in), then it can be released by the garbage collector. Now *B* has nothing pointing to it, so can be released, and finally *C* can be released as well.

More complicated arrangements of references can be harder to deal with:

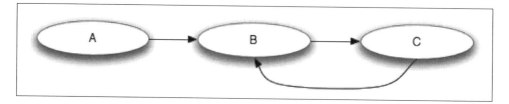

Now we have added a property to object *C* that refers back to *B*. In this case, when *A* is released, *B* still has a pointer to it from *C*. This **reference loop** needs to be handled specially by JavaScript, which must notice that the entire loop is isolated from the variables that are in scope.

Accidental reference loops

Closures can cause reference loops to be inadvertently created. As functions are objects that must be kept in memory, any variables they have in their closing environment are also kept in memory:

```
function outerFn() {
  var outerVar = {};
  function innerFn() {
    $.print(outerVar);
  }
  outerVar.fn = innerFn;
  return innerFn;
};
```

Here, an object named `outerVar` is created and referenced from within the inner function `innerFn()`. Then, a property of `outerVar` that points to `innerFn()` is created, and `innerFn()` is returned. This creates a closure on `innerFn()` that refers to `outerVar`, which in turn refers back to `innerFn()`.

However, the loop can be even more insidious than this:

```
function outerFn() {
  var outerVar = {};
  function innerFn() {
    $.print('hello');
  }
  outerVar.fn = innerFn;
  return innerFn;
};
```

Here, we have changed `innerFn()`, so that it no longer refers to `outerVar`. However, this does not break the loop! Even though `outerVar` is never referred to from `innerFn()`, it is still in `innerFn()`'s **closing environment**. All variables in the scope of `outerFn()` are *implicitly* referred to by `innerFn()` due to the closure. Therefore, closures make it easy to accidentally create these loops.

The Internet Explorer memory leak problem

All of this is generally not an issue because JavaScript is able to detect these loops and clean them up when they become orphaned. Some versions of Internet Explorer, however, have difficulty handling one particular class of reference loops. When a loop contains both DOM elements and regular JavaScript objects, IE cannot release either one because they are handled by different memory managers. These loops are never freed until the browser is closed, which can eat up a great deal of memory over time. A common cause of such a loop is a simple event handler:

```
$(document).ready(function() {
  var button = document.getElementById('button-1');
  button.onclick = function() {
    $.print('hello');
    return false;
  };
});
```

When the `click` handler is assigned, this creates a closure with `button` in the closing environment. However, `button` now contains a reference back to the closure—the `onclick` property itself. Thus, the resulting loop cannot be released by Internet Explorer even when we navigate away from the page.

In order to release the memory, we would need to break the loop, such as by getting rid of the `onclick` property before the window is closed (taking care not to introduce a new loop between `window` and its `onunload` hander). Alternatively, we could rewrite the code to avoid the closure:

```
function hello() {
  $.print('hello');
  return false;
}
$(document).ready(function() {
  var button = document.getElementById('button-1');
  button.onclick = hello;
});
```

As the `hello()` function no longer closes over `button`, the reference only goes one way (from `button` to `hello`) and there is no loop and, therefore, no memory leak.

The good news

Now we will write the same code, but using normal jQuery constructs as follows:

```
$(document).ready(function() {
  var $button = $('#button-1');
  $button.click(function() {
    $.print('hello');
    return false;
  });
});
```

Even though a closure is still created, causing the same kind of loop as before, we do not get an IE memory leak from this code. Fortunately, jQuery is aware of the potential for leaks, and manually releases all of the event handlers that it assigns. As long as we faithfully adhere to using jQuery event binding methods for our handlers, we need not fear leaks caused by this particular common idiom.

This does not mean that we are completely out of the woods; we must continue to take care when we are performing other tasks with DOM elements. Attaching JavaScript objects to DOM elements can still cause memory leaks in Internet Explorer; jQuery just helps make this situation far less prevalent.

As a result of this, jQuery gives us another tool to help avoid these leaks. In *Chapter 12, Advanced DOM Manipulation*, we saw that the .data() method allows us to attach information to DOM elements in much the same way as we can with **expando** properties. Since this data is not stored directly as an expando (jQuery uses an internal map to store the data using IDs it creates), the reference loop is never formed and we sidestep the memory leak issue. Whenever an expando seems like a convenient data storage mechanism, we should consider .data() a safer alternative.

Summary

JavaScript closures are a powerful language feature. They are often quite useful in hiding variables from other code, so that we don't tread on variable names being used elsewhere. Due to jQuery's frequent reliance on functions as method arguments, they can also be inadvertently created quite often. Understanding them allows us to write more efficient and concise code, and with a bit of care and the use of jQuery's built-in safeguards, we can avoid the memory-related pitfalls they can introduce.

B
Testing JavaScript with QUnit

Throughout this book, we have written a lot of JavaScript code, and we have seen the many ways in which jQuery helps us write this code with relative ease. Yet, whenever we have added a new feature, we have had to take the extra step of manually checking our web page to ensure that everything is working as expected. While this process may work for simple tasks, as projects grow in size and complexity, manual testing can become quite onerous. New requirements can introduce "regression bugs" that break parts of the script that previously worked well. It is far too easy to miss these bugs that don't specifically relate to the latest code changes because we naturally only test for what we have just done.

What we need instead is an automated system that runs our tests for us. The **QUnit** testing framework is such a system. While there are many other testing frameworks, and they all have their own benefits, we recommend QUnit for most jQuery projects because it is written and maintained by the jQuery project. In fact, jQuery itself uses QUnit (running nearly 5,000 tests!).

Downloading QUnit

The best place to find QUnit is in the GitHub repository at `https://github.com/jquery/qunit/`. You don't need to know how to use Git or have a GitHub account to download QUnit; just click on the **Downloads** button and choose either the `.tar.gz` or `.zip` file to save to your computer, as shown in the following screenshot:

Once the file is downloaded, we can expand (unzip) the archived files and then copy the `qunit.js` and `qunit.css` files from the `qunit` subfolder into a folder within our own project.

Setting up the document

Once we have the QUnit files in place, we can set up the test HTML document. In a typical project, this file would be named `index.html` and placed in the same test subfolder as `qunit.js` and `qunit.css`. For this demonstration, however, we will put it in a parent directory.

The `<head>` of the document contains a `<link>` tag for the CSS file and `<script>` tags for jQuery, QUnit, the JavaScript we will be testing (`B.js`) and the tests themselves (`test/test.js`). The `<body>` tag consists of six main elements, each with an ID that is used by QUnit for running and displaying the results of the tests. A file with similar markup in the downloaded QUnit's `test` folder can be used as a template for getting started.

In order to demonstrate QUnit, we will use portions of *Chapter 2, Selecting Elements* and *Chapter 6, Sending Data with Ajax*:

```
<!DOCTYPE html>
<html>
<head>
  <meta charset="UTF-8" />
  <title>Appendix B Tests</title>
```

```
<link rel="stylesheet" href="qunit.css" media="screen">

<script src="jquery.js"></script>
<script src="test/qunit.js"></script>
<script src="B.js"></script>
<script src="test/test.js"></script>

</head>
<body>
    <h1 id="qunit-header">Appendix B Tests</h1>
    <h2 id="qunit-banner"></h2>
    <div id="qunit-testrunner-toolbar"></div>
    <h2 id="qunit-userAgent"></h2>
    <ol id="qunit-tests"></ol>
    <div id="qunit-fixture">

      <!-- Test Markup Goes Here -->

    </div>
</body>
</html>
```

Since the *Chapter 2* code that we will test depends on the DOM, we want the test markup to match what we are using on the actual page. We can simply copy and paste the HTML content that we used in *Chapter 2*, which should replace the `<!-- Test Markup Goes Here -->` comment.

Organizing tests

QUnit provides two levels of grouping named after their respective function calls: `module()` and `test()`. The **module** is like a general category under which the tests will be run; the test is actually a *set* of tests that takes a callback in which all of that test's specific **unit tests** are run. We will group our tests by the chapter topic, placing the code in our `test/test.js` file:

```
module('Selecting');

test('Child Selector', function() {
  // tests go here
});
test('Attribute Selectors', function() {
  // tests go here
});
module('Ajax');
```

It is not necessary to set up the file with the test structure, but it is good to have an overall structure in mind. Notice that our modules and tests do not need to be placed inside a $(document).ready() call because QUnit, by default, waits until the window has loaded before it begins running the tests. With this very simple setup, loading the test HTML results in a page that looks like this:

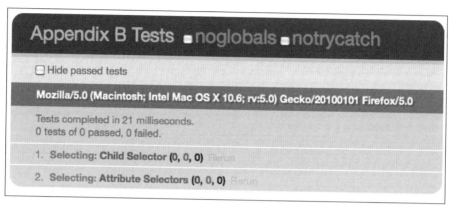

Note that the module name is light blue and the test name is darker blue. Clicking on either one will expand the results of that set of tests, which are collapsed by default when all pass (or, in this case, when they have no tests). The Ajax module does not appear yet because we haven't written any tests for it.

Adding and running tests

In **test-driven development**, we write tests before writing code. This way, we can observe that a test fails, add new code, and then see that the test passes, verifying that our change has the intended effect.

Let's start by testing the child selector that we used in *Chapter 2* to add a horizontal class to all <li> elements that are children of <ul id="selected-plays">:

```
test('Child Selector', function() {
    expect(1);
    var topLis = $('#selected-plays > li.horizontal');
    equal(topLis.length, 3, 'Top LIs have horizontal class');
});
```

Here, we have actually introduced two tests. We begin with the `expect()` test, which instructs QUnit how many tests we expect to run in this set. Then, because we are testing our ability to select elements on the page, we use the `equal()` test to compare the number of top-level `<li>` elements against the number 3. If the two are equal, the test passes:

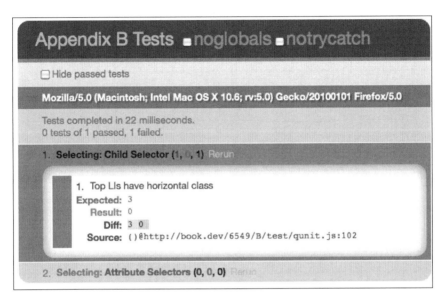

Of course, the test fails because we have not yet written the code to add the `horizontal` class. It is simple to add that code, though. We do so in the main script file for the page, which we named `B.js`:

```
$(document).ready(function() {
  $('#selected-plays > li').addClass('horizontal');
});
```

When we run the test now, it passes:

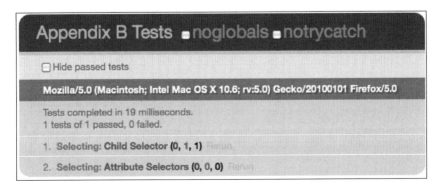

Now the **Selecting: Child Selector** test shows no failing tests and one passing test out of a total of one test. We can add a couple of attribute selector tests as well:

```
module('Selecting', {
  setup: function() {
    this.topLis = $('#selected-plays > li.horizontal');
  }
});

test('Child Selector', function() {
  expect(1);
  equal(this.topLis.length, 3,
    'Top LIs have horizontal class');
});

test('Attribute Selectors', function() {
  expect(2);
  ok(this.topLis.find('.mailto').length == 1, 'a.mailto');
  equal(this.topLis.find('.pdflink').length, 1, 'a.pdflink');
});
```

Here we have introduced another type of test: `ok()`. This one takes two arguments: an expression that should evaluate to a "truthy" value, and a description. Also, note that we have moved the local `topLis` variable out of the **Child Selector** test and into the module's `setup()` callback function. The `module()` takes an optional second argument, which is a map that can include a `setup()` and a `teardown()` function. Within these functions, we can use the `this` keyword to assign variables once for all of a module's tests.

Again, the new tests will fail without the corresponding working code, so let's include that in the script as follows:

```
$(document).ready(function() {
  $('#selected-plays > li').addClass('horizontal');
  $('a[href^="mailto:"]').addClass('mailto');
  $('a[href$=".pdf"]').addClass('pdflink');
});
```

If we expand the newly passing test set, we can see the difference in output between the `ok()` and `equal()` tests, as shown in the following screenshot:

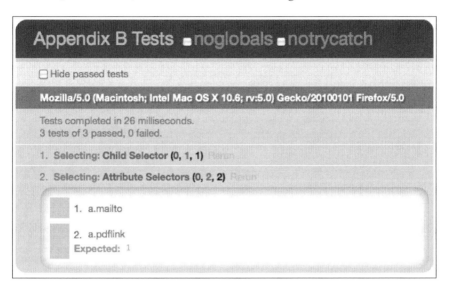

In addition to indicating that both of the tests have passed with the green color, the `equal()` test details the expected result. As it provides more information, the `equal()` test is typically preferred over the `ok()` test.

Asynchronous testing

Testing asynchronous JavaScript, such as Ajax requests, presents an additional challenge. The rest of the tests must pause while the asynchronous test occurs and then they must begin again when it is complete. This type of scenario is by now very familiar; we have seen such asynchronous operations in effects queues, Ajax callback functions, and promise objects. In QUnit, we use a special test set named `asyncTest()`. It looks like the regular `test()` set, except that it will pause the running of tests until we resume them with a call to the special `start()` function:

```
asyncTest('JSON', function() {
  $.getJSON('B.json', function(json, textStatus) {
    // add tests here
  }).always(function() {
    start();
  });
});
```

Here we are simply requesting JSON from `B.js` and allowing the tests to continue once the request has completed, whether it succeeds or fails. For actual tests, we are going to check the `textStatus` to ensure that the request is successful and check the value of one of the objects within the response JSON array as follows:

```
asyncTest('JSON', function() {
  expect(2);
  var backbite = {
    "term": "BACKBITE",
    "part": "v.t.",
    "definition": "To speak of a man as you find him when he
      can't find you."
  };

  $.getJSON('B.json', function(json, textStatus) {
    equal(textStatus, 'success', 'Request successful');
    deepEqual(json[1], backbite,
      'result array matches "backbite" map');
  }).always(function() {
    start();
  });
});
```

For testing the response value, we use yet another test function, `deepEqual()`. Normally, when two objects are compared, they are considered not equal unless they actually refer to the same memory. If we want to compare the object contents instead, `deepEqual()` meets the need. This function walks through two objects to ensure that they have the same properties and that those properties have the same values.

Other types of tests

QUnit comes with a number of other test functions as well. Some, such as `notEqual()` and `notDeepEqual()` are simply the inverses of functions we have used, while others such as `strictEqual()` and `raises()` have more distinct uses. More information about these functions, as well as details and additional examples regarding QUnit in general, are linked from the GitHub repository (`https://github.com/jquery/qunit/`).

Practical considerations

The examples in this appendix have been necessarily simple. In practice, we can write tests that ensure the correct operation of quite complicated behaviors.

Ideally, we keep our tests as brief and simple as possible, even when the behaviors they are testing are intricate. By writing tests for a few specific scenarios, we can build reasonable certainty that we are fully testing the behavior even though we do not have a test for every possible set of inputs.

However, it is possible that an error is observed in our code even though we have written tests for it. When tests pass and yet an error occurs, the correct response is not to immediately fix the problem, but rather to first write a new test for the behavior that fails. This way, we not only verify that the problem is solved when we correct the code, but also introduce an additional test that will help us avoid regressions in the future.

QUnit can be used for **functional testing** in addition to **unit testing**. While unit tests are designed to confirm the correct operation of code units (methods and functions), functional tests are written to ensure appropriate interface responses to user input. For example, in *Chapter 12* we implemented a table-sorting behavior. We could write a unit test for a sorting method verifying that once the method is called the table is sorted. Alternately, a functional test could simulate a user's click on a table heading and then observe the result to check that the table is indeed sorted. Dedicated functional testing frameworks such as **Selenium** (`http://seleniumhq.org/`) can be used for more advanced scenarios.

In order to ensure consistent results for our tests, we need to work with sample data that is reliable and unchanging. When testing the jQuery code that is applied to a dynamic site, it can be beneficial to capture and store a static version of the page to run tests against. This approach also isolates your code's components, making it easier to determine whether errors are caused by the server-side or the browser-side code.

Further reading

These considerations are certainly not an exhaustive list. Test-driven development is a deep topic, and a short appendix is not enough to cover it fully. Some online resources containing more information on the topic include:

- The QUnit documentation site (`http://docs.jquery.com/Qunit`)
- Jörn Zaefferer's *Automating JavaScript Testing with QUnit* (`http://msdn.microsoft.com/en-us/scriptjunkie/gg749824.aspx`)
- Elijah Manor's *jQuery Test-Driven Development* (`http://msdn.microsoft.com/en-us/scriptjunkie/ff452703.aspx`)
- Bob McCune's *Unit Testing Best Practices* (`http://www.bobmccune.com/2006/12/09/unit-testing-best-practices/`)

Many books on the topic also exist, such as Kent Beck's *Test Driven Development: By Example* and Christian Johansen's *Test-Driven JavaScript Development*.

Summary

Writing tests with QUnit can be an effective aid in keeping our jQuery code clean and maintainable. We have seen just a few ways that we can implement tests in a project to ensure that our code is functioning the way we intend it to. By testing small, discrete units of code, we can mitigate some of the problems that occur when projects become more complex. At the same time, we can more efficiently test for regressions throughout a project, saving us valuable programming time.

C
Quick Reference

This appendix is intended to be a quick reference for the jQuery API, including selector expressions and methods. A more detailed discussion on this topic is available in this book's companion volume, *jQuery Reference Guide,* and on the jQuery documentation site: `http://docs.jquery.com`.

Selector expressions

The jQuery factory function `$()` is used to find elements on the page to work with. This function takes a string composed of CSS-like syntax, called a selector expression. Selector expressions are discussed in detail in *Chapter 2, Selecting Elements*.

Simple CSS

Selector	Matches
`*`	All elements
`#id`	The element with the given ID
`element`	All elements of the given type
`.class`	All elements with the given class
`a, b`	Elements that are matched by a or b
`a b`	Elements b that are descendants of a
`a > b`	Elements b that are children of a
`a + b`	Elements b that immediately follow sibling elements a
`a ~ b`	Elements b that follow sibling elements a

Position among siblings

Selector	Matches
`:nth-child(index)`	Elements which are the `index`th child of their parent element (1-based)
`:nth-child(even)`	Elements which are an even child of their parent element (1-based)
`:nth-child(odd)`	Elements which are an odd child of their parent element (1-based)
`:nth-child(formula)`	Elements which are the nth child of their parent element (1-based); formulas are of the form `an+b` for integers `a` and `b`
`:first-child`	Elements which are the first child of their parent
`:last-child`	Elements which are the last child of their parent
`:only-child`	Elements which are the only child of their parent

Position among matched elements

Selector	Matches
`:first`	The first element in the result set
`:last`	The last element in the result set
`:not(a)`	All elements in the result set that are not matched by a
`:even`	Even elements in the result set (0-based)
`:odd`	Odd elements in the result set (0-based)
`:eq(index)`	A numbered element in the result set (0-based)
`:gt(index)`	All elements in the result set after (greater than) the given index (0-based)
`:lt(index)`	All elements in the result set before (less than) the given index (0-based)

Attributes

Selector	Matches
[attr]	Elements that have the attribute attr
[attr="value"]	Elements whose attr attribute are value
[attr!="value"]	Elements whose attr attribute are not value
[attr^="value"]	Elements whose attr attribute begin with value
[attr$="value"]	Elements whose attr attribute end with value
[attr*="value"]	Elements whose attr attribute contain the substring value
[attr~="value"]	Elements whose attr attribute is a space-delimited set of strings, one of which is value
[attr|="value"]	Elements whose attr attribute is either equal to value or begins with value followed by a hyphen

Forms

Selector	Matches
:input	All <input>, <select>, <textarea>, and <button> elements
:text	<input> elements with type="text"
:password	<input> elements with type="password"
:file	<input> elements with type="file"
:radio	<input> elements with type="radio"
:checkbox	<input> elements with type="checkbox"
:submit	<input> elements with type="submit"
:image	<input> elements with type="image"
:reset	<input> elements with type="reset"
:button	<input> elements with type="button", and <button> elements
:enabled	Enabled form elements
:disabled	Disabled form elements
:checked	Checked checkboxes and radio buttons
:selected	Selected <option> elements

Other custom selectors

Selector	Matches
`:header`	Header elements (e.g. `<h1>`, `<h2>`)
`:animated`	Elements with an animation in progress
`:contains(text)`	Elements containing the given text
`:empty`	Elements with no child nodes
`:has(a)`	Elements containing a descendant element matching `a`
`:parent`	Elements that have child nodes
`:hidden`	Elements that are hidden, either through CSS or because they are `<input type="hidden" />`.
`:visible`	The inverse of `:hidden`
`:focus`	The element that has the keyboard focus

DOM traversal methods

After creating a jQuery object using `$()`, we can alter the set of matched elements we are working with by calling one of these DOM traversal methods. DOM traversal methods are discussed in detail in *Chapter 2*.

Filtering

Traversal Method	Returns a jQuery object containing
`.filter(selector)`	Selected elements that match the given selector
`.filter(callback)`	Selected elements for which the callback function returns `true`
`.eq(index)`	The selected element at the given 0-based index
`.first()`	The first selected element
`.last()`	The final selected element
`.slice(start, [end])`	Selected elements in the given range of 0-based indices
`.not(selector)`	Selected elements that do not match the given selector
`.has(selector)`	Selected elements that have a descendant matching `selector`

Descendants

Traversal Method	Returns a jQuery object containing
.find(selector)	Descendant elements that match the selector
.contents()	Child nodes (including text nodes)
.children([selector])	Child nodes, optionally filtered by a selector

Siblings

Traversal Method	Returns a jQuery object containing
.next([selector])	The sibling immediately following each selected element, optionally filtered by a selector
.nextAll([selector])	All siblings following each selected element, optionally filtered by a selector
.nextUntil([selector], [filter])	All siblings following each selected element, up to and not including the first element matching selector, optionally filtered by an additional selector
.prev([selector])	The sibling immediately preceding each selected element, optionally filtered by a selector
.prevAll([selector])	All siblings preceding each selected element, optionally filtered by a selector
.prevUntil([selector], [filter])	All siblings preceding each selected element, up to and not including the first element matching selector, optionally filtered by an additional selector
.siblings([selector])	All siblings, optionally filtered by a selector

Ancestors

Traversal Method	Returns a jQuery object containing
`.parent([selector])`	The parent of each selected element, optionally filtered by a selector
`.parents([selector])`	All ancestors, optionally filtered by a selector
`.parentsUntil([selector], [filter])`	All ancestors of each selected element, up to and not including the first element matching `selector`, optionally filtered by an additional selector
`.closest(selector)`	The first element that matches the selector, starting at the selected element and moving up through its ancestors in the DOM tree
`.offsetParent()`	The positioned parent (for example, relative, absolute) of the first selected element

Collection manipulation

Traversal Method	Returns a jQuery object containing
`.add(selector)`	Selected elements, plus any additional elements that match the given selector
`.andSelf()`	The selected elements, plus the previous set of selected elements on the internal jQuery stack
`.end()`	The previous set of selected elements on the internal jQuery stack
`.map(callback)`	The result of the callback function when called on each selected element
`.pushStack(elements)`	The specified elements

Working with selected elements

Traversal Method	Description
.is(selector)	Determine whether any matched element is matched by the given selector expression
.index()	Get the index of the matched element in relation to its siblings
.index(element)	Get the index of the given DOM node within the set of matched elements
$.contains(a, b)	Determine whether DOM node b contains DOM node a
.each(callback)	Iterate over the matched elements, executing callback for each element
.length	Get the number of matched elements
.get()	Get an array of DOM nodes corresponding to the matched elements
.get(index)	Get the DOM node corresponding to the matched element at the given index
.toArray()	Get an array of DOM nodes corresponding to the matched elements

Event methods

In order to react to user behavior, we need to register our handlers using these event methods. Note that many DOM events only apply to certain element types; these subtleties are not covered here. Event methods are discussed in detail in *Chapter 3*.

Binding

Event Method	Description
.ready(handler)	Bind handler to be called when the DOM and CSS are fully loaded
.bind(type, [data], handler)	Bind handler to be called when the given type of event is sent to the element
.one(type, [data], handler)	Bind handler to be called when the given type of event is sent to the element; removes the binding when the handler is called
.unbind([type], [handler])	Remove the bindings on the element (for an event type, a particular handler, or all bindings)
.live(type, handler)	Bind handler to be called when the given type of event is sent to the element, using event delegation
.die(type, [handler])	Remove the bindings on the element previously bound with .live()
.delegate(selector, type, [data], handler)	Bind handler to be called when the given type of event is sent to a descendant element matching selector
.delegate(selector, handlers)	Bind a map of handlers to be called when the given types of events are sent to a descendant element matching selector
.undelegate(selector, type, [handler])	Remove the bindings on the element previously bound with .delegate()

Shorthand binding

Event Method	Description
.blur(handler)	Bind handler to be called when the element loses keyboard focus
.change(handler)	Bind handler to be called when the element's value changes
.click(handler)	Bind handler to be called when the element is clicked
.dblclick(handler)	Bind handler to be called when the element is double-clicked
.error(handler)	Bind handler to be called when the element receives an error event (browser-dependent)

Event Method	Description
.focus(handler)	Bind handler to be called when the element gains a keyboard focus
.focusin(handler)	Bind handler to be called when the element, or a descendant, gains a keyboard focus
.focusout(handler)	Bind handler to be called when the element, or a descendant, loses keyboard focus
.keydown(handler)	Bind handler to be called when a key is pressed and the element has keyboard focus
.keypress(handler)	Bind handler to be called when a keystroke occurs and the element has keyboard focus
.keyup(handler)	Bind handler to be called when a key is released and the element has keyboard focus
.load(handler)	Bind handler to be called when the element finishes loading
.mousedown(handler)	Bind handler to be called when the mouse button is pressed within the element
.mouseenter(handler)	Bind handler to be called when the mouse pointer enters the element; not affected by event bubbling
.mouseleave(handler)	Bind handler to be called when the mouse pointer leaves the element; not affected by event bubbling
.mousemove(handler)	Bind handler to be called when the mouse pointer moves within the element
.mouseout(handler)	Bind handler to be called when the mouse pointer leaves the element
.mouseover(handler)	Bind handler to be called when the mouse pointer enters the element
.mouseup(handler)	Bind handler to be called when the mouse button is released within the element
.resize(handler)	Bind handler to be called when the element is resized
.scroll(handler)	Bind handler to be called when the element's scroll position changes
.select(handler)	Bind handler to be called when text in the element is selected
.submit(handler)	Bind handler to be called when the form element is submitted
.unload(handler)	Bind handler to be called when the element is unloaded from memory

Special shorthands

Event Method	Description
.hover(enter, leave)	Bind enter to be called when the mouse enters the element, and leave to be called when the mouse leaves it
.toggle(handler1, handler2, ...)	Bind handler1 to be called when the mouse is clicked on the element, followed by handler2 and so on for subsequent clicks

Triggering

Event Method	Description
.trigger(type, [data])	Trigger handlers for the event on the element, and execute the default action for the event
.triggerHandler(type, [data])	Trigger handlers for the event on the element without executing any default actions

Shorthand triggering

Event Method	Description
.blur()	Trigger the blur event
.change()	Trigger the change event
.click()	Trigger the click event
.dblclick()	Trigger the dblclick event
.error()	Trigger the error event
.focus()	Trigger the focus event
.keydown()	Trigger the keydown event.
.keypress()	Trigger the keypress event
.keyup()	Trigger the keyup event
.select()	Trigger the select event
.submit()	Trigger the submit event

Utility

Event Method	Description
`$.proxy(fn, context)`	Create a new function that executes with the given context

Effect methods

These effect methods may be used to perform animations on DOM elements. Effect methods are discussed in detail in *Chapter 4*.

Predefined effects

Effect Method	Description
`.show()`	Display the matched elements
`.hide()`	Hide the matched elements
`.show(speed, [callback])`	Display the matched elements by animating height, width, and opacity
`.hide(speed, [callback])`	Hide the matched elements by animating height, width, and opacity
`.toggle([speed], [callback])`	Display or hide the matched elements
`.slideDown([speed], [callback])`	Display the matched elements with a sliding motion
`.slideUp([speed], [callback])`	Hide the matched elements with a sliding motion
`.slideToggle([speed], [callback])`	Display or hide the matched elements with a sliding motion
`.fadeIn([speed], [callback])`	Display the matched elements by fading them to opaque
`.fadeOut([speed], [callback])`	Hide the matched elements by fading them to transparent
`.fadeToggle([speed], [callback])`	Display or hide the matched elements with a fading animation
`.fadeTo(speed, opacity, [callback])`	Adjust the opacity of the matched elements

Custom animations

Effect Method	Description
`.animate(attributes, [speed], [easing], [callback])`	Perform a custom animation of the specified CSS attributes
`.animate(attributes, options)`	A lower-level interface to `.animate()`, allowing control over the animation queue

Queue manipulation

Effect Method	Description
`.queue([queueName])`	Retrieve the queue of functions on the first matched element
`.queue([queueName], callback)`	Add `callback` to the end of the queue
`.queue([queueName], newQueue)`	Replace the queue with a new one
`.dequeue([queueName])`	Execute the next function on the queue
`.clearQueue([queueName])`	Empty the queue of all pending functions
`.stop([clearQueue], [jumpToEnd])`	Stop the currently running animation, then start queued animations, if any
`.delay(duration, [queueName])`	Wait `duration` milliseconds before executing the next item in the queue
`.promise([queueName], [target])`	Return a promise object to be resolved once all queued actions on the collection have finished

DOM manipulation methods

DOM manipulation methods are discussed in detail in *Chapter 5*.

Attributes and properties

Manipulation Method	Description
`.attr(key)`	Get the attribute named `key`
`.attr(key, value)`	Set the attribute named `key` to `value`
`.attr(key, fn)`	Set the attribute named `key` to the result of `fn` (called separately on each matched element)
`.attr(map)`	Set attribute values, given as key-value pairs

Manipulation Method	Description
`.removeAttr(key)`	Remove the attribute named `key`
`.prop(key)`	Get the property named `key`
`.prop(key, value)`	Set the property named `key` to `value`
`.prop(key, fn)`	Set the property named `key` to the result of `fn` (called separately on each matched element)
`.prop(map)`	Set property values, given as key-value pairs.
`.removeProp(key)`	Remove the property named `key`
`.addClass(class)`	Add the given class to each matched element.
`.removeClass(class)`	Remove the given class from each matched element
`.toggleClass(class)`	Remove the given class if present, and add it if not, for each matched element
`.hasClass(class)`	Return `true` if any of the matched elements has the given class
`.val()`	Get the value attribute of the first matched element
`.val(value)`	Set the value attribute of each element to `value`

Content

Manipulation Method	Description
`.html()`	Get the HTML content of the first matched element
`.html(value)`	Set the HTML content of each matched element to value
`.text()`	Get the textual content of all matched elements as a single string
`.text(value)`	Set the textual content of each matched element to `value`

CSS

Manipulation Method	Description
`.css(key)`	Get the CSS attribute named `key`
`.css(key, value)`	Set the CSS attribute named `key` to `value`
`.css(map)`	Set CSS attribute values, given as key-value pairs

Dimensions

Manipulation Method	Description
.offset()	Get the top, and left, pixel coordinates of the first matched element, relative to the viewport
.position()	Get the top, and left, pixel coordinates of the first matched element, relative to the element returned by .offsetParent()
.scrollTop()	Get the vertical scroll position of the first matched element
.scrollTop(value)	Set the vertical scroll position of all matched elements to value
.scrollLeft()	Get the horizontal scroll position of the first matched element
.scrollLeft(value)	Set the horizontal scroll position of all matched elements to value
.height()	Get the height of the first matched element
.height(value)	Set the height of all matched elements to value
.width()	Get the width of the first matched element
.width(value)	Set the width of all matched elements to value
.innerHeight()	Get the height of the first matched element, including padding, but not border
.innerWidth()	Get the width of the first matched element, including padding, but not border
.outerHeight(includeMargin)	Get the height of the first matched element, including padding, border, and optional margin
.outerWidth(includeMargin)	Get the width of the first matched element, including padding, border, and optional margin

Insertion

Manipulation Method	Description
.append(content)	Insert content at the end of the interior of each matched element
.appendTo(selector)	Insert the matched elements at the end of the interior of the elements matched by selector
.prepend(content)	Insert content at the beginning of the interior of each matched element
.prependTo(selector)	Insert the matched elements at the beginning of the interior of the elements matched by selector
.after(content)	Insert content after each matched element
.insertAfter(selector)	Insert the matched elements after each of the elements matched by selector
.before(content)	Insert content before each matched element
.insertBefore(selector)	Insert the matched elements before each of the elements matched by selector
.wrap(content)	Wrap each of the matched elements within content
.wrapAll(content)	Wrap all of the matched elements as a single unit within content
.wrapInner(content)	Wrap the interior contents of each of the matched elements within content

Replacement

Manipulation Method	Description
.replaceWith(content)	Replace the matched elements with content
.replaceAll(selector)	Replace the elements matched by selector with the matched elements

Removal

Manipulation Method	Description
.empty()	Remove the child nodes of each matched element
.remove([selector])	Remove the matched nodes (optionally filtered by selector) from the DOM
.detach([selector])	Remove the matched nodes (optionally filtered by selector) from the DOM, preserving jQuery data attached to them
.unwrap()	Remove the element's parent

Copying

Manipulation Method	Description
.clone([withHandlers])	Make a copy of all matched elements, optionally also copying event handlers

Data

Manipulation Method	Description
.data(key)	Get the data item named key associated with the first matched element
.data(key, value)	Set the data item named key associated with each matched element to value
.removeData(key)	Remove the data item named key associated with each matched element

Ajax methods

We can retrieve information from the server without requiring a page refresh by calling one of the following Ajax methods. Ajax methods are discussed in detail in *Chapter 6*.

Issuing requests

Ajax Method	Description
`$.ajax(options)`	Make an Ajax request using the provided set of options; this is a low-level method that is usually called through other convenience methods
`.load(url, [data], [callback])`	Make an Ajax request to `url`, and place the response into the matched elements
`$.get(url, [data], [callback], [returnType])`	Make an Ajax request to `url` using the GET method
`$.getJSON(url, [data], [callback])`	Make an Ajax request to `url`, interpreting the response as a JSON data structure
`$.getScript(url, [callback])`	Make an Ajax request to `url`, executing the response as JavaScript
`$.post(url, [data], [callback], [returnType])`	Make an Ajax request to `url` using the POST method

Request monitoring

Ajax Method	Description
`.ajaxComplete(handler)`	Bind `handler` to be called when any Ajax transaction completes
`.ajaxError(handler)`	Bind `handler` to be called when any Ajax transaction completes with an error
`.ajaxSend(handler)`	Bind `handler` to be called when any Ajax transaction begins
`.ajaxStart(handler)`	Bind `handler` to be called when any Ajax transaction begins, and no others are active
`.ajaxStop(handler)`	Bind `handler` to be called when any Ajax transaction ends, and no others are still active
`.ajaxSuccess(handler)`	Bind `handler` to be called when any Ajax transaction completes successfully

Configuration

Ajax Method	Description
`$.ajaxSetup(options)`	Set default options for all subsequent Ajax transactions
`$.ajaxPrefilter([dataTypes], handler)`	Modify the options on each Ajax request before it is processed by `$.ajax()`
`$.ajaxTransport(transportFunction)`	Define a new transport mechanism for Ajax transactions

Utilities

Ajax Method	Description
`.serialize()`	Encode the values of a set of form controls into a query string
`.serializeArray()`	Encode the values of a set of form controls into a JavaScript data structure
`$.param(map)`	Encode an arbitrary map of values into a query string
`$.globalEval(code)`	Evaluate the given JavaScript string in the global context
`$.parseJSON(json)`	Convert the given JSON string into a JavaScript object
`$.parseXML(xml)`	Convert the given XML string into an XML document

Deferred objects

Deferred objects and their promises allow us to react to the completion of long-running tasks with a convenient syntax. They are discussed in detail in *Chapter 11*.

Object creation

Function	Description
`$.Deferred([setupFunction])`	Returns a new deferred object
`$.when(deferreds)`	Returns a promise object to be resolved when the given deferred objects are resolved

Methods of deferred objects

Method	Description
`.resolve([args])`	Sets the state of the object to resolved
`.resolveWith(context, [args])`	Sets the state of the object to resolved, while making the keyword `this` refer to `context` within callbacks
`.reject([args])`	Sets the state of the object to resolved
`.rejectWith(context, [args])`	Sets the state of the object to resolved, while making the keyword `this` refer to `context` within callbacks
`.promise([target])`	Returns a promise object corresponding to this deferred object

Methods of promise objects

Method	Description
`.done(callback)`	Execute `callback` when the object is resolved
`.fail(callback)`	Execute `callback` when the object is rejected
`.always([callback])`	Execute `callback` when the object is resolved or rejected
`.then(doneCallbacks, failCallbacks)`	Execute `doneCallbacks` when the object is resolved, or `failCallbacks` when the object is rejected
`.isRejected()`	Return `true` if the object has been rejected
`.isResolved()`	Return `true` if the object has been resolved
`.pipe([doneFilter], [failFilter])`	Return a new promise object which is resolved when the original promise is, optionally after filtering the object's status through a function

Miscellaneous properties and functions

These utility methods do not fit neatly into the preceding categories, but are often very useful when writing scripts using jQuery.

Properties of the jQuery object

Property	Description
`$.support`	Return a map of properties indicating whether the browser supports various features and standards

Arrays and objects

Function	Description
`$.each(collection, callback)`	Iterate over `collection`, executing `callback` for each item
`$.extend(target, addition, ...)`	Modify the object `target` by adding properties from the other supplied objects
`$.grep(array, callback, [invert])`	Filter `array` by using `callback` as a test
`$.makeArray(object)`	Convert `object` into an array
`$.map(array, callback)`	Construct a new array consisting of the result of `callback` being called on each item
`$.inArray(value, array)`	Determine the position of value in array or return -1 if value is not in array
`$.merge(array1, array2)`	Combine the contents of `array1` and `array2`
`$.unique(array)`	Remove any duplicate DOM elements from `array`

Object introspection

Function	Description
`$.isArray(object)`	Determine whether `object` is a true JavaScript array
`$.isEmptyObject(object)`	Determine whether `object` is empty
`$.isFunction(object)`	Determine whether `object` is a function
`$.isPlainObject(object)`	Determine whether `object` was created as an object literal or with `new Object`
`$.isWindow(object)`	Determine whether `object` represents a browser window
`$.isXMLDoc(object)`	Determine whether `object` is an XML node
`$.type(object)`	Get the JavaScript class of `object`

Other

Function	Description
`$.trim(string)`	Remove whitespace from the ends of `string`
`$.noConflict([removeAll])`	Revert $ to its pre-jQuery definition
`$.noop()`	A function that does nothing
`$.now()`	The current time, in seconds since the epoch

Index

A

default parameter values 212
    parameter maps 211
micro-optimization 237
MIME type 152
MIT License 12
module 359
module() function 359
mouseenter event 67, 255
mouse events 79
mouseleave event 67, 255
mouseout event handler 66
multiple functions
    adding, to jQuery plugin 202-205
multiple properties
    animating, at once 99-101
multi-property easing 280, 281

N

namespace collisions 348
namespace pollution 341
Narrow Column button 55
negation pseudo-class 30
nextPage event 261 263
nodeList 238
non-class attributes
    manipulating 114, 115
    value callbacks 115-117
notDeepEqual() test function 364
notEqual() test function 364

O

object creation functions
    $.Deferred([setupFunction]) 384
    $.when(deferreds) 384
object instance 17
object introspection
    functions 386
object introspection functions
    $.isArray(object) 386
    $.isEmptyObject(object) 386
    $.isFunction(object) 386
    $.isPlainObject(object) 386
    $.isWindow(object) 386
    $.isXMLDoc(object) 386
    $.type(object) 386
Objective-C 353

object literal 80, 145
object-oriented programming 347
observer functions, Ajax requests 165-167
ok() test 363
outerFn() function 342, 343
outerWidth() method 100

P

page load
    tasks, performing on 47
pageNum variable 254
parseFloat() 296
Pascal 343
performance
    measuring 308
PHP
    URL 155
plain JavaScript
    versus jQuery 19, 20
plugin architecture 181
plugin design recommendations 223
Plugin Repository
    about 181
    URL 181
plugins
    about 11
    custom selector plugins 186, 187
    Cycle plugin 182
    Cycle plugin, downloading 182
    Cycle plugin, referencing 182
    global function plugins 187
    searching 181
    using 182
pointers 353
POST request
    performing 160
practical considerations, QUnit 364, 365
predefined effect methods, DOM
    .fadeIn([speed], [callback]) 377
    .fadeOut([speed], [callback]) 377
    .fadeToggle([speed], [callback]) 377
    .fadeTo(speed, opacity, [callback]) 377
    .hide() 377
    .hide(speed, [callback]) 377
    .show() 377
    .show(speed, [callback]) 377

Thank you for buying
Learning jQuery Third Edition

About Packt Publishing

Packt, pronounced 'packed', published its first book "*Mastering phpMyAdmin for Effective MySQL Management*" in April 2004 and subsequently continued to specialize in publishing highly focused books on specific technologies and solutions.

Our books and publications share the experiences of your fellow IT professionals in adapting and customizing today's systems, applications, and frameworks. Our solution based books give you the knowledge and power to customize the software and technologies you're using to get the job done. Packt books are more specific and less general than the IT books you have seen in the past. Our unique business model allows us to bring you more focused information, giving you more of what you need to know, and less of what you don't.

Packt is a modern, yet unique publishing company, which focuses on producing quality, cutting-edge books for communities of developers, administrators, and newbies alike. For more information, please visit our website: www.packtpub.com.

About Packt Open Source

In 2010, Packt launched two new brands, Packt Open Source and Packt Enterprise, in order to continue its focus on specialization. This book is part of the Packt Open Source brand, home to books published on software built around Open Source licences, and offering information to anybody from advanced developers to budding web designers. The Open Source brand also runs Packt's Open Source Royalty Scheme, by which Packt gives a royalty to each Open Source project about whose software a book is sold.

Writing for Packt

We welcome all inquiries from people who are interested in authoring. Book proposals should be sent to author@packtpub.com. If your book idea is still at an early stage and you would like to discuss it first before writing a formal book proposal, contact us; one of our commissioning editors will get in touch with you.

We're not just looking for published authors; if you have strong technical skills but no writing experience, our experienced editors can help you develop a writing career, or simply get some additional reward for your expertise.

Learning jQuery

ISBN: 978-1-847192-50-9   Paperback: 380 pages

Better Interaction Design and Web Development with
Simple JavaScript Techniques

1. Create better, cross-platform JavaScript code

2. Learn detailed solutions to specific client-side
    problems

3. For web designers who want to create
    interactive elements for their designs

4. For developers who want to create the best
    user interface for their web applications.

Learning jQuery 1.3

ISBN: 978-1-847196-70-5   Paperback: 444 pages

Better Interaction Design and Web Development with
Simple JavaScript Techniques

1. An introduction to jQuery that requires
    minimal programming experience

2. Detailed solutions to specific client-side
    problems

3. For web designers to create interactive elements
    for their designs

4. For developers to create the best user interface
    for their web applications

5. Packed with great examples, code, and clear
    explanations

Please check **www.PacktPub.com** for information on our titles

jQuery 1.4 Reference Guide

ISBN: 978-1-849510-04-2   Paperback: 336 pages

This book and eBook is a comprehensive exploration of the popular JavaScript library

1. Quickly look up features of the jQuery library

2. Step through each function, method, and selector expression in the jQuery library with an easy-to-follow approach

3. Understand the anatomy of a jQuery script

4. Write your own plug-ins using jQuery's powerful plug-in architecture

jQuery 1.4 Animation Techniques: Beginners Guide

ISBN: 978-1-849513- 30-2   Paperback: 344 pages

Quickly master all of jQuery's animation methods and build a toolkit of ready-to-use animations using jQuery 1.4

1. Create both simple and complex animations using clear, step-by-step instructions, accompanied with screenshots

2. Walk through each of jQuery's built-in animation methods and see in detail how each one can be used

3. Over 50 detailed examples of different types of web page animations

Please check **www.PacktPub.com** for information on our titles

2797641R00230

Made in the USA
San Bernardino, CA
05 June 2013